Islamic Law & Wisdom – 1
FAITH AND MORALITY

A fresh insight into Islam, its beliefs, moral commands, and the wisdom behind these beliefs and commands, and how it relates to the true essence of the religion, which is purifying oneself.

Publisher: Ghamidi Center of Islamic Learning - Al-Mawrid US
ISBN: 978-1-966600-31-2

Address: 3620 N Josey Ln, Suite 230 Carrollton, TX 75007
Website: www.ghamidicenter.com
Email: info@ghamidi.org

Chapter 1

Introduction to the Course

Introduction

- Our beloved Prophet Muhammad (peace be upon him) emphasized that seeking religious knowledge is obligatory for every Muslim, regardless of gender.
- Following the assertion of our Prophet, the purpose of this course is to provide its students with the required knowledge, offering fresh insight into Islam, its beliefs, its practices, and the wisdom behind them.
- In this two-part course, students will learn about Islam, its core beliefs, and teachings to appreciate the true essence of the directives given by Allah SWT: the purification of oneself.
- Every lecture or discussion will be a sincere effort to understand how these beliefs and directives play a significant role in self-development and personal growth.
- Students will be asked to evaluate the subject matter rationally. The first part of the course will focus on articles of faith and their relationship to our social lives, with a brief introduction to rituals.
- The second part will focus on the laws given by Allah SWT for Muslims to lead their lives in this world.

Objectives:

- The primary objective of this course is to explore the objectivity behind Islamic beliefs and understand how the articles of faith are closely intertwined with our daily lives. The effort is to know that it is ok to rationalize the commandments of Allah SWT and the reasons for the success criteria in Allah's eyes. At the end of this course, the students will be able to:
  - Rationally evaluate the reasoning behind the articles of faith and their requirements.
  - Understand how the objective of Islam, purification, is at the center of every commandment given by Allah SWT
  - Learn how to use the tools given by Allah SWT in the form of ethics and morality to achieve success in the Hereafter.

Structure of the course

- The course is structured into two main modules:
  - The first module covers faith (beliefs) and morality, which have not changed since the time of Adam.
  - The second module deals with religious laws and the rationales behind them, which vary across time and place.

Faith and Morality
Part 1

- A deeper look into **Faith & Morality** in Islam.
- Rationally evaluate the reasoning behind the Articles of Faith and moral commandments.
- Understand how purification is at the center of every commandment.
- How to achieve success in the Hereafter.

Islamic Law and Wisdom
Part 2

- A deeper look into the Laws given in Islam.
- Academically and rationally evaluate the laws.
- Significance of the directives of Islam, their objectives, and Western interpretation.
- Understand how laws achieve the target of purification and success in the Hereafter.

Why are you a Muslim?

Why revisit Islam?

- Islam is the most misunderstood religion on Earth, not only by non-Muslims but also by Muslims themselves.
- Most of us are not Muslims by choice.
- The sources of Islam are the Quran (the sacred text) and Sunnah (the sacred acts), but their interpretation has always been a human endeavor.
- Arguments and reasoning based on the original sacred sources should serve as the basis for accepting or rejecting an interpretation.
- It is only then that the wisdom behind God's religious instructions can be fully appreciated.

**This journey is
<u>unavoidable</u>**

- Islam claims to be the universal religion sent for all places and times.
- God has stated clearly that He will only accept Islam for eternal salvation.
- The Quran claims to be humanity's answer to its supplications 1400 years ago.
- If we want to live our lives as Muslims, then it is incumbent upon us to understand what we believe and practice.

> We must make a sincere effort to understand the beliefs, moral code, and practices of Islam in the light of the Quran and how they relate to our lives.

Why should you learn about Islam?

- Before telling anyone about Islam, it is your responsibility to learn about Islam for your own sake. You should comprehend what you believe and practice.
- To know exactly what Allah wants from you.
- To counter Islamophobia around us at the personal level.
- To be aware of the innovations introduced into Islam.
- To be the ambassador of Islam with confidence wherever you live and work.
- It will help you connect with your heritage and feel part of the global Muslim community.
- Today's society exposes people to a wide range of values and ideologies, and learning about Islam provides you with a strong foundation to remain rooted in your faith. Having a clear sense of Islamic identity equips you to handle peer pressure, harmful trends, and misleading ideologies with confidence.
- To teach true religion to your children.

> If you had to explain Islam to a non-Muslim friend in 2 minutes, what would you say?

Few things to know

- Muslims always say "Peace and blessings of Allah be upon him," with the name of Prophet Muhammad. In the slides, it is omitted for editing purposes, but we should say that we mention his name.
- Allah (The Most-High) is the only True God. In this course, God and Allah are used interchangeably and mean the same.
- Islam is the message for all Muslims, regardless of their gender. In this course, you may find references in the Quran and the Hadith that use the masculine gender only. As in many other languages, in Arabic, when both genders are addressed, masculine pronouns are used.

Islamic Resources

Join Ask Ghamidi
A community-driven discussion portal to ask, answer, share, and learn

https://www.ghamidi.org/app/

Meezan Lectures – English
By Dr. Shehzad Saleem

https://www.youtube.com/playlist?list=PL3yXG2ufxd6USiyYQVHtzpXAnMvXC4-C9

Islam – A Comprehensive Introduction
Meezan translation by Dr. Shehzad Saleem

https://archive.org/details/mizan-english-ghamidi/Islam%20A%20comprehensive%20introduction%20-%20Javaid%20Ahmed%20Ghamidi%20%28English%20translation%20of%20Mizan%29/page/n5/mode/1up

Important Notes

- You are required to attend all classes unless you have a valid reason to skip.
- Please send a note (or ask your parents) to your teacher on Google Classroom if you will skip a session.
- Attendance will be taken at the beginning of every class. Arriving in class 5 minutes after the start will be considered tardy.
- Three (3) tardies will be counted as one absence.
- Attendance will be counted toward your final assessment.
- Every student will be assessed via:
    - Participation in the class
    - Multiple Quizzes
    - Assignments
    - Semester Exam
    - End-of-Year Exam

Chapter 2

True Religion

This chapter introduces Islam, its essence, content, main objective, and what God demands of us.

Definition of Religion understood from the Quran

General Definition of Religion

A belief concerning the supernatural, sacred, or divine, and the practices and institutions associated with such a belief.

Definition understood from the Quran

The Quran does not specifically define religion, but the scholars of Islam have understood the religion of God from the Quran as such:

> As a created being, it is incumbent upon me to **worship** my **Creator** and the Creator of this Universe. We call Him God.

> This worship demands a relationship with the Creator, whose rights must be fulfilled.

> This relationship prescribes metaphysical and ethical bases, determines worship rituals, and stipulates limits (within the religious framework) that the servant abides by in life.

- Universal morality, worship rituals such as prayers and fasting, and law (Shariah) are all rooted in God's relationship with His believers.
- According to the Quran, God's religion has been Islam for the entire humanity since the time of Adam, and it encompasses everything that exists in this universe. God **never** gave any other religion.

Should Muslims make such a big claim that Islam is the only TRUE religion given by God?

Islam and its essence

Definition of Islam

The word Islam comes from the root *Salama*. It means submitting yourself to God, which in essence means submitting your free will to God with humility and servility.

The essence of Islam

- In a word, the essence of religion in Quranic terms is "*ibadah*" (worship) of God.
- It is "worship" that the Creator of this world desires from His "servants."
- God said in the Quran:

  And I created jinn and mankind <u>only</u> to 'worship' Me. (51:56)

- The word 'worship' is used in Islam in two aspects:
    - It is specifically used for rituals we perform as part of religion, such as prayers and fasting (Ibadaat).
    - In a broader sense, it describes an attitude that is the opposite of arrogance and rebellious behavior. An attitude that shows humility and servility in front of God as His creation and acts according to that.
- In this verse, the word *Ibadah* is used in its broader sense and does not simply mean rituals like prayers, etc.
- This expands a believer's scope of worship.

Examples of Worship

- Studying to earn pure living.
- Spending time with family because Allah said so.
- Changing opinion after knowing the truth.
- Helping less fortunate people.
- Playing sports to remain healthy.
- Earning Halal to take care of the family.
- Gaining the knowledge of your religion.

The worship rituals

- Muslims generally think of Islam as a collection of rituals and practices.
- What we just understood about the concept of *Ibadah* changes how we should view worship rituals.
- Worship rituals are just symbolic expressions of the actual "worship," which is the inner sense of humility and servility before God in every matter of life.
- The inner sense of humility and servility should result in the following:
  - Humbleness with no sign of arrogance, pride, or vanity
  - God consciousness with no element of disobedience
  - Trust in God with no ungratefulness
  - Development of goodness and no sign of oppression against anyone
- The symbolic expressions of the above behavior must be reflected in our worship rituals.
- For example, prayers or salah embody humility, and fasting embodies obedience.

- When God reminded us in the Quran, He means the total submission that He requires from us:

إِنَّ الدِّينَ عِنْدَ اللَّهِ الْإِسْلَامُ

The only true religion in God's sight is Islam (3:19)

وَمَنْ يَبْتَغِ غَيْرَ الْإِسْلَامِ دِينًا فَلَنْ يُقْبَلَ مِنْهُ وَهُوَ فِي الْآخِرَةِ مِنَ الْخَاسِرِينَ

…. and he who chooses a religion other than Islam, it will not be accepted by him, and in the hereafter, he will surely be among the losers. (3:85)

Concept of Worship in Ahadith

- This concept is well explained by the Messenger of God, Prophet Muhammad, in the following narrations:

Some of the people from among the Companions said to him: Messenger of Allah, the rich have taken away (all the) reward. They observe prayer as we do; they keep the fasts as we keep, and they give charity out of their surplus riches. Upon this, the Prophet said: Has Allah not prescribed for you (a course) by following which you can (also) do charity? In every declaration of the glorification of Allah (i. e. saying *Subhan Allah*), there is a charity, and every *Takbir* (i. e. saying *Allah-O-Akbar*) is a charity, and every praise of His (saying *al-Hamdu Lillah*) is a charity, and every declaration that He is One (*La Ilaha ill-Allah*) is a charity, and enjoining of good is a charity, and forbidding of that which is evil is a charity, and in man's sexual Intercourse (with his wife) **there is a charity**. The Companions said: Messenger of Allah, is there a reward for him who satisfies his sexual passion among us? He said: Tell me, if he were to devote it to something forbidden, would it not be a sin on his part? Similarly, if he were to devote it to something lawful, he should have a reward for it. **(Sahih Muslim #1006)**

Kaab ibn Ujrah reports that a person passed by us. The companions, noticing his strength and vigor, commented: O Prophet, if only this person were [utilizing his ability] in the path of Allah! The Prophet has been reported to have said: If he has left his home to earn for his young children, then he is **on the path of Allah**. If he has left his home to earn for his elderly parents, then he is **on the path of Allah**. If he has left his home to earn sufficient for himself, then he is **on the path of Allah**. If he has left his home to earn for showing and boasting, he is on the path of Shaytan!'
(Al Mujamul Kabir, vol.12, Hadith #282)

If it's all about the inner sense of humility, then why can't just feeling humble inside be enough?

History and Sources of Islam

History of Islam

- When talking to non-Muslims or even Muslims, you may get a sense as if Islam, as a religion, was started by Prophet Muhammad in the 6th century in the Arabian Peninsula. That is completely against the picture that the Quran paints for us about Islam and its origin.

شَرَعَ لَكُمْ مِنَ الدِّينِ مَا وَصَّى بِهِ نُوحًا وَالَّذِي أَوْحَيْنَا إِلَيْكَ وَمَا وَصَّيْنَا بِهِ إِبْرَاهِيمَ وَمُوسَى وَعِيسَى أَنْ أَقِيمُوا الدِّينَ وَلَا تَتَفَرَّقُوا فِيهِ

He has prescribed for you (O Muhammad) the same religion which He prescribed for Noah, and which We have now revealed to you and which We enjoined on Abraham, Moses, and Jesus, with the assertion: "Adhere to this religion [in your lives] and do not create any divisions in it. (42:13)

- The Quran insists that Prophet Muhammad did not bring any new religion, and He had chosen many people before Prophet Muhammad for His religion.

اِنَّ اللهَ اصْطَفَى اٰدَمَ وَ نُوْحًا وَّ اٰلَ اِبْرٰهِيْمَ وَ اٰلَ عِمْرٰنَ عَلَى الْعٰلَمِيْنَ

No doubt, God chose Adam and Noah, Abraham's family, and Imran's family over all the nations [to guide their nations]. (3:33)

- In light of this information from God, one can easily conclude that Judaism and Christianity are offshoots of Islam. These nations formed their own religion after rejecting the Messenger sent to them. For example, Jews rejected Jesus as their messenger and formed Judaism; Prophet Musa taught them the same Islam as Prophet Muhammad.

Sources of Islam

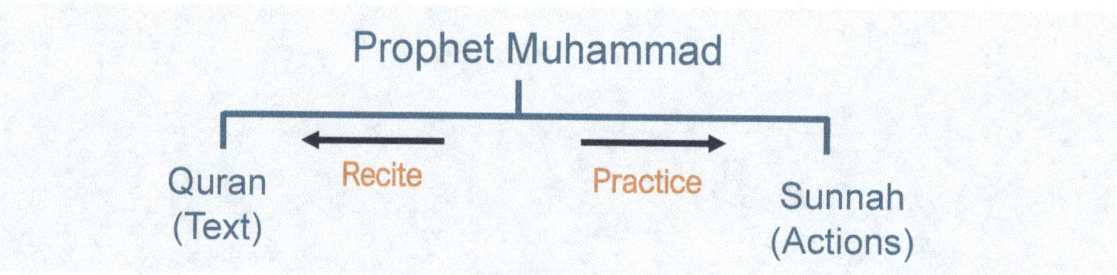

- If religion is a body of beliefs, morals, and laws, then there must be a source for all of it.
- According to God, for us now, Prophet Muhammad is the ONLY source of Islam. For something to be part of the religion of Islam, it must be given or sanctioned by Prophet Muhammad.
- Prophet Muhammad gave us this religion in two forms, which serve as our sources and form the corpus of religious knowledge: the Quran and the Sunnah.
- Generally, Muslims attribute the Sunnah to Prophet Muhammad, but they also attribute the Quran to him. We did not receive this Quran directly. Prophet Muhammad received it and gave it to us, which makes him the source of it for us as well.

Quran	Sunnah
- The last book of Islam revealed to Prophet Muhammad by God.	- The tradition and practices of Prophet Ibrahim.
- Preserved in its original language and continuously transmitted first orally and then in written form through generations without any gaps.	- Prophet Muhammad instituted it after reviving and reforming it and adding certain practices, and now he is the source of it for us.
- Verbatim words of God.	- Transmitted through perpetual practice through generations without any gaps.
- Source for beliefs, morality guidelines, and some laws.	- Source for rituals and most of the laws.

The scope of the Quran

- Allah and His attributes.
- The case for Monotheism and the case against Polytheism.
- System of belief and its components.
- The stories of previous nations and the moral lessons they hold for the direct addressees and us.
- The role of previous scriptures.
- Instructions about wars and incidents during the time of the Prophet Muhammad.
- Instructions for the new nation that will lead humanity until the Day of Judgment.
- Importance of following the Prophet and his Sunnah and the Shariah given through it.

The scope of the Sunnah

- All Rituals that are prescribed in Shariah.
- The details of those Rituals are in two forms:
  - Mandatory
  - Optional
- All other practices outside of rituals, such as saying Salam and maintaining hygiene, etc.
- The majority of the laws (*Shariah*) are part of Sunnah.

> **Note:** Some units of prayers in the five daily prayers are also referred to as 'sunnah prayers'; however, this term is explicitly associated with the Hanafi school of thought. Sunnah (with capital S) is one of the sources of Islam and must not be confused with 'sunnah prayers' associated with Hanafi Fiqh.

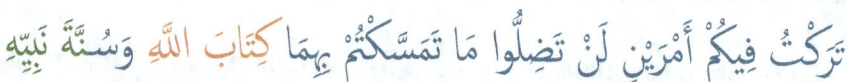

I have left two matters with you. As long as you hold to them, you will never go astray. They are the Book of Allah and the Sunnah of His Prophet. (Muwatta, Imam Malik, Book of Decree)

Hadith and its relationship with the sources

- The historical record of Prophetic sayings, actions, and approvals reported by a few people.
- It further explains and demonstrates what is already present in the primary sources of Islam: the Quran and Sunnah.
- Naturally, companions began writing down their interactions with Prophet Muhammad and recording them for their own benefit.
- They naturally transmitted that knowledge through generations, sometimes verbally and sometimes in written form (their personal notes).
- Practically turned into a body of knowledge after a couple of hundred years of the prophet's death.
- The great scholars of Islam spent decades researching and sifting through hundreds of thousands of reports, grading them into different categories so we can be a little more certain whether a narration was actually said by the Prophet.
- It's a treasure because his divinely guided wisdom and understanding of religion are preserved in the hadith.
- Through hadith, we learn about his life, personality, daily activities, exemplary practice of Islam, character, morals, and wise statements.

An Example Chain

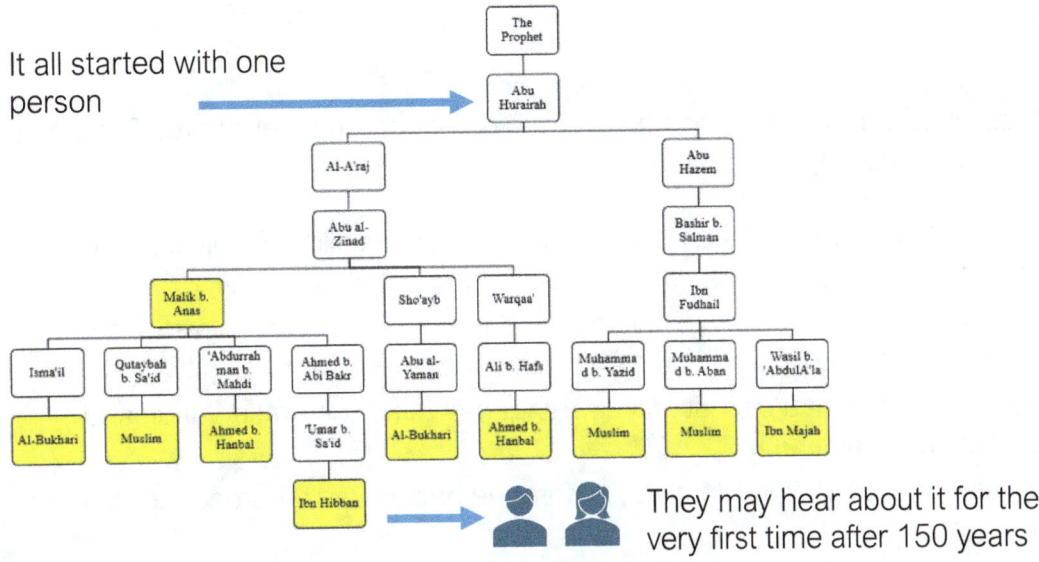

It all started with one person

They may hear about it for the very first time after 150 years

Difference between Sunnah and Hadith

- Hadith is often misunderstood to be a synonym for the word Sunnah.
- In classical Islamic scholarship, the distinction is well understood and used accordingly.
- The science of hadith decides its relative authenticity. It can be relatively more authentic, a little less authentic, not reach the prophet, or even fabricated.
- Sunnah gives us the religion through perpetual practice of the generations after Prophet Muhammad, while Hadith provides us with the record of the exemplary way our Prophet practiced that religion.

Sunnah (the actual religion)	What does hadith provide? *Exemplary way*
Prayers	How did Prophet pray?
Fasting	What did he eat in the morning, and what were his daily activities during the fast?
Sacrifice animal	What animal he sacrificed and how did he do it?
Perform Hajj	How many times did he do it, and how did he perform the steps already mentioned in Sunnah?

Why can't hadith be an independent source?

يَا أَيُّهَا الرَّسُولُ بَلِّغْ مَا أُنزِلَ إِلَيْكَ مِن رَّبِّكَ ۖ وَإِن لَّمْ تَفْعَلْ فَمَا بَلَّغْتَ رِسَالَتَهُ

O Messenger, deliver what has been revealed to you from your Lord; if you do not, you have not conveyed His message. (5:67)

- Prophet Muhammad was entrusted with the responsibility of delivering and explaining the religion to all people around him, and he fulfilled it.
- Anything in the main body of religion (Islam) cannot be given to just one person and left to his/her discretion to communicate to the broader community.
- Prophet Muhammad did not make arrangements for the preservation and dissemination of hadith.
- People were practicing Islam way before the hadith was recorded, scrutinized, and compiled.
- Hadith can only clarify or dispel misunderstandings within the main body of Islam, as already received through the Quran and the Sunnah.

Purpose of Divine Books & Messengers

- Most Prophets and Messengers received revelation in written form (books). However, not every prophet or messenger needs to receive a new divine text.
- For religious laws, some are asked to follow the laws that came with the prophet or messenger before them, if they are intact.
- The Quran clearly states the purpose of the divine books, including the Quran.
- Their purpose is to act as a judge between what is right and what is wrong in religion, so that people can resolve their differences through them.
- For example, today the Quran will render a verdict in matters of religion.
- The details on this topic will come in the chapter on the Quran.

Responsibility of *Indhar*

With the chain of prophethood and revelation having ceased, the responsibility of Indhar (warning people about the Day of Judgment) now lies with the scholars of Muslim nations till the day of judgment, and this Indhar must be done through the Quran (Surah 9, Verse 122 & Surah 6, Verse 19)

Purpose of Messengers and Prophets

- They are chosen by God, after receiving divine revelation, and teach the truth to their direct addressees.
- Gives glad tidings of a good fate in the Hereafter to those who accept it – *Bashaarah*.
- Warns those who reject it that a bad consequence awaits them – *Indhar*.
- 'Messengers' among them, after being rejected, practically enforce the sovereignty of the truth upon their people by implementing God's Judgment in this very world.
- With the signs of the truth that they have directly observed, they present the truth and the guidance to the people with full certainty, and that is called *Shahadah*.
- The details of this topic will be provided in the chapter on the Messengers and Prophets.

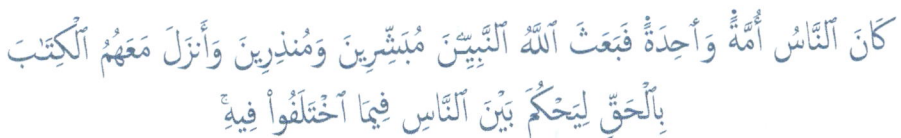

Mankind was once a community (then differences arose among them), so Allah sent forth prophets as bearers of glad tidings and as warners. And with them, He sent His Book as the truth so that it may settle differences between people (2:213)

وَلِكُلِّ أُمَّةٍ رَّسُولٌ ۖ فَإِذَا جَاءَ رَسُولُهُمْ قُضِيَ بَيْنَهُم بِالْقِسْطِ وَهُمْ لَا يُظْلَمُونَ

And for each community, there is a messenger. Then, when their messenger comes, their fate is decided with justice, and they are not wronged (10:47)

إِنَّا أَرْسَلْنَا إِلَيْكُمْ رَسُولًا شَاهِدًا عَلَيْكُمْ كَمَا أَرْسَلْنَا إِلَىٰ فِرْعَوْنَ رَسُولًا

O Quraysh, We have sent a messenger to you to bear witness before you, just as we sent a messenger to the Pharaoh. (73:15)

لَقَدْ أَرْسَلْنَا رُسُلَنَا بِالْبَيِّنَاتِ وَأَنزَلْنَا مَعَهُمُ الْكِتَابَ وَالْمِيزَانَ لِيَقُومَ النَّاسُ بِالْقِسْطِ

Indeed, we have sent messengers with clear signs, and with them we sent down our book, which is the criterion (judge between right and wrong), so that people are able to adhere to justice as a result (57:25)

The content of Islam

- When understanding any religion, it is important to distinguish what is within its scope and what is not.
- It is important to note that Islam is also sometimes used to imply the outer aspect of religion. A person who does certain acts is called a Muslim.
- However, the entire content of Islam has a scope, and it is comprised of two main content types:

Al-Hikmah

- The metaphysical and ethical basis of the worship prescribed by religion – matters of faith (beliefs) and morality.
- Remains the same for all prophets and their nations.
- It reminds us of the wisdom behind the law.

Al-Kitab (Law)

- Contains the laws (Shariah) suitable for the time, including rituals and limits.
- Changes due to evolution in human civilizations and societies.
- Current laws are based on the laws given to Prophet Ibrahim, and then sanctioned by Prophet Muhammad, which have been shaped into the Sunnah since then.

Al-Hikmah	Al-Kitab (Law)
• Worship Allah SWT alone	• Daily prayers and its procedure
• Don't consume other people's wealth unjustly	• Interest/Riba is outlawed
• Spend on the poor and in the path of Allah	• Pay your Zakah at the rate of X%
• Do not go near obscenity or adultery, it is an act of Satan	• 100 lashes for someone who commits adultery
• Do not follow Satan and consider him your open enemy	• Perform Hajj and its practices including stoning Satan

Why is understanding the wisdom behind any given law so important?

Al-Kitaab and Al-Hikmah

- Whenever Al-Kitaab and Al-Kitaab appeared together in the Quran, they encompassed the entire content of the religion.
- Some of the verses are presented below:

هُوَ الَّذِي بَعَثَ فِي الْأُمِّيِّينَ رَسُولًا مِنْهُمْ يَتْلُو عَلَيْهِمْ آيَاتِهِ وَيُزَكِّيهِمْ وَيُعَلِّمُهُمُ الْكِتَابَ وَالْحِكْمَةَ

It is He who has sent among the unlettered a Messenger from amongst themselves who recites to them His verses and purifies them, and [for this purpose] he instructs them in Shariah (the law) and in Hikmah (Faith and Morality). (62:2)

وَأَنْزَلَ اللَّهُ عَلَيْكَ الْكِتَابَ وَالْحِكْمَةَ وَعَلَّمَكَ مَا لَمْ تَكُنْ تَعْلَمُ ۚ وَكَانَ فَضْلُ اللَّهِ عَلَيْكَ عَظِيمًا

And God has revealed to you al-Kitab and al-Hikmah and in this manner taught you what you did not know before, and great is God's favor upon you. (4:113)

وَاذْكُرُوا نِعْمَتَ اللَّهِ عَلَيْكُمْ وَمَا أَنْزَلَ عَلَيْكُمْ مِنَ الْكِتَابِ وَالْحِكْمَةِ يَعِظُكُمْ بِهِ ۚ وَاتَّقُوا اللَّهَ وَاعْلَمُوا أَنَّ اللَّهَ بِكُلِّ شَيْءٍ عَلِيمٌ

And remember the favors He has bestowed upon you, and the al-Kitab and al-Hikmah which He has revealed to you, of which He instructs you, and keep fearing Allah, and know that He has knowledge of all things.(2:231)

- The word Al-Kitaab is used in many places in the Quran to refer to the law.
- In Surah Bani Israel (17), verses 22-39, God listed all matters of belief (in the one true God) and morality, and, in the end, called them the matters of *Al-Hikmah*.

ذَٰلِكَ مِمَّا أَوْحَىٰ إِلَيْكَ رَبُّكَ مِنَ الْحِكْمَةِ

..... these are from the counsels of wisdom which your Lord has revealed to you. (17:39)

Over time, people tend to overlook aspects of *Al-Hikmah* (wisdom) and pay more attention to *Al-Kitab* (the law). This reduces religion to mere rules, and the essence of those laws is lost.

Divine Books (content summary)

- The three major divine books that are still with us are Torah, the Gospel, and the Psalms. They were revealed on Prophet Mosa, Eisa, and Dawood, respectively.
- There is a major theme in every divine book, but the Quran is unique in that it encompasses all major themes in a single place.
- Since the Quran is the last revelation and is protected and preserved, it is the guardian over all books when it comes to understanding the religion.

Torah	Gospel	Psalm
is mostly law and practices	is full of wisdom, some history	is a collection of duas

Quran

Law, wisdom, duas, history

- God called the Quran 'Muhaymin' among other divine books, meaning the Guardian or Protector. All religious texts and other Divine Books must be understood in the light of the Quran, provided the Quran addresses that topic.

وَأَنزَلْنَا إِلَيْكَ الْكِتَابَ بِالْحَقِّ مُصَدِّقًا لِّمَا بَيْنَ يَدَيْهِ مِنَ الْكِتَابِ وَمُهَيْمِنًا عَلَيْهِ ۖ فَاحْكُم بَيْنَهُم بِمَا أَنزَلَ اللَّهُ ۖ وَلَا تَتَّبِعْ أَهْوَاءَهُمْ عَمَّا جَاءَكَ مِنَ الْحَقِّ

And [O Prophet!] We have revealed the Book with the truth, confirming it before it and standing as a guardian over it. Therefore, give judgment among them according to the guidance revealed by God and do not yield to their whims by swerving from the truth revealed to you. (5:48)

Objective of Islam

- The content of Islam is very closely related to its objective.
- Every instruction given in the Quran and Sunnah is for one objective: *Tazkiyah* (**purification** of the self).
- It demands that our beliefs and deeds be developed in the right direction that helps us attain **purification**.
- Our objective should be entering paradise, and according to the Quran, paradise is prepared for 'purified souls'.
- There is no instruction, teaching, practice, or law within Islam that is not targeted to achieve the objective of purification. If an instruction does not meet this criterion, it cannot be part of Islam.
- The picture below depicts that relationship.

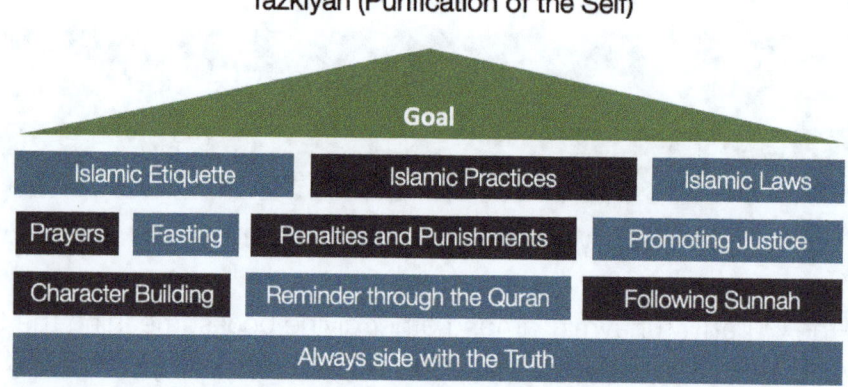

Tazkiyah (Purification of the Self)

Target	Instructions
Purification of **Soul**	Beliefs and worship rituals
Purification of **Food**	Dietary laws and nature's guidance
Purification of **Morals**	Guidance on morality and laws
Purification of **Body**	Laws and practices related to cleanliness

It is He who has sent among the unlettered a Messenger from amongst themselves who recites to them His verses and purifies them, and [for this purpose] he instructs them in Shariah (the law) and in Hikmah (Faith and Morality). (62:2)

Eeman – The inner aspect of Islam

- Islam sometimes signifies the outer aspect of the religion, which is manifested through practicing certain rituals like prayers, fasting, Hajj, etc.
- On the other hand, Eeman (faith) signifies the inner aspect of Islam, which is not easily manifest and usually remains in the heart of a Muslim, yet it shapes how we behave in our lives.
- The Foundation of Islam is upon the belief in **FIVE** things, which are the inner aspects called *Eeman.*
- Our Eeman is usually manifest through our attitude towards life and the actions that we take.

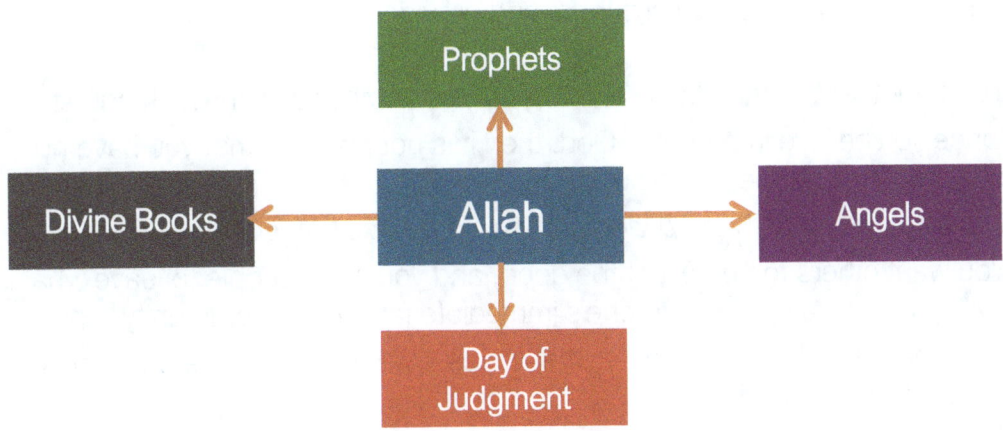

- Although as Muslims we believe in five things, in essence, it's all centered around the belief in Allah.
- What we must believe in can only come from Allah and His Prophets. No one else can guide us in what to believe.
- Similarly, no one can add ANYTHING to these five beliefs, because they will determine our fate on the Day of Judgment.

The Fate (Qada and Qadr)

- Another aspect that scholars include in the list of Eeman is fate (*Qadr*). *Qadr* means that Allah knows everything about the past, present, and future, including our lives, and it's all written in a Big Book.
- If you look carefully, it is actually part of the belief in Allah. It is one of the Attributes of Allah that He knows everything.

Requirements of Eeman

Righteous deeds

- Once you believe in one True God, then it is not possible that your actions are not righteous.
- These deeds result from a person's morals being purified and "healthy".
- Their bases and inclination towards them are in our nature, and collectively, they are admirable. We are all born good and want to be good.
- Shariah only urges us toward them and provides guidance to them.

Urging one another to truthfulness and urging one another to remain steadfast

- Once you believe in one True God, then it is not possible that you have no concern for other people around you.
- It is also termed as "*Amr bi al-maroof wa nahi an al-Munkar*".
- You want others to be part of the good, and you want people to leave what is evil. And it usually relates to one's immediate family and community.
- It distinguishes Islam from other theologies – we advise people on what is good and what is evil.

Contingent Requirements (Only when circumstances demand)

Migration to another land due to persecution

- This is required when it is difficult to comply with the basic teachings of Islam, and even to worship God or declare your beliefs.

Supporting the cause of Islam (Nusrah)

- This is required and is related to protecting and disseminating the message of Islam with whatever money/resources a person has.

Adhering to justice

- This is required when someone needs to make a judgment or give testimony. No emotions, vested interests, or biases should divert the person from being just in all worldly and religious matters.

- The Quran lists, in a few places, what we are supposed to believe to become a believer.

آمَنَ الرَّسُولُ بِمَا أُنْزِلَ إِلَيْهِ مِنْ رَبِّهِ وَالْمُؤْمِنُونَ كُلٌّ آمَنَ بِاللَّهِ وَمَلَائِكَتِهِ وَكُتُبِهِ وَرُسُلِهِ لَا

نُفَرِّقُ بَيْنَ أَحَدٍ مِنْ رُسُلِهِ ۚ وَقَالُوا سَمِعْنَا وَأَطَعْنَا ۖ غُفْرَانَكَ رَبَّنَا وَإِلَيْكَ الْمَصِيرُ

The Messenger has believed in what has been revealed to him by His Lord, and so do those who follow [him]. They all professed faith in **God**, His **angels**, His **books**, and His **messengers**. [They affirm:] "We do not discriminate between any of God's messengers," and they said: "We heard and have obeyed. Lord! We seek Your forgiveness, and [believe that on the Day of Judgment] to You shall we **return**." (2:285)

- In a famous hadith called Hadith-e-Jibrael, Prophet Muhammad said something like this:

أَنْ تُؤْمِنَ بِاللَّهِ وَمَلَائِكَتِهِ وَكُتُبِهِ وَرُسُلِهِ وَالْيَوْمِ الْآخِرِ وَتُؤْمِنَ بِالْقَدَرِ خَيْرِهِ وَشَرِّهِ

Eeman is that you believe in **God**, His **Angels**, His **Books**, His **Messengers**, the **Hereafter**, and the **good and evil fate** [ordained by your God].
(Sahih Muslim, the book of faith)

- The requirements of Eeman signify how a Muslim should live their life. Once we say that "we believe in Allah," then we sign an unwritten covenant with our Lord, and these requirements and conditions emerge from that covenant.
- The Quran described this minimum requirement of Eeman necessary for salvation in Surah Al-Asr.

وَ الْعَصْرِ إِنَّ الْإِنْسَانَ لَفِي خُسْرٍ

إِلَّا الَّذِينَ آمَنُوا وَ عَمِلُوا الصَّالِحَاتِ وَ تَوَاصَوْا بِالْحَقِّ ۙ وَ تَوَاصَوْا بِالصَّبْرِ

Time (historically from the time of Adam to Muhammad) bears witness that these people shall definitely be in a state of loss. Yes, except those who professed faith, did righteous deeds, and urged one another to the truth, and urged one another to remain steadfast on the truth. (103:1-3)

The correct religious attitude

- One might ask: What is the relationship between Eeman (inner aspect) and Islam (outer aspect)?
- Eeman should shape our Islam and lead to excellence in everything we do.
- In other words, the correct attitude that the follower of Islam should adopt is called *Ihsan*. *Ihsan* means to do something in the best possible way.
- This will only happen when your Eeman is strong.

- Although related to the instructions of our religion, this is usually required in every sphere of our lives.
- Excellence is 'doing the best possible way', which means the acts are carried out in a manner that a complete balance is maintained between their form and spirit.

- Prophet Muhammad said that when performing a religious act, consider yourself standing before God – this ultimately leads to sincerity in those acts.
- However, remember: strive for excellence, **not** perfection.

A Misunderstanding related to *Ihsan*

There is a misunderstanding among one school of thought in Islam that "*Ihsan* is a level that a person would achieve as a result of practicing religion and getting closer to Allah".

This is not true. It's an attitude towards the acts you do, not a level. One day you will do well; another day, you may not do as well.

How Ehsan is implemented in these examples with strong Eeman

- We must perform our Salah with gratitude and a sense of remembrance of Allah.
- We should give charity with sincerity, taking into account our current situation and financial circumstances.
- Treat your parents kindly, with love and gratitude.
- Sacrificing time and money when society hits a calamity to gain the pleasure of Allah.

Summarizing Eeman and Islam

- The following verses from the Quran and hadith capture Eeman and Islam beautifully.

وَمَن يَعْمَلْ مِنَ ٱلصَّـٰلِحَـٰتِ مِن ذَكَرٍ أَوْ أُنثَىٰ وَهُوَ مُؤْمِنٌ فَأُو۟لَـٰٓئِكَ يَدْخُلُونَ ٱلْجَنَّةَ وَلَا يُظْلَمُونَ نَقِيرًا ۝ لِلَّهِ وَهُوَ مُحْسِنٌ وَٱتَّبَعَ مِلَّةَ إِبْرَٰهِيمَ حَنِيفًا ۗ وَمَنْ أَحْسَنُ دِينًا مِّمَّنْ أَسْلَمَ وَجْهَهُ وَٱتَّخَذَ ٱللَّهُ إِبْرَٰهِيمَ خَلِيلًا

And whosoever does good works, whether men or women, and he or she is a believer, such will enter into paradise and they will not be wronged even to the extent of a speck on the date seed. And who has the better religion than the one who submits to God, such that he does I'hsan, and follows the faith of Abraham, who was devoted to [God]. (4:124-125)

Hadith-e-Jibrael

We were sitting with the Messenger of Allah; one day, a man appeared with very white clothes and black hair. There were no signs of travel on him, and we did not recognize him. He sat in front of the Prophet, rested his knees against his, and placed his hands on his thighs. The man said, "O Muhammad, tell me about Islam." The Prophet said, "Islam is to testify there is no God but Allah and that Muhammad is the Messenger of Allah, to establish prayer, to give charity, to fast the month of Ramadan, and to perform pilgrimage to the House if a way is possible." The man said, "You have spoken truthfully." We were surprised that he asked him and said he was truthful. He said, "Tell me about faith." The Prophet said, "Faith is to believe in Allah, his angels, his books, his messengers, the Last Day, and to believe in providence, its good and its evil." The man said, "You have spoken truthfully. Tell me about excellence." The Prophet said, "Excellence is to worship Allah as if you see him, for if you do not see Him, He surely sees you." The man said, "Tell me about the final hour." The Prophet said, "The one asked does not know more than the one asking." The man said, "Tell me about its signs." The Prophet said, "The slave girl will give birth to her mistress, and you will see barefoot, naked, and dependent shepherds compete in the construction of tall buildings." Then, the man returned, and I remained. The Prophet told me, "O Umar, do you know who he was?" I said, "Allah and His messenger know best." The Prophet said, "Verily, Gabriel came to teach you your religion."

Pick one well-known religion of your choice and compare it with Islam in the following concepts:

1. God or A Supreme Being
2. Key figure or personality
3. Life after death
4. Salvation – what is required at a minimum to be successful in life after death (if there is such a concept)
5. How life should be lived in this world to get closer to God
6. A book or any divinely inspired scripture
7. Main rituals
8. Importance of actions or deeds

Chapter 3

Final Message

This chapter introduces religion in general, the questions it seeks to answer, parallel philosophies, the Abrahamic religions, and how Islam stands out as the only true divine religion in the world.

The Need for Religion

General Definition of Religion

A belief concerning the <u>supernatural, sacred, or divine</u>, and the practices and institutions associated with such a belief.

- The need for religion rises from the fact that when we pay attention to our being and try to answer a few questions that human beings have been looking for an answer to since time immemorial.

Our being:

- Three things differentiate us from other creatures: moral sense, aesthetic sense, and intellect.
- They are manifested in every sphere of my life. For example, to satisfy our powerful aesthetic sense, we create and appreciate various forms of art. We observe a phenomenon and derive or conclude an unobservable phenomenon using our intellect.
- This a priori knowledge of appreciating art is within us and manifests in our work of art.

Our questions:

- I am certain that I am a created being, so who created me?
- How did I and this universe begin?
- Death is imminent, and the most puzzling question is: what is it?
- Is this life the beginning and the end?
- What happens when people die?
- Why is this universe so perfectly designed with precise math behind it?
- Why do I share such a strong moral sense with everyone?

Note: Any theory, philosophy, or thought that does not claim <u>a metaphysical source</u> is considered outside of this definition. For example, Atheism may be a movement or 'ism', but cannot be treated as a religion, regardless of people practicing it like a religion.

Human needs and quests

- Humans have many fundamental needs that they have often addressed using their intellect and collective ability as a society,

Human Need	Answer
Sickness and diseases	Medical science and medicines
Injustice, crime, misuse of free will	Governments and Criminal Justice System
Ease of trade	Banks, Financial systems
Relationships and socialization	Marriage, social clubs, gatherings, parties
Defend against aggression	Arms, Weapons, Missiles, Fighter jets

- Similarly, when it comes to answering the big questions, humans have sought out philosophies and dogmas.

Human Need	Answer
Unanswered questions about my existence and purpose	Religion and philosophies

Who has the answers?

- All philosophies and religions that humans have "founded" so far are simply in the pursuit of answering these fundamental questions.
- The need for religion always sprang from these questions.
- Finding the right, most logical answer and gaining access to the TRUTH have been the efforts of human beings.
- Revealed religions say that God Himself provided the answers and must be looked at as one answer among many.

Among all the answers, we must find out which answer **makes the most sense and is closest to our natural inclinations.**

Revealed vs 'Other' Religions

- In the world, there are only two types of religions. If anything does not have a metaphysical source, then it can be called anything but religion.

- The picture below shows the major divisions and the types of religions:

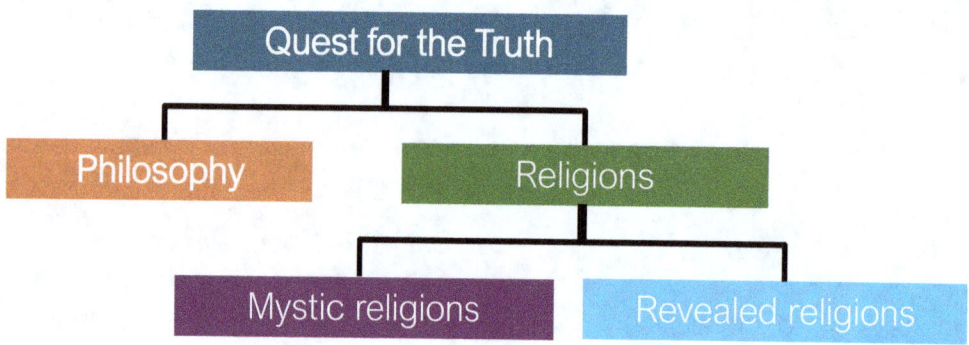

Difference between Mystic and Revealed religion

Mystic religions
A human being wants to establish a 'communication channel' with the Ultimate Truth through certain practices and tries to get answers

Revealed religions
God selects someone from human beings to provide guidance to the Ultimate Truth with the answers

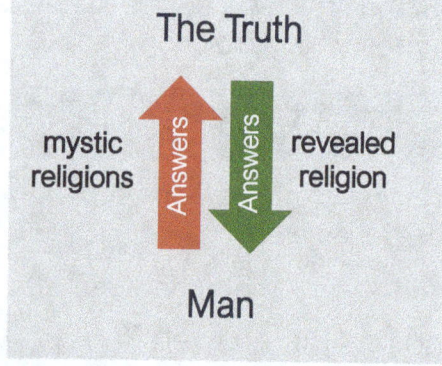

Sufism in Islam

- Sufism emerged in the 8th century as an ascetic and mystical movement, partly in response to the growing Fiqhi traditions of the early Islamic empire.

- It claims the mystical dimension of Islam, focused on the inner, spiritual journey to achieve a direct, personal experience of God's love and presence.

- It claims to emphasize purifying the heart, transcending the ego, and seeking a deeper connection with the divine.

Revealed vs 'Other' Religions

- The following tables compare Philosophy and two types of religions. Mystic religions are also religions because they claim a divine source.

Philosophy	• Reason and intellect are at the center of everything in pursuit of the answers. • Greek philosophy plays a critical role in this branch. • Modern philosophies, including science, continue to find the answers. • Notable figures in this branch include Aristotle, Plato, Socrates, Confucius, Hume, Kant, and Descartes.
Mystic Religions	• Belief in a Deity or Absolute Truth. • 'Becoming part of that Truth' is the ultimate goal. • Access to the Deity and 'enlightenment' is possible through contemplation, self-surrender, and mystical practices. • It has roots in almost every religion, but Buddhism represents it best.
Revealed Religions	• Claim a Divine Source. • The source of guidance and instruction on various matters of life is revelation from a Supreme Being. • Concepts of Prophets, Angels, Divine Books, the Hereafter, and other unseen matters that cannot be understood on their own. • **Examples:** Islam, Judaism, and Christianity, and their various branches.

- The Quran claims that **only** Allah allows and decides whom He should communicate with.

وَمَا كَانَ لِبَشَرٍ أَنْ يُكَلِّمَهُ اللَّهُ إِلَّا وَحْيًا أَوْ مِنْ وَرَاءِ حِجَابٍ أَوْ يُرْسِلَ رَسُولًا فَيُوحِيَ بِإِذْنِهِ مَا يَشَاءُ ۚ إِنَّهُ عَلِيٌّ حَكِيمٌ

It is not fitting for a man that Allah should speak to him except by inspiration (in the heart), from behind a veil, or by sending a messenger to reveal, with Allah's permission, what Allah wills: for He is Most High Most Wise. (42:51)

"I am spiritual but not religious" group

What is this group?

- A growing number of people claim they are "good people" or "spiritual" people, but do not believe in any 'organized religion' or at least not practicing the religion they originally associated with
- They are also known as "unaffiliated".
- Their claim is that they don't have to follow any 'organized religion' as long as they are 'good'.
- This includes a large swath of people – some do not believe in any higher power or God-like figure, while others do.
- Atheists, Agnostics, "Nothing in particular," Naturalists, so-called Christians and Muslims, and more
- Everyone is "spiritual" or "good" in his/her own terms, with the meaning only he/she understand.
- What attracts them is the emphasis on individual freedom, subjective experience, and open-mindedness.

Root of the problem

- There are many reasons for this group's growth.
- First of all, the 'religious people' tried to 'solve' world problems through religion, which religion never came to solve in the first place.
- They presented religion as an 'alternative' to solving the world's problems, such as economic or political issues.
- Secondly, the non-religious people are intimidated by the behavior and the attitude of religious people, especially leaders of organized religions.
- They feel aversion to rigid dogma (strict rules), authority, and perceived hypocrisy, which often drives people away from religious institutions.
- Religious institutions carry a history of abuse, scandal, and conflict, such as the sex abuse crisis in the Catholic Church or religiously motivated violence. Many find spirituality an appealing alternative because it is not tied to a potentially corrupt or hypocritical organization.
- In summary, **non-affiliated life is a reaction**, not a thoughtful conclusion.
- "Freedom" of choosing a lifestyle becomes more relevant and appealing.
- It is much easier to be "spiritual" than "religious" – it's cool.

Dangers of a-religious life

- Negating any organized religion means negating a LOT.
- In reality, when a-religious people say they are "good," they are "piggybacking" on religious goodness (from human and religious history) without carrying the baggage of religion.
- No organized religion implies:
    - No God
    - No accountability
    - No ultimate justice
    - No objective morality
    - No higher purpose
    - No significance of human values
    - No hope
    - No motivation to do good

Things to consider

- Believing there is no organized religion is a recipe for existential disaster, as shown above.
- This leads to complacency and self-centeredness.
- No common societal aims or goals.
- Being "good" is subjective and can lead to egotism.
- Truth and God's Will become irrelevant.
- A sense of 'accountability' before God is seriously lacking.
- People can blend Buddhism, Taoism, Judaism, Sufism, and other beliefs to "make" their own. The objectivity is lost.
- Unknowingly connotate that God is 'irresponsible' and never communicates to us after creating us.

Identify some benefits of non-affiliation with any organized religion.

Atheism

- Sometimes researchers group atheists, agnostics, humanists, freethinkers, unaffiliated/nones into the atheist category.
- Many people do not believe in a god but still do not call themselves atheists.
- A survey from University of Kentucky psychologists Will Gervais and Maxine Najle found that as many as 26% of Americans may be atheists ("maybe" indicates that all sorts of people are included in this survey).
- The actual number of 'convinced atheists' is way smaller. It is more correct to say that affiliation with organized religions is declining.
- In his article "Unbelief Comes in Shades", Phil Zuckerman, a sociologist specializing in secular studies, has shown through research that non-religious people are not a monolithic group but a very diverse group.

Main Argument

- "Atheists don't have to give any arguments on atheism because the burden of proof is on the one who believes in something positively."

Specific Arguments to justify their position

- There is inadequate scientific evidence for God's existence – there is no persuasive "reason" to believe in God.
- An all-good and all-powerful God and pain/suffering/injustice cannot coexist, also called the problem of evil.
- There are so many "versions" of God; all cannot be true at the same time.
- There is incoherence in many religious concepts, like free will and an All-Knowing God.
- As natural sciences advance and explain things, the need for the supernatural diminishes.
- Historical "evidence" suggests that any belief in God emerged from the psychological and sociological factors/needs of human beings, natural forces, finding comfort, etc.

How can you refute: "Atheists don't have to give any arguments on atheism because the burden of proof is on the one who believes in something positively."

Is Atheism really growing?

- We often hear this statement that Atheism is growing fast. But factually, it is not true.

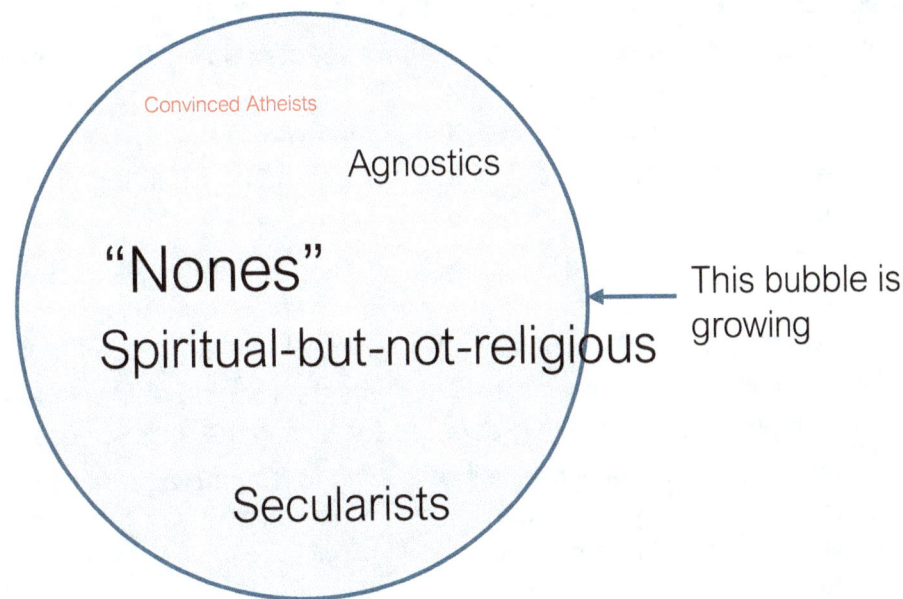

- So the current statement is that affiliation with organized religions is declining.

- As a sociologist specializing in secular studies, Phil Zuckerman has shown through research that non-religious people are not a monolithic group. Many groups come under this umbrella, and convinced atheists are a minority. According to him, the "Unbelief" comes in shades.

- While the broader "nones" category is growing, strict self-identified atheism may be growing more slowly or remaining stable. In the U.S., while the non-religious population is rising, some estimates place the strictly self-identified atheist population at a much lower percentage (0.7%–1.6%) than the overall "nones" segment.

- Barna research indicates that younger generations, such as Gen Z, are much less likely to identify with a religion than previous generations. However, other studies have reported that some in Gen Z are turning toward religion, potentially leveling off the decline of Christianity. However, none of these stats indicate that they are now tuned toward atheism.

Analysis of the arguments

Argument#1: Scientific Evidence

- Science, based on observations, is just one source of knowledge. God is outside the physical universe, so direct observation of Him is impossible.
- On the other hand, inference is a fundamental aspect of scientific reasoning, enabling scientists to move from raw data and observations to meaningful conclusions that advance our understanding of the world. Examples:
  - Observation: The coastlines of South America and Africa fit together like pieces of a puzzle.
  - Reliable Inference: These continents were once connected as part of a supercontinent.
  - Observation: Global temperatures have been rising over the past century.
  - Reliable Inference: Human activities, such as the burning of fossil fuels, are contributing to the increase in greenhouse gases in the atmosphere.
- Science lacks answers to many realities of this world that are as real as physical things—morals, personality, why things happen in a certain way, our conscience, innate knowledge of good and evil, etc.

Argument#2: The problem of evil

- Life is created as a test because of the free will granted to us by God. If He intervenes, the grand scheme of the test will fail.

Argument#3: Versions of God

- God's religion has always been Islam since the time of the first human being. It is humans who corrupted the message and introduced innovation in God's religion.

Argument#4: Incoherence in religion

- The seemingly incoherent concepts can be easily understood in the light of the grand scheme God presented in the Quran.

Argument#5: The development of natural sciences

- The development of natural sciences only explains the phenomena behind natural processes. It does not negate the existence of God.

Argument#6: Historical "evidence"

- Written human history dates back only 5,000 to 6,000 years. However, humans' actual history can be traced back millions of years. We cannot infer the origins of the concept of God from 5000-year-old history.

Religion and Science

- There is no conflict between religion and science because their realms are completely different.
- The conflict is created by a group of people who want to reject God or religion.
- Science does not answer any of the following questions, which are very critical to us as human beings, and we have been searching for answers.
- It's only religion that answers these questions to some extent satisfactorily.

Questions	Science Answers
Our purpose in life and on this earth?	X
What is death and why do we die?	X
What happens to "me" after my death?	X
Where did I get my conscience from?	X
Why is there universal good and evil?	X
What is sleep and why do I see dreams?	X
Why is there a comprehensive harmony in the universe?	X
Where did this universe come from?	X
Where does mother-child love come from?	X

Relevance of religion in modern times

- One of the biggest reasons this question has risen in modern times is that today's religious people are trying to present religion in comparison to modern philosophies and science.
- If any of the questions listed in the table before are relevant to us, then religion is relevant.
- Science has emerged from the belly of philosophy, a human endeavor, and has attempted to answer these questions, but it can never answer them.
- So far, only religion answers these questions most logically, and this premise is what makes it remain relevant across time and ages.
- If, at any point in time, other philosophies, including science, can answer these questions, we should stop and analyze.

Islam, Judaism, and Christianity

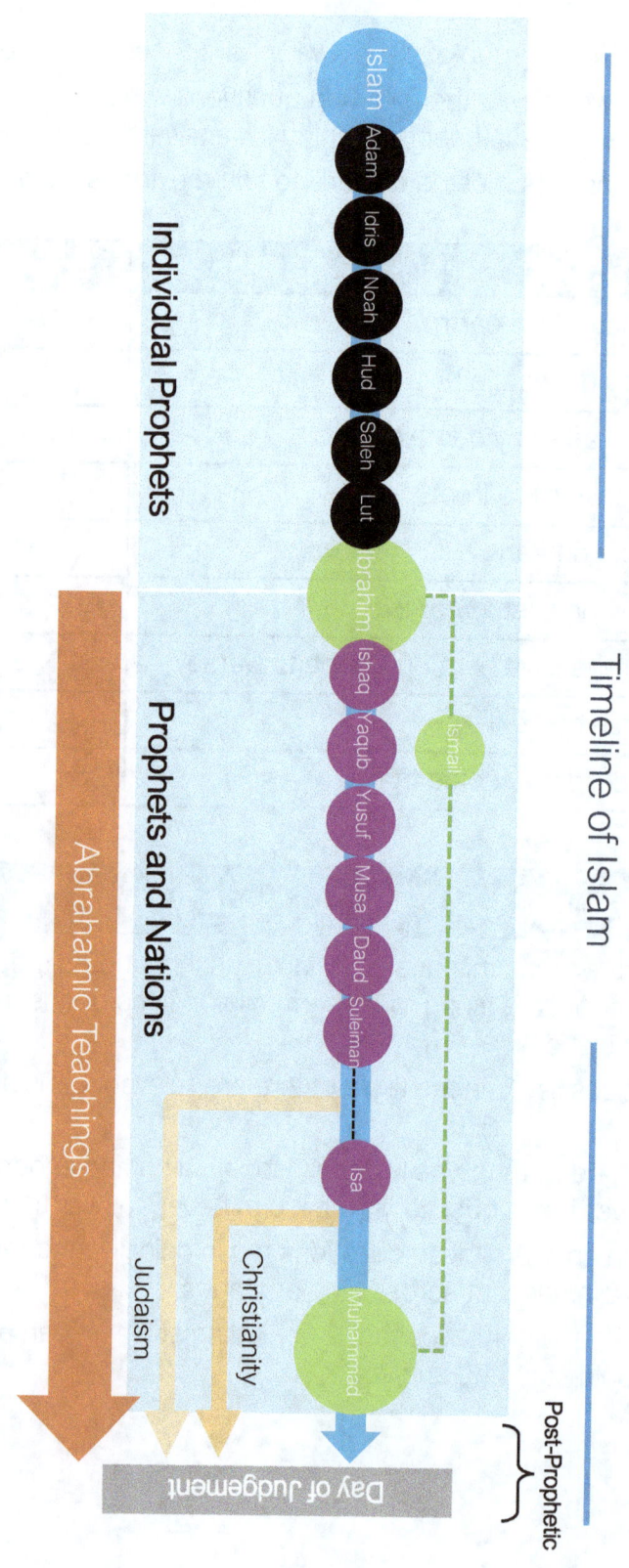

Abrahamic religion(s) and Islam

- The history of Islam and its timeline are presented in the previous page.
- Islam started with the first conscious human being on earth, and Adam was the first Prophet of God.
- Up until Prophet Ibrahim, only individual prophets were sent to nations.
- After Prophet Ibrahim, this responsibility was shared by two nations: first, the Children of Israel and then the Children of Ismael.
- God asked Prophet Ibrahim to settle one of his sons in the land of Palestine and the other in the land of Hijaz (Arabia).
- Today's Muslims, Jews, and Christians have a common root – the legacy of Ibrahim.
- Jews, due to their tribal and race superiority complex (chosen nation of God), and association with Musa, tried to interpolate the scriptures and distanced Ismail and his progeny from Ibrahim. They never accepted Muhammad as a prophet because they were 'keen' to receive the last prophet from among them.
- They did not accept Jesus either and tried to kill him.
- Christians, due to their preaching and interaction with Romans and their pagan beliefs, exaggerated the personality of Jesus and introduced beliefs that were more appealing to Pagans. They, as a nation, did not accept Prophet Muhammad despite being foretold in their scriptures.
- From an Islamic point of view, Judaism and Christianity are misguided groups of Islam. God never sent any other religion other than Islam on Earth. Islam is never associated with a group of people.
- Now, until the Day of Judgment, the Quran is the ultimate source of Islam.
- Similarly, the two nations, the Children of Israel and the Children of Ismael, will continue to be signs of God's religion on earth. If they uphold the Quran and its teachings, they will prosper among all nations, and if they continue to create divisions among Muslims and do not uphold the teachings of the Quran, they will suffer at the hands of other nations.

Why Islam is the ONLY divine religion

The following are the reasons, unique to Islam, that make it the ONLY divine religion today. Even a non-Muslim would agree to these because these are the facts, not claims:

1. The FINAL practices and religious texts exist in their original form in the light of history, with no signs of alteration.
2. Its final book is a verbatim speech of God with nothing added by Prophet Muhammad.
3. The only religion that claims to be given from the first human until the day of judgment, which is a very plausible argument, and God must not change His mind about religion.
4. Teachings are closest to the nature of human beings.
5. Quran – a living miracle given to Muhammad, a Bedouin, over a period of 23 years, with no sign of progression in thought and message, with zero inconsistency.
6. Prophet Muhammad never claimed authorship of any writings before the Quran. In his first 40 years, he spent among the Quraish, where poetry was very common.
7. The Quran was revealed over 23 years, yet there are no inconsistencies in its message, unlike any book written by a human being.
8. Prophet Muhammad predicted certain results at the beginning of his mission, which came true exactly as he said in less than 20 years
9. Messengers demonstrated multiple times a manifestation of God's judgment in this world – the last one happened 1400 years ago
10. Basic human values that the world is struggling with today were part of Islam 1400 years ago – human rights is just one example (see the next page for more).
11. Islam is the only religion that promotes deliberation and questioning in faith and teachings.

Had it been from anyone other than Allah, they would have found in it many inconsistencies (4:82)

Write a short survey that analyzes the key reasons and arguments people give for leaving the organized religion with which they have been associated their entire lives. Look at the argument, good or bad, from their point of view, as they use it as a justification for the decision they have made.

Analyze each reason and evaluate them on merit, and present a counterargument if you have any.

Chapter 4

Faith in Islam

This chapter introduces the concept of Faith (Eeman) in Islam and its relationship to our actions and deeds.

The role of Faith (*Eeman*) in religion

- The word "***Eeman***" comes from the root word for "safety" – in a comprehensive way, *Eeman* safeguards from the corruption of the heart from diseases, misdeeds that our limbs can commit, delusion in this world, the punishment of God in the hereafter, despair, and sadness, devil and corruption of the soul, etc

- *Eeman* is not single-dimensional – our intuition, senses and observation, intellectual reasoning, inference, historical evidence, the testimony of prophets and messengers, the consensus of humanity, etc., all corroborate with faith

- **Our Faith in Allah:** It is accepting Al-Mighty God with the certitude of the heart through strong conviction, which exists with all the conditions and effects of humility, trust, and acknowledgment. One who surrenders his/her heart and mind in such a condition is called Mu'min (Believer). Words and actions should testify to it.

- The Foundation of Islam is upon the belief in <u>FIVE</u> things: God, Prophets, Hereafter, Books, and Angels.

- Anyone who professes faith with his/her tongue is a Muslim. On the other hand, Faith is not static; it grows stronger and weaker inside someone's heart.

- The Quran states that there should be no compulsion in religion, or in other words, faith.

Islam does not promote "blind faith"

There is a common misconception that "Islam demands blind faith and discourages its adherents from questioning."

- There is <u>no</u> concept of blind faith in Islam. By contrast, the Quran constantly invites its readers to ponder, contemplate, and reason about the core matters of belief, i.e., belief in God and related matters.

- The Quran demands "*Eeman bi Al-Ghaib*" – Faith in the unseen through intellectual reasoning without insisting on seeing it.

- Eeman bi Al-Ghaib does not mean to act without thinking or pondering matters of faith.

- However, as human beings, we have limits on what we can comprehend. The Quran asks us not to follow matters of faith we cannot comprehend. For e.g., angels. It makes sense that one would believe in angels, but there is no way we can comprehend their nature or anything related to them.

Faith in God is a 'word of purity.'

- The Quran describes strong belief in God as a pure word of faith that bears its fruits.

أَلَمْ تَرَ كَيْفَ ضَرَبَ ٱللَّهُ مَثَلاً كَلِمَةً طَيِّبَةً كَشَجَرَةٍ طَيِّبَةٍ أَصْلُهَا ثَابِتٌ وَفَرْعُهَا فِى ٱلسَّمَآءِ تُؤْتِى أُكُلَهَا كُلَّ حِينٍ بِإِذْنِ رَبِّهَا وَيَضْرِبُ ٱللَّهُ ٱلْأَمْثَالَ لِلنَّاسِ لَعَلَّهُمْ يَتَذَكَّرُونَ

Have you not reflected on how God has mentioned the example of the **word of purity**? Its example is like that of a pure tree with deep roots in the earth, and branches spread in the sky; it yields its fruit every season by God's directive. [This is a parable of the pure word], and God mentions such parables to men so that they may take heed. (Surah Ibrahim:24-25)

- "Word of Purity" refers to the word or declaration of Faith (Eeman), which is "La Ilaha Illallah (There is no God but Allah)".
- When Faith in God is deeply and firmly implanted in human nature, it is not like a plant sprouting from dung with no root, and a slight calamity can uproot it like the word of Disbelief. It has firm and deeply set roots so that even if a storm passes upon it (all types of trials of knowledge and action), it is not even slightly disturbed.
- By comparing the word of faith to such a tree, the Quran first makes evident that its roots are not only deeply and firmly implanted in human nature but also that it is the most highly valued by God. In other words, the status it occupies in the heavens and earth is unparalleled.
- The second reality that is explained is that it receives nourishment and strength from within human nature and from providence as well. This always keeps it lush and healthy.
- The blessings and benefits a believer bestows on his own life and, through it, on others who, in some way, come into contact with him, are akin to a tall, shady tree that benefits everyone under it.

Quran promotes thinking and pondering

Numerous verses in the Quran promote reflection and contemplation, contrary to the common perception about Islam that it promotes blind faith. A few examples are presented below:

These people remember Allah while standing or sitting or [lying] on their sides and **ponder over the creation of the heavens and the earth**, [saying], "Our Lord, You did not create this without any purpose. (3:191)

An example of this worldly life is rain. We sent it down from the sky; then, thick vegetation sprouted from the earth because of it – that which humans and animals also eat. Then the earth became lush, beautifying itself, and the inhabitants of the earth thought they were in complete control of it. Suddenly, our verdict came over it [at some time] by night or by day. Then We chopped it to the ground in such a manner as if nothing was there yesterday. This is how we explain our verses **to those who ponder.** (10:24)

And He has subjected to you whatever is in the heavens and earth – all from Him. Indeed, these are **signs for people who reflect.** (45:13)

And of His signs is that He created for you from yourselves mates that you may find happiness and tranquility in them, and He placed between you affection and mercy. Indeed, these are **signs for people who ponder** (30:21)

Allah takes the souls at the time of their death, and for those who do not die, [He takes] them during their sleep. Then, He keeps those for which He has decreed death and releases the others for a specified term. Indeed, these are **signs for people who reflect.** (39:42)

Why can't God make things easy for us by showing Himself?

Relationship between Faith and Actions

- The Quran paired faith and righteous deeds hundreds of times to show their mutual dependence.
- Pure faith in the Almighty is a prerequisite for accepting righteous deeds – according to the Quran, deeds have no basis without it.
- As a quality of a believer, every virtue must emanate from Faith.
- According to the Quran, neither faith alone nor righteous deeds alone would help on the Day of Judgment.
- Words and deeds provide proof for the faith hidden in the heart:
    - Speaking the truth, speaking gently, saying kind words, and becoming an advocate of justice.
    - Charity, security, and safety for others, modesty, respect for elders, kindness to neighbors, and generosity towards guests.
    - Constantly practicing faith through knowledge (remembering God through reading His revelation and witnessing His signs in this world) and actions keep it strong.

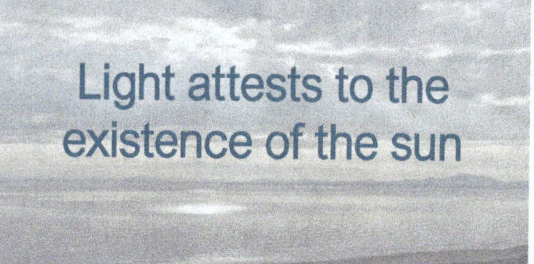

- The relationship between faith in the heart and the actions of the limbs is beautifully described in the hadith below:

When an adulterer commits Zina, he is not a believer at that time; when a thief commits theft, he is not a believer at that time; and when a drinker consumes liquor, he is not a believer at that time (Sahih Muslim: 45, 202)

- Meaning, how is it even possible that someone accepts Allah as their Lord and then commits these evil deeds?

Faith and Actions

- Similarly, the Quran beautifully describes how faith and action are interrelated.

إِنَّمَا ٱلْمُؤْمِنُونَ ٱلَّذِينَ إِذَا ذُكِرَ ٱللَّهُ وَجِلَتْ قُلُوبُهُمْ وَإِذَا تُلِيَتْ عَلَيْهِمْ ءَايَٰتُهُۥ زَادَتْهُمْ إِيمَٰنًا وَعَلَىٰ رَبِّهِمْ يَتَوَكَّلُونَ ٱلَّذِينَ يُقِيمُونَ ٱلصَّلَوٰةَ وَمِمَّا رَزَقْنَٰهُمْ يُنفِقُونَ أُو۟لَٰٓئِكَ هُمُ ٱلْمُؤْمِنُونَ حَقًّا لَّهُمْ دَرَجَٰتٌ عِندَ رَبِّهِمْ وَمَغْفِرَةٌ وَرِزْقٌ كَرِيمٌ

True believers are those whose hearts are filled with awe at the mention of God, and when His revelations are recited before them, <u>their faith grows stronger</u>, and they are those who put their trust in their Lord alone, are diligent in their prayer, and spend [in Our cause] what We have given them. Such are the true believers. For them, the priorities are ranked before God, forgiveness, and respectable sustenance. (Surah Anfal:2-4)

- Similarly, the Quran painted a picture of deeds not backed by pure faith in God.

مَّثَلُ ٱلَّذِينَ كَفَرُوا۟ بِرَبِّهِمْ أَعْمَٰلُهُمْ كَرَمَادٍ ٱشْتَدَّتْ بِهِ ٱلرِّيحُ فِى يَوْمٍ عَاصِفٍ لَّا يَقْدِرُونَ مِمَّا كَسَبُوا۟ عَلَىٰ شَىْءٍ ذَٰلِكَ هُوَ ٱلضَّلَٰلُ ٱلْبَعِيدُ

The deeds of people who disbelieve in the Almighty are **like ashes subjected to severe wind** on a stormy day. They shall gain nothing from what they do. This is straying far into error. (Surah Ibrahim:18)

وَٱلَّذِينَ كَفَرُوٓا۟ أَعْمَٰلُهُمْ كَسَرَابٍۭ بِقِيعَةٍ يَحْسَبُهُ ٱلظَّمْآنُ مَآءً حَتَّىٰٓ إِذَا جَآءَهُۥ لَمْ يَجِدْهُ شَيْـًٔا وَوَجَدَ ٱللَّهَ عِندَهُۥ فَوَفَّىٰهُ حِسَابَهُۥ وَٱللَّهُ سَرِيعُ ٱلْحِسَابِ

And as for the disbelievers, their deeds are **like a mirage in a desert**. The thirsty thought that it was water [leaped towards it] until he found nothing when he came near it: He found God there. Then He took his account, and swift is God in taking account. (Surah Nur:39)

Consider a few life situations where having faith or no faith can make a significant difference, and compare the actions.

Chapter 5

Beliefs in Islam

This is a very important chapter that details Islam's core beliefs. In the course of explanation, it also evaluates other concepts related to religion.

Creator Debate

- Before we talk about the belief in God in Islam, let's look at the bigger picture.
- There is a common understanding that Atheists do not believe in the existence of a creator. This is not correct. The correct statement would be that Atheists do not believe in the existence of a Creator God as a person who interacts with human beings.
- Undoubtedly, this is our daily observation that we are **created beings,** and this universe is created.
- The debate is about who the Creator is. For the creator of this universe, there are only two possibilities:

Universe has a Creator	OR	Universe itself is the Creator

- There is no third possibility that exists today.
- Atheists simply believe that this universe has the potential to create itself, including energy, matter, life in matter, and consciousness in matter.
- The most widely accepted theory, called the Big Bang theory, is that the universe began about 13.8 billion years ago from an extremely hot, dense point (a singularity), not as an explosion in space, but as an expansion of space.
- Science is not certain about the origin of that "singularity," and the Big Bang is considered the beginning of everything, including time and space.
- On the other hand, Muslims believe that the Universe has a Creator.
- As soon as you get into the Creator debate, the following question is asked:

Q: Who created the Creator?

A. He is not a creation

The concept of God

Source of belief in God

- Recognition of an Almighty (a Supreme Being) is innate in human nature.
- That's why the concept of God is never a 'strange' concept for any human being and always appears to answer a natural need within them.
- That concept of God may be a mythological god or a supernatural force, but it exists.
- The Quran alluded to the reason why human beings have such a powerful instinct for a Creator.

وَإِذْ أَخَذَ رَبُّكَ مِنْ بَنِى ءَادَمَ مِن ظُهُورِهِمْ ذُرِّيَّتَهُمْ وَأَشْهَدَهُمْ عَلَىٰ أَنفُسِهِمْ أَلَسْتُ بِرَبِّكُمْ قَالُواْ بَلَىٰ
شَهِدْنَآ أَن تَقُولُواْ يَوْمَ ٱلْقِيَٰمَةِ إِنَّا كُنَّا عَنْ هَٰذَا غَٰفِلِينَ

And remember when your Lord brought forth from the loins of the progeny of Adam, their children, and made them testify against themselves. He said: **"Am I not your Lord?"** They replied: "We bear witness that You are." This We did lest you should say on the Day of Judgement: "We had no knowledge of that" (Surah Aaraf:172)

- The above incident, called the **Incident of the Pledge**, as the Quran puts it, caused the recognition of a Supreme Power (God) to be stamped on the human heart and ingrained in the soul.
- However, the incident is erased from memory so that this life may be a trial. This is similar to the incident of our birth, which we can never recall, but we still recognize the fact that we were born from a mother's womb.

- There are many other things besides the concept of a divine God that are ingrained in us, including the concept of good and evil and an understanding of shapes, distances, quantity, etc.
- According to the Quran, this inner testimony about God is so powerful and indisputable that God will hold the person accountable for His Lordship.
- However, this matter remains between God and the person because we don't know what's inside a person's heart.

God is a human need

- It is interesting to note that humans have a need within them (an inner world), and they have something outside (exists even in its crude form) that meets that inner need.
- People who believe in science claim that we evolved based on what was in the outer world. However, it's the other way. God has placed everything that a human being and other creatures need.
- Some examples are given below:

Need inside a human being	What meets the needs
Thirst	Water
Hunger	Food
Love and Care	Parents and relatives
Sexual desire & need	Opposite gender, marriage
Socialization	Society, friends, people
Aesthetics	Art, Beauty, Creativity
Rest, peace, tranquility	Home, Night, Sleep

- Similarly:

Desire to worship, big questions, sense of purpose, justice, helplessness, goodness	GOD

God is a <u>fundamental belief</u> that is found in our **Fitrah** (original disposition)

Pick one of the topics above, investigate, and write a small essay on what evolutionary biologists say about their origin. Also include fundamental morality and the need for God in the list.

Evidence for GOD

- The convergence of evidence occurs when multiple independent sources of data or evidence all point to the same conclusion. In this case, the strength of that conclusion increases exponentially.
- That's exactly what happens when we look at the evidence of God.

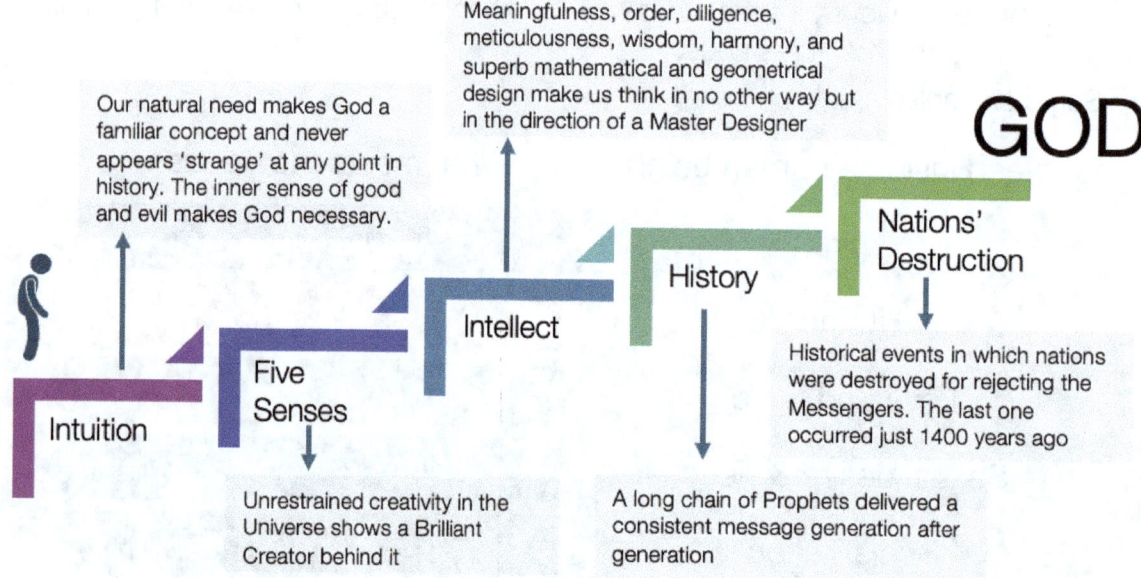

A slight contemplation on the existence of God reveals:

1. It's the only concept shared by the entire humanity from time immemorial. History is unaware of any time when the concept of God or god(s) did not exist. From time immemorial, the concept has existed in one form or the other.
2. It's like the thirst inside, when it finds complete compatibility with the water outside.
3. Unrestrained Creativity, meaningfulness, and order in the universe show a brilliant Creator.
4. Its diligence and meticulousness are stunning, and it possesses great wisdom and harmony.
5. It shows a superb mathematical and geometrical design.
6. The life events and occurrences are completely compatible with the concept of a test or trial that God told us we are in.
7. We all want Justice that we mostly don't get in this life.
8. The chain of Prophets and Messengers delivered a uniform, consistent message from the first Prophet, Adam.
9. Events that occurred among past nations. They were destroyed for rejecting messengers.
10. And finally, the miraculous book of the Quran is with us.

GOD (Allah)

Belief in GOD

- Knowing that human beings have been looking for answers, God categorically declared that the mystery of this universe cannot be solved without looking through the light of God.

- That does not mean we should not explore this universe. Exploring the universe and believing in God are mutually exclusive; neither should hinder the other.

- However, God demands that, for someone to benefit from the guidance of the Quran and the Messengers, they should first appreciate the inner guidance (in the form of intuition) that God gives them.

- That inner guidance must not be corrupted with biases and opinions that are already formed before coming to the Quran.

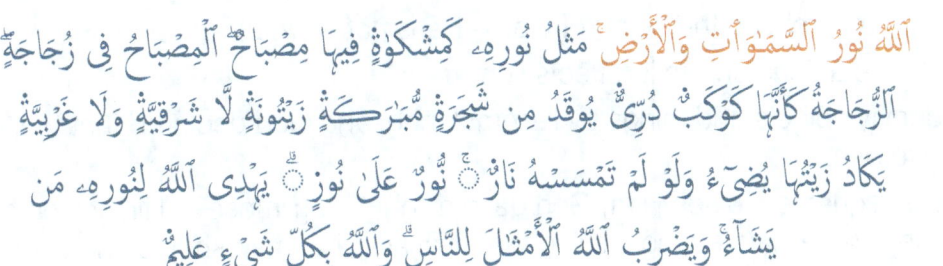

[Belief in] Allah is the light of the heavens and the earth! [In the heart of a person] the similitude of His light is like a niche in which there is a lamp – the lamp is in a glass, the glass as if it were a brilliant star – that is being kindled by the oil of a blessed olive tree that is neither of the eastern nor of the western [side]: its oil would all but light up, even though no fire touched it. Light upon light! Allah guides to His light whomever He wishes. [This is a similitude]. And Allah strikes these similitudes [to guide] people. [He deals with each person the way he deserves it]. And Allah has knowledge of everything. (Surah Nur:35)

The Real Question

The real question should NOT be: "Does God Exist?"

The real question should be: What reasons does one have to reject God's existence?

His Being

- After believing in God, the first natural question that comes to our mind is "how is He?"
- God knows that we can never find the answer to this question so in the Quran He declared:

There is NOTHING like Him (Shoora:11)

- No mind can comprehend the being of God – He is not a creation.
- Eyes cannot see a thing unless it reflects light.
- Also, we identify objects and things by resemblance, and God declared that there is nothing like Him.
- When Moses requested to see Him, God gave a lightning glimpse of Himself on a mountain, and Moses fainted, conveying the message that man should know his limitations when grappling with the nature of being of God. Even mountains, the most solid and mightiest structure on earth, cannot bear the slightest vision of God.
- Humans are so limited in their sensory and biological capabilities that even a slight change in the distance between the Sun and Earth can make life impossible for them.
- Believers are promised sight of Him (in whatever capacity He allows) on the Day of Judgment as a gift from Him.

 *ALLAH* (Al-ILAH) – this name has been used throughout Arab history as a remnant of the Abrahamic religion **and** is used by Arabic-speaking Christians and Jews as well as by Muslims. This is not the personal name of God, but the name the Arabs used, so God adopted it in the Quran. The Quran says that we can call Him by any good name.

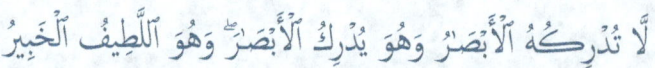

No eyes can comprehend Him, though He comprehends all eyes. He is subtle and all-knowing. (Surah Anaam:103)

We know God through His attributes

- We can comprehend His attributes to some extent—we possess them.
- Knowledge, mercy, power, providence, wisdom, kindness, generosity, forgiveness, patience, etc.
- Human beings possess the consciousness of their own self; that's why they can comprehend these attributes.
- Only people who ponder and reflect can realize this, and if they forget, God's guidance is always there to remind.
- People who reflect on themselves and what's around them (both are required) can testify to the fact that God is not merely the first cause but manages affairs with intention, knowledge, and infinite wisdom.
- In the Quran, God mentioned that the universe, including human existence, is the consequence of:

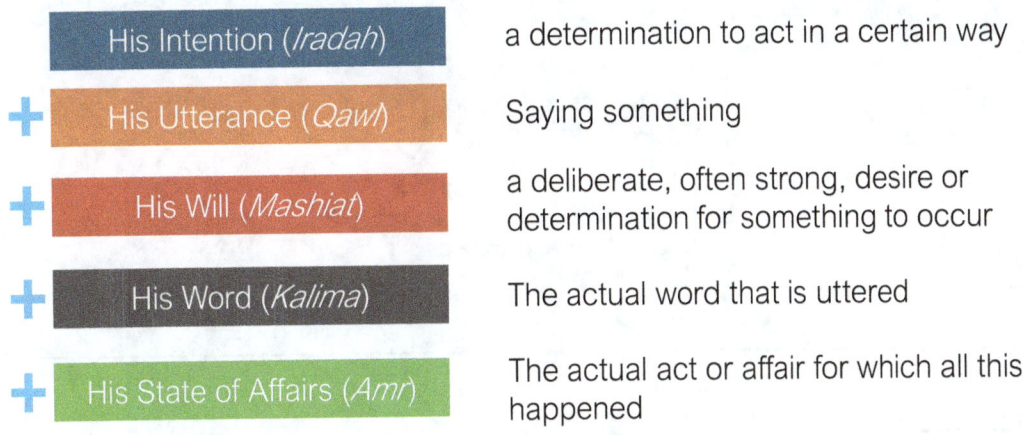

His Intention (*Iradah*)	a determination to act in a certain way
+ His Utterance (*Qawl*)	Saying something
+ His Will (*Mashiat*)	a deliberate, often strong, desire or determination for something to occur
+ His Word (*Kalima*)	The actual word that is uttered
+ His State of Affairs (*Amr*)	The actual act or affair for which all this happened

- When we act and do something, we pretty go through the same process as described above. The only difference is that God only instructs things to follow a process and complete something. Their potential to completion is within that thing.
- This can be understood easily through the example of a software program. All the potential of what the program would do is written in the program. The programmer only executes a command to run it.

اِنَّمَآ اَمْرُهٗٓ اِذَآ اَرَادَ شَيْئًا اَنْ يَّقُوْلَ لَهٗ كُنْ فَيَكُوْنُ

Such are His matters that when He decides to accomplish something, He only says: "Be." And it happens (or starts to happen). (36:82)

Note: The occurrence might take thousands of years.

Remembering God in our Lives

How to keep ourselves spiritually alive?

- A very common problem that every Muslim faces is: "We often forget Allah and find ourselves spiritually dead inside. How to keep that relationship with God alive all the time?"

- God told us how to do it. It's a three-step process:

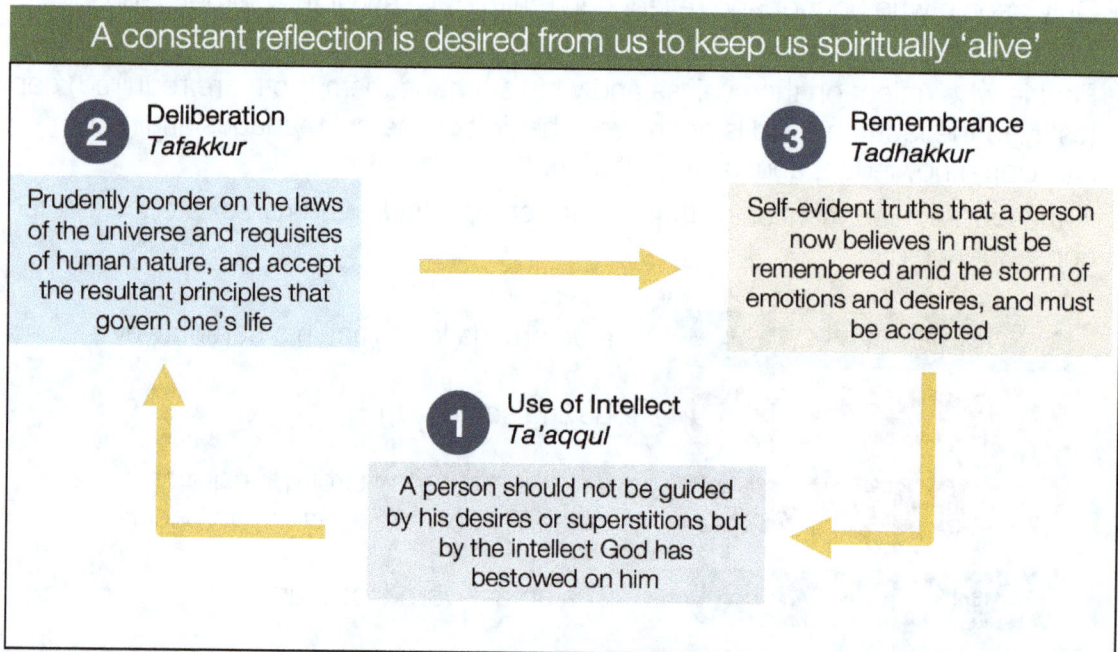

A constant reflection is desired from us to keep us spiritually 'alive'

2 Deliberation
Tafakkur

Prudently ponder on the laws of the universe and requisites of human nature, and accept the resultant principles that govern one's life

3 Remembrance
Tadhakkur

Self-evident truths that a person now believes in must be remembered amid the storm of emotions and desires, and must be accepted

1 Use of Intellect
Ta'aqqul

A person should not be guided by his desires or superstitions but by the intellect God has bestowed on him

Use of Intellect

- A person must use their intellect when it comes to religion. God never said that one should follow their forefathers, their desires, or wishful thinking when looking at religion.

Deliberate

- Deliberation is more than just thinking. A person should not take everything around them for granted. Just imagine the process an apple undergoes before it reaches our mouths for consumption. So much and so many people are involved.

Remember

- Remembrance is also key in keeping the relationship with God alive. We should not just realize the facts and truths once but always remember them when the storm of emotions and desires tries to take over us. God's bounties must be remembered even when we lose something dear to us.

Deliberations

- If one deliberates on one's surroundings and on the world within him, everything bears testimony that God is not merely the first cause and an eternal entity; He is, in fact, a being who has intention and knowledge and has all noble attributes.

Matter and Soul	- Both Matter (physical) and Soul (metaphysical) are plagued with weaknesses, decay, and deterioration. They can't create themselves. - A remarkable universe and its various phenomena are created just for them to get benefits from – to show that someone who is Powerful and Wise has created these wonders for them. - It appears that the entire universe is serving this small population of human beings on one small planet, Earth.
Potential and Knowledge	- Knowledge is nothing but "becoming aware of hidden potentials," and every new knowledge bears witness to these potentials. - The extreme organization found in the knowledge and potential points to a Wise and Knowledgeable God.
Beyond Time and Space	- In our concept of time, this Creator, Living and Self-Sustaining, is Eternal. He is the First and the Last; nothing is before or after Him. He is Apparent, and nothing is above Him. He is Hidden, and there is nothing below Him. - All these attributes, without the concept of a **Distinct Being** behind them, are meaningless. That's why even after the destruction of this entire Universe, He shall continue to exist.

أَمْ خُلِقُوا مِنْ غَيْرِ شَيْءٍ أَمْ هُمُ الْخَالِقُونَ ۞ أَمْ خَلَقُوا السَّمٰوٰتِ وَ الْأَرْضَ ۞ بَلْ لَّا يُوقِنُونَ

Were they created without a Creator, or were they their own creators? Have they created the heavens and the earth? [No] in fact they [in reality] lack certainty (Surah Tur:35-36)

كُلُّ مَنْ عَلَيْهَا فَانٍ ۞ وَيَبْقَى وَجْهُ رَبِّكَ ذُو الْجَلَالِ وَالْإِكْرَامِ

Everything is mortal. Only the person of Your Majestic and Glorious God will remain forever

Who is our God?

- Only God can introduce Himself, and He did that in the Quran. So, instead of running our imaginations, it is important that we go to the Quran and ask this question.
- The God of the Quran is All-Powerful, All-Mighty, and All-Knowing.

اللَّهُ لَا إِلَهَ إِلَّا هُوَ الْحَيُّ الْقَيُّومُ ۚ لَا تَأْخُذُهُ سِنَةٌ وَلَا نَوْمٌ ۚ لَهُ مَا فِي السَّمَاوَاتِ وَمَا فِي الْأَرْضِ ۗ مَن ذَا الَّذِي يَشْفَعُ عِندَهُ إِلَّا بِإِذْنِهِ ۚ يَعْلَمُ مَا بَيْنَ أَيْدِيهِمْ وَمَا خَلْفَهُمْ ۖ وَلَا يُحِيطُونَ بِشَيْءٍ مِّنْ عِلْمِهِ إِلَّا بِمَا شَاءَ ۚ وَسِعَ كُرْسِيُّهُ السَّمَاوَاتِ وَالْأَرْضَ ۖ وَلَا يَئُودُهُ حِفْظُهُمَا ۚ وَهُوَ الْعَلِيُّ الْعَظِيمُ

God, there is no god but He, the Living, the Sustainer. Neither slumber nor sleep overtakes Him. All that is in the heavens and the earth belongs to Him. Who can intercede with Him for someone except by His permission? He knows what lies before them and what is after them, and without His will, they cannot grasp any part of His knowledge. His dominion prevails in the heavens and the earth, and their protection/maintenance does not wear Him slightly, and He is the Exalted and the Glorious One. (Surah Baqarah:255)

قُلْ أَئِنَّكُمْ لَتَكْفُرُونَ بِالَّذِي خَلَقَ الْأَرْضَ فِي يَوْمَيْنِ وَتَجْعَلُونَ لَهُ أَندَادًا ۚ ذَٰلِكَ رَبُّ الْعَالَمِينَ وَجَعَلَ فِيهَا رَوَاسِيَ مِن فَوْقِهَا وَبَارَكَ فِيهَا وَقَدَّرَ فِيهَا أَقْوَاتَهَا فِي أَرْبَعَةِ أَيَّامٍ سَوَاءً لِّلسَّائِلِينَ ثُمَّ اسْتَوَىٰ إِلَى السَّمَاءِ وَهِيَ دُخَانٌ فَقَالَ لَهَا وَلِلْأَرْضِ ائْتِيَا طَوْعًا أَوْ كَرْهًا قَالَتَا أَتَيْنَا طَائِعِينَ فَقَضَاهُنَّ سَبْعَ سَمَاوَاتٍ فِي يَوْمَيْنِ وَأَوْحَىٰ فِي كُلِّ سَمَاءٍ أَمْرَهَا ۚ وَزَيَّنَّا السَّمَاءَ الدُّنْيَا بِمَصَابِيحَ وَحِفْظًا ۚ ذَٰلِكَ تَقْدِيرُ الْعَزِيزِ الْعَلِيمِ

Ask them: "Do you disbelieve in Him and associate partners with Him who created the earth in two days? The Lord of the Universe is He. And [after creating the earth] He set up on it the mountains towering high above it and placed His blessings upon it (earth) and for all the needy according to their needs provided it with sustenance with correct measure – all this in four days. Then He turned towards the sky, which was in the form of smoke, and He said to it and the earth: "Obey the directive willingly or unwillingly." Both said: "We come forth willingly." Then He made seven heavens in two days, and to each heaven, He assigned its task. And We decked the lowest heaven with brilliant stars and made it fully secure. All this is the design of the Mighty One, the All-knowing. (Surah Fussilat:9-12)

His Attributes

- His attributes are not like ours – the aspect of finesse, dignity, and balance should not be overlooked when understanding His attributes:
  - Powerful but with Mercy, Affection, and Justice
  - Angry and Furious against oppression and injustice, but being Wise
  - Merciful and Forgiving, but still be Just
- We cannot claim that human beings have such a balance in their attributes. For example, a mother might be merciful to her child but will definitely ignore justice.
- Because of this perfection, man, while fearing God, leaps towards Him for this very reason and tries to seek refuge in Him. That's why many Muslim supplications start with "Allahumma Aa'udhu Bik" (O Lord, I seek refuge in You). Because we have the assurance that we will never be dealt injustice, and that He will protect me in this world and the next if I am sincere towards Him.
- Any perception of God must have the following:

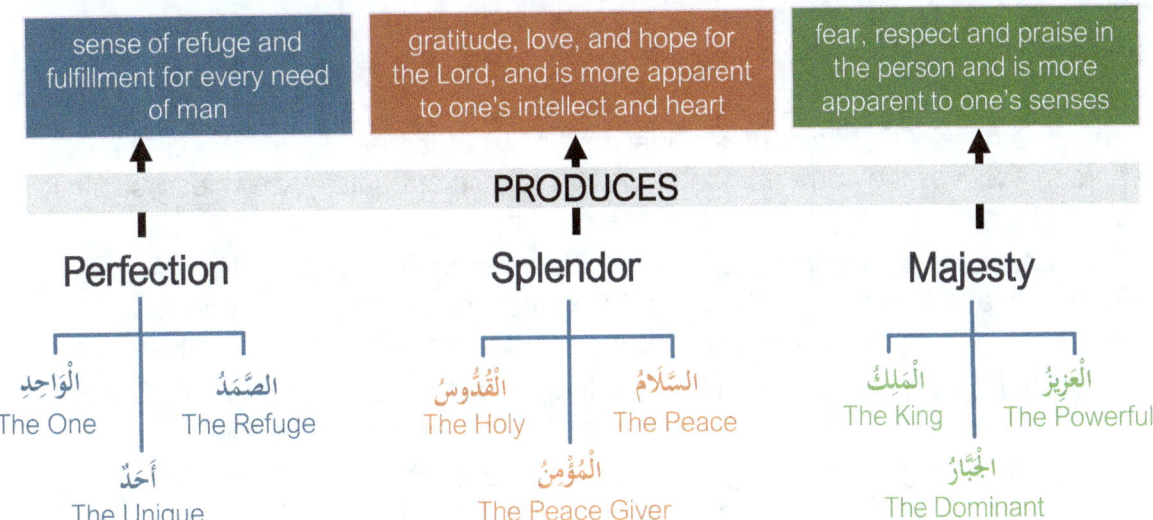

- Some of the names or attributes of God that give rise to this perception are listed above because God Himself uses them in the Quran.
- However, the Quran also says that all good names are His, and He can be called by any good and beautiful name.

قُلِ ادْعُوا اللَّهَ أَوِ ادْعُوا الرَّحْمَٰنَ ۖ أَيًّا مَّا تَدْعُوا فَلَهُ الْأَسْمَاءُ الْحُسْنَىٰ

Tell them: "You may call upon Him by using Allah or Rahman; by whatever name you call Him, His are the most gracious names. (Surah Bani Israel:110)

Our perception of God matters

- Perceptions of God are incredibly diverse; some envision a being of immense kindness and love, while others see an angry, punishing figure.
- There are consequences of how we imagine Him to be.
- Prophet Muhammad said in one of the hadith:

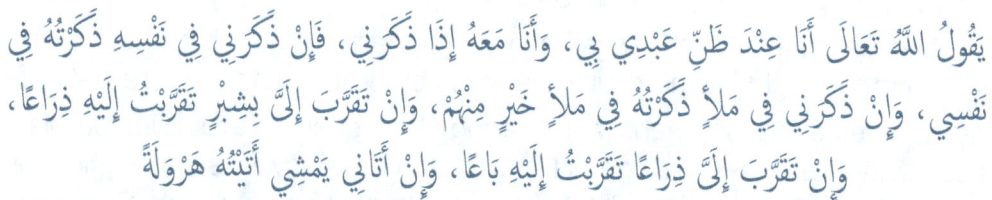

Allah says: **'I am just as My slave thinks I am**, and I am with him if He remembers Me. If he remembers Me in his heart, I too, remember him; and if he remembers Me in a group of people, I remember him in a group that is better than those people; and if he comes one span nearer to Me, I go one cubit nearer to him; and if he comes one cubit nearer to Me, I go a distance of two outstretched arms nearer to him; and if he comes to Me walking, I go to him running. [Sahih al-Bukhari #7405]

- The greatness of God becomes evident from His attributes of perfection. When a person acquires the correct understanding of these attributes, he professes faith in a God Who is unique, peerless, and one of a kind.
- The conception of God in one's heart should be of someone who is Kind, Merciful, Forgiving, and Compassionate, but at the same time Just and does not allow injustice to go unchecked, sometimes in this world and ultimately in the Hereafter.
- When in difficulty, a person should know that He is the rock of shelter for all; to Him solely belong the heavens and the earth and whatever is between them.
- When committing sins and being unjust to someone, one should know that there is nothing in this world that is hidden from Him; no affair of this world is beyond His jurisdiction and control.
- He is beyond what is beyond, yet He is closer to man than his life-vein; His knowledge and wisdom encompass everything; He even knows what is concealed in the hearts.
- When prayers become a burden, know that everything needs Him, but He needs no one; matter, plants, and animals all prostrate before Him, and are busy in celebrating His praises and glorifying Him; His power is immense, and He is all-embracing, and every particle of this universe is subservient to His will.

This is the Lord we worship

With a correct understanding of these attributes, one professes faith in a God Who is:

- Immensely Powerful
- Undisputable Owner of the heavens and the earth and whatever is in between them
- All-embracing
- Unique
- Peerless
- All creation prostrates before Him
- He is immortal
- He does what He Wills
- He can destroy anything at any time
- All need Him and He needs no one
- Nothing is hidden from Him
- He does what He wishes
- Absolute Sovereign with no partners
- The Refuge
- He is beyond this Universe, yet He is very close
- All creation celebrates His Praises
- Every affair is under His Jurisdiction and Control
- His command supersedes all commands
- He is free of fault, blemishes and allegations
- He can re-create
- He bestows honor and humiliation
- He knows what is hearts
- His knowledge and wisdom encompass everything
- All creation Glorifies Him
- All creation is subservient to His Will
- His intentions supersede all intentions

What is *Shirk*?

- Oneness of God is at the core of every belief in Islam, and that's why *Shirk*, or associating someone with God, is considered an unforgivable crime against God.
- In the fundamental testimony of Islam, it is required to deny every other deity first before affirming one true God.

There is no one worthy of worship but Allah

- Associating other gods with God Almighty is termed polytheism (*Shirk*). *Shirk* is a term that the Quran uses for this concept.
- A concept or belief will be considered *Shirk* if it has any of the following types of association:

Types of Shirk

Type 1: to regard someone as having the **exact nature** as that of God, or to regard God as having the exact nature as someone; or

- Christians and their concept of Jesus and Mary
- Polytheists of Arabia and their concept of angels
- Mystical beliefs about the nature of this universe

Type 2: to regard someone as having a **role in the creation** or in running the **affairs** of the creatures and, in this manner, make someone God's peer to some extent in one way or another

- Hinduism about Brahma, Vishnu, and Shiva
- *Ghaus, Qutub, Abdal, Daata,* etc, in Mystic culture

Polytheists of Arabia

- The Quran called the Polytheists of Arabia "Mushrik".
- They adopted "*Shirk*" as their religion by believing in the partners of Allah.
- They never considered these idols (mostly Angels) as gods, but rather as something that could bring them closer to God and bless them in their daily lives.
- Some of these idols were of goddesses whom they considered daughters of God and believed would bring them closer to God; Laat, Manaat, and Uzzah were among them.

The Quran's response to Polytheism

قُلْ هُوَ اللهُ أَحَدٌ ۚ اللهُ الصَّمَدُ ۚ لَمْ يَلِدْ وَ لَمْ يُوْلَدْ ۚ وَ لَمْ يَكُنْ لَّهُ كُفُوًا أَحَدٌ

Declare [O Prophet]: "In reality, God is One and Alone. God is everyone's support. He is neither father nor son, and there is none like Him." (112)

- The attribute of *Tawḥid (oneness)* is the most explained and emphasized attribute in the Quran. God has left no margin for error in explaining this concept.
- The argument that nullifies polytheism is that no one has any basis for associating partners with God.
- At more than one place, the Quran has demanded from its addressees to present, if they can, any grounds for polytheism, whether based on intellect or on divine sources.
- Only God Himself could have informed us whether He had any associates, and the only way to know God's will in this regard was through the Divine books He revealed, as well as the traditions and narratives transmitted generation after generation by His prophets and messengers. None of these contains anything that substantiates polytheism in any way.

قُلْ أَرَءَيْتُمْ مَّا تَدْعُوْنَ مِنْ دُوْنِ اللهِ أَرُوْنِيْ مَاذَا خَلَقُوْا مِنَ الْأَرْضِ أَمْ لَهُمْ شِرْكٌ فِى السَّمٰوٰتِ ۚ اِيْتُوْنِيْ بِكِتٰبٍ مِّنْ قَبْلِ هٰذَآ أَوْ أَثٰرَةٍ مِّنْ عِلْمٍ اِنْ كُنْتُمْ صٰدِقِيْنَ

Tell them: Have you ever reflected that those whom you call besides God, just show me what they have created in the earth, or do they have some share in the heavens [that they be made deities?] Present before me a book before this or any tradition based on knowledge, if you are truthful. (26:4)

إِنَّ رَبَّكُمُ اللَّهُ الَّذِي خَلَقَ السَّمَاوَاتِ وَالْأَرْضَ فِي سِتَّةِ أَيَّامٍ ثُمَّ اسْتَوَىٰ عَلَى الْعَرْشِ يُغْشِي اللَّيْلَ النَّهَارَ يَطْلُبُهُ حَثِيثًا وَالشَّمْسَ وَالْقَمَرَ وَالنُّجُومَ مُسَخَّرَاتٍ بِأَمْرِهِ ۗ أَلَا لَهُ الْخَلْقُ وَالْأَمْرُ ۗ تَبَارَكَ اللَّهُ رَبُّ الْعَالَمِينَ

Your Lord is the God who created the heavens and the earth in six days and then ascended His throne. He covers the day with the night, which swiftly follows it. And He created the sun, moon, and stars, subservient to His command. Make it clear: He is the Creator, and He runs the affairs as well. Blessed is God, Lord of the Universe. (Surah Aaraf:54)

Evidence from nature

- Seemingly opposing and conflicting elements of nature (day and night, heavens and earth, life and death, rain and drought, ship and sea, clouds and winds) display a harmony and unity that create a perfect systematic order and an overall purpose in the universe.

- This systematic order and harmony are not possible if there is more than one God.

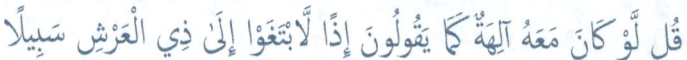

قُل لَّوْ كَانَ مَعَهُ آلِهَةٌ كَمَا يَقُولُونَ إِذًا لَّابْتَغَوْا إِلَىٰ ذِي الْعَرْشِ سَبِيلًا

Say (O Muhammad): If there were other gods along with Him, as they say, then they had sought a way against the Lord of the Throne. (Surah Bani Israel:42)

Shirk is an unforgivable crime

- The Quran calls Shirk *Zulm* (Injustice) because of not being grateful to the Creator, who deserves gratitude and worship.

- Pure monotheism is the most significant and fundamental requirement of justice that humans can dispense.

- Human beings involved in Shirk have no basis, foundation, or evidence in favor of Shirk that suggests that God has given this status to any of His creation.

- God considers Shirk as a pure lie that is imposed on Him without any proof.

- God has declared in the Quran that it is such a great injustice that it is an unforgivable sin.

Predestination (good and "evil" fate)

- The second topic closely related to the belief in God is the concept of Predestination (scholars of Islam call it "*Qada*" and "*Qadr*").
- One of God's attributes is All-Knowing, which means He cannot be unaware of the good or bad that happens to us.
- However, the matter is not that simple and must be understood properly. It is the most complex matter in religion.

What is predetermined?

- In some cases, we are predestined, but in all those cases where our moral judgments are involved, we are free – otherwise, the test is meaningless.
- Our family, birthplace, features, talents, country environments, etc., are all fixed, and that is the playing field God has chosen for us to be tested on.
- We have no say in any of the above.
- Our talents are predetermined, but how we polish and grow them is left to us.
- All the 'factors' above will be considered when we are judged.
- Some of them may be impacting our moral judgments and will be considered in the final judgment. For example, the moral judgment of a person born in a criminal family will be very different from that of a person born in an upright family.

Our free will

- Our moral choices are not predetermined – God only KNOWS by His infinite knowledge what we are going to choose, as He transcends time.
- The strategies and plans we make in our lives are crucial and always work, but sometimes God intervenes out of His infinite Wisdom and Grand Scheme, putting us through a test.
- The concurrence of the outcome of our deed and God's Will is needed.
- A farmer who fails to meet the requirements for his crops to grow will have nothing to reap. But if the farmer does everything he needs to reap the fruit, it still must concur with God's Will. If an Earthquake hits his field, it simply means that his and God's plans did not concur. This could be because it was required in the Grand Scheme of things, and at the same time, it became a test for him on how he behaves in this circumstance.

Example of Free Will and our choices

- The modern world provides a better explanation of fate than at any other time. For example, the outcome in a well-designed computer game is predetermined, but at no moment in the game are my efforts and choices enforced on me. There is a "space" that I play in of my own free will. Only the programmer knows the consequences of my actions and how I will move forward.

Video Games and Fate – Simple Example

Playing a game – Another example

- If your teacher asks each of you to choose one thing from the chart on the right.
- And he knows in my mind what you are going to choose (maybe his intuition, knowledge of your personality, or maybe he is a god).
- He writes it down on a piece of paper.
- Your choice matches what he has written on the paper for you.

The important questions?

What impact did the teacher have on your decision to choose?

What should be our attitude towards Predestination?

Allah's Dealings and Practices

- We are fortunate that God has elaborated in the Quran on what unalterable principles He deals with us.
- He has different principles for individuals and nations.
- They are called **Sunnatullah (The practices of Allah)**.
- As with God's attributes, knowledge of these dealings and practices is crucial to our lives.
- It helps us understand life situations and reflect on our moral condition. It helps us understand the correct perspective in every situation we face.

What is Free Will

- The concept of fundamental good and evil is absolute and universal.
- We are created with a noble nature, and we have the natural ability to distinguish good from evil because **we are given free will**.
- The differences we sometimes see among people and cultures are in their application, not in the fundamentals. For example, between two people, both know what justice is. However, they might differ in the application of whether one is committing injustice against the other.
- Exercising our free will is a '**grant**' which we see as a 'right' – but God controls the outcomes.
- It's our adherence to virtues — or our avoidance of them— that plays a decisive role first in our character, while God's grace and his respite/leeway come later.
- The "reward" (positive or negative) is tied to my "intention" and "ability" to act on it - not on the success or failure of that action.
- God's all-embracing knowledge of our fate does not contradict our ability to choose between right and wrong – He knows that a person will take or leave guidance according to the law of guidance He has set.
- God is the embodiment of good; e.g., He created this universe as a manifestation of His Mercy. Something can only be called good if it is in accordance with the attributes of God, who is All-Good.
- Good is eternal because God is eternal, and He does not command anything that is not in accordance with His attributes.
- E.g., we like the truth, but our liking for the truth cannot be real if we are not satisfied and confident that God also likes the truth.
- We cannot love a God whom we think is not just and does not like the truth, which is the foundation of our relationship with God.

God allows evil committed by human beings

- There are two types of evil as we see it as human beings:
    - Evil is committed by human beings because of their free will.
    - Misfortunes that occur in the world where humans are partially or not at all involved.
- The first type of evil, in its actual form, emanates from the ill use of our free will, and God allows it for retribution and test – our free will is not unlimited.
- In a society, He **allows the first type of evil** to test the righteous and the wicked.
- The best we can say is that God sometimes allows the first type of evil as a necessary means of completing his plan for the world.
- However, He interferes in such cases as well.
- Imagine a person planned to kill another human being. He planned everything perfectly, left his home to kill, and could not kill because something happened on the scene right at that moment when he was about to attack the person. For us, it was a "failed plan" or "a lucky guy," but in reality, God intervened.

Unfortunate events are not evil

- Other misfortunes, which we also call evil, are sometimes in the grand scheme of things for tests and sometimes come to bring good out of it – E.g., the death of loved ones, the suffering of children, storms, and earthquakes, etc.
- We see this as evil, but it is hard to say whether the results of such misfortune are really evil. They will all be good in the end.
- Natural disasters are a fundamental part of the divine system of trial (test) for humanity, and must not be confused with divine punishment for the immediate victims.
- Natural disasters also serve as a reminder of human vulnerability and the temporary nature of this world, prompting reflection, patience, and spiritual growth.
- In Surah Al-Kahf, through the story of Prophet Musa and the wise man (Al-Khidr), God taught us that sometimes we only look at the apparent picture of an event and conclude things that are completely opposite to the actual reasons and wisdom behind it.
- No one has the power to stop the Will of God, but He materializes it with justice and wisdom – He is not a blind power.

> Issues on which the Almighty will hold us accountable are those in which we have the freedom to choose and where we exercise our free will. We will not be held accountable for anything that is beyond our control.

God's Actions

- God does not act contrary to what He practices and has set as principles for Himself – Justice and Wisdom.
- Justice is central to God's attributes and to His religion; for us as humans, our intellect should be the judge of what is just and what is not.
- All actions and deeds emanating from God are regarded as just – this fact is validated by intellect and universal truths.
- In the Quran, certain acts are attributed to God; the real objective is to attribute them to specific laws, principles, and practices that underlie these acts.
- For example, when He says, "He guides whoever He wills," it simply means that both the course and the outcome will occur according to the process/practice He has set for guidance and misguidance.
- Similarly, when He says "He never guides the corrupt", He means that it is due to their corrupt behavior and evil intentions that they are unable to get the guidance and remain blind to the truth.

His actions are centered around justice

- God not only adheres to justice when dealing with us and this world in this life or next, but He also demands justice from us.
- Justice means "to put things in their right place". Once we act against justice, we see the world spiral into corruption and moral destruction.

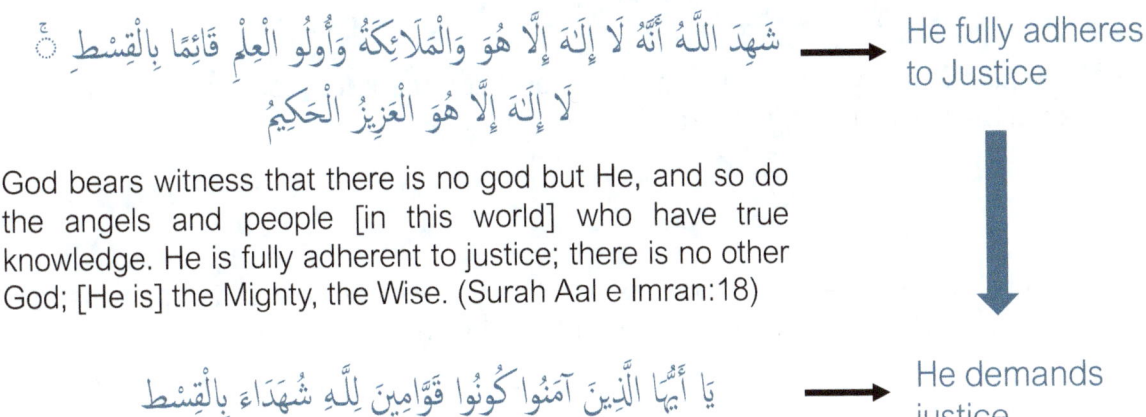

شَهِدَ اللَّهُ أَنَّهُ لَا إِلَهَ إِلَّا هُوَ وَالْمَلَائِكَةُ وَأُولُو الْعِلْمِ قَائِمًا بِالْقِسْطِ

لَا إِلَهَ إِلَّا هُوَ الْعَزِيزُ الْحَكِيمُ

He fully adheres to Justice

God bears witness that there is no god but He, and so do the angels and people [in this world] who have true knowledge. He is fully adherent to justice; there is no other God; [He is] the Mighty, the Wise. (Surah Aal e Imran:18)

يَا أَيُّهَا الَّذِينَ آمَنُوا كُونُوا قَوَّامِينَ لِلَّهِ شُهَدَاءَ بِالْقِسْطِ

He demands justice

O you who believe, stand firmly for Allah as witnesses to justice … (Surah Maida:8)

- In the next few sections, we will go over some of the actions or Sunnah of God that we see in our lives, and God has explained them in the Quran.

1 – Tests and Trials

- The **only** reason this universe that we live in was created is for **Test and Trial**.
- It is a universal phenomenon and not restricted to Muslims.
- The Quran insists that the only reason this factory of life and death is created is to see who performs better in his/her deeds.
- The tests and trials are according to a person's environment, situation, capabilities, and knowledge.
- Abundance or the lack of provisions is not a sign of God's pleasure or otherwise.
- The abundance of worldly pleasures and provisions is deceptive and dangerous.
- A special set of tests and trials comes in the lives of the Prophets and their companions to separate them from people of weak faith or hypocrites.
- If we understand God's scheme about tests and trials, we can have the **right perspective on everything** that happens to us.

الَّذِي خَلَقَ الْمَوْتَ وَالْحَيَاةَ لِيَبْلُوَكُمْ أَيُّكُمْ أَحْسَنُ عَمَلًا ۚ وَهُوَ الْعَزِيزُ الْغَفُورُ

[He] Who created death and life that He might test you as to which of you is best regarding deeds. And He is also Mighty and Forgiving. (Surah Mulk:2)

إِنَّا جَعَلْنَا مَا عَلَى الْأَرْضِ زِينَةً لَّهَا لِنَبْلُوَهُمْ أَيُّهُمْ أَحْسَنُ عَمَلًا

We have placed everything on this earth as an adornment for it so that We can test who is the best in their deeds. (Surah Kahf:7)

كُلُّ نَفْسٍ ذَائِقَةُ الْمَوْتِ ۗ وَنَبْلُوكُم بِالشَّرِّ وَالْخَيْرِ فِتْنَةً ۖ وَإِلَيْنَا تُرْجَعُونَ

Every soul shall taste death, and we are inflicting you with sorrow and happiness to test you, and to Us shall you return. (Surah Al Anbiya:35)

> The beauty of this test is that there is no cheating possible in this test, as the test is unique to each person

Wisdom behind trials

- It's only a matter of perspective; otherwise, every trial has hidden benefits for us.
- There are two types of tests that everyone is going through, without exception:

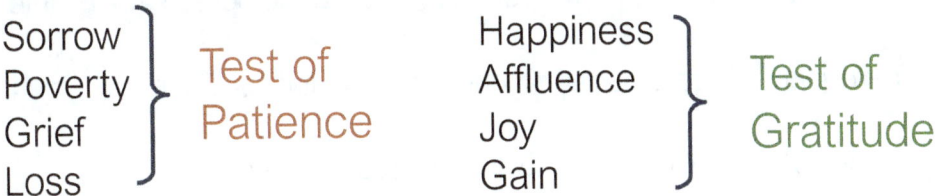

The test of Gratitude

- The test of patience is easy to understand.
- However, most people do not consider affluence and an easy life as a test. In reality, it is a bigger test than the patience required in adverse situations.
- This test is experienced during times of ease, prosperity, and the reception of God's blessings and bounties. God wants to test our attitude in times of ease. Many people fail this test:
  - Becoming arrogant and proud due to one's wealth or abilities.
  - Attributing success solely to oneself and forgetting the divine source of the blessings.
  - Using God's blessings for worldly desires and disobedience (e.g., corruption, extravagance).

Benefits of Trials

- Most of the time, our inner abilities come out during tough times, not when we are at ease.
- We can act our entire lives hypocritically, but our true selves are revealed in times of trial. It is said that if you want to see someone's true personality, travel with them.
- We may say a lot with our tongues about our belief in God and how strong it is, but when we are put to the test of patience or gratitude, our true faith is tested. In other words, the words attest to deeds.
- It is only because of tests and trials that knowledge and society progress. Imagine if there were no sickness, would medical science have progressed? Or if there were no suffering when walking for miles, would we have made cars, trains, and airplanes?
- The collective suffering humanity faces is a blessing in disguise.

2 – Guidance and Error

- One aspect of the trial is to adhere to the straight path and not go astray in religious guidance – it requires patience.
- This guidance towards one Lord and His path is an **inner guidance** fortified by the signs in the heavens and the earth around him, once the person attains intellectual maturity.
- The entire religion of God is based on our natural inclinations and is rooted in our nature.
- A person can have two types of behavior towards this inner guidance:

If one cherishes the inner guidance

- If the person values and treasures this 'inner' guidance and acts towards it, God increases in him the desire for guidance, and faith continues to settle in his heart.
- It is because of this inner guidance that a person is able to recognize the external guidance when it comes through prophets and their books.
- Though the Quran conditions guidance on the Will of God, it is actually this law that prevails. If a person cherishes the inner guidance, the external guidance becomes evident and clear.
- Angels and righteous people provide further guidance to the person if he continues to value it and remains grateful and steadfast.

If one neglects/evades the inner guidance

- On the other hand, a person may evade or neglect inner guidance, refuse to use intellect, and deliberately deviate from the truth.
- God shows His signs and warnings both inside and outside as reminders.
- If the person persists in defiance and shows no sign of turning back, God then leaves Him to wander in the darkness of error and misguidance
- In Quranic terms, that person commits "*zulm*" (injustice) to himself.
- Persistence increases stubbornness and selfishness, and that person is deprived of the ability to think and understand in the proper manner.
- Satan and his agents support this person in everything he does.
- If he is even mischievous and spreads corruption as a result, then God finally seals his heart for any guidance.

Quran describes the law

- God describes this law of guidance and error on multiple occasions. God attributes guidance and misguidance to Him, but if one reads the verse carefully, the law is apparent.

لَا إِكْرَاهَ فِي الدِّينِ ۖ قَد تَّبَيَّنَ الرُّشْدُ مِنَ الْغَيِّ ۚ فَمَن يَكْفُرْ بِالطَّاغُوتِ وَيُؤْمِن بِاللَّهِ فَقَدِ اسْتَمْسَكَ بِالْعُرْوَةِ الْوُثْقَىٰ لَا انفِصَامَ لَهَا ۗ وَاللَّهُ سَمِيعٌ عَلِيمٌ

There is no compulsion in religion. Distinct is the way of guidance from error. He who turns away from the forces of evil and believes in Allah has grasped a firm handhold that will never break. Allah hears all and knows everything. (Surah Baqarah:256)

إِنَّ الَّذِينَ كَفَرُوا سَوَاءٌ عَلَيْهِمْ أَأَنذَرْتَهُمْ أَمْ لَمْ تُنذِرْهُمْ لَا يُؤْمِنُونَ خَتَمَ اللَّهُ عَلَىٰ قُلُوبِهِمْ وَعَلَىٰ سَمْعِهِمْ ۖ وَعَلَىٰ أَبْصَارِهِمْ غِشَاوَةٌ ۖ وَلَهُمْ عَذَابٌ عَظِيمٌ

Those who have decided to reject [this Book], it is the same to them whether you warn them or not; they will not believe. Allah has now sealed their hearts and their ears [as per His law], and on their eyes is a veil, and great is the penalty that awaits them [on the Day of Judgment] (Surah Baqarah:7)

وَمَن يَعْشُ عَن ذِكْرِ الرَّحْمَٰنِ نُقَيِّضْ لَهُ شَيْطَانًا فَهُوَ لَهُ قَرِينٌ

And whosoever turns away from the remembrance of Al-Rahman, we appoint a Satan over him, and he becomes his companion (Surah Zukhruf:36)

إِنَّ هَٰذِهِ تَذْكِرَةٌ فَمَن شَاءَ اتَّخَذَ إِلَىٰ رَبِّهِ سَبِيلًا وَمَا تَشَاءُونَ إِلَّا أَن يَشَاءَ اللَّهُ ۚ إِنَّ اللَّهَ كَانَ عَلِيمًا حَكِيمًا يُدْخِلُ مَن يَشَاءُ فِي رَحْمَتِهِ ۚ وَالظَّالِمِينَ أَعَدَّ لَهُمْ عَذَابًا أَلِيمًا

This [Quran] is only a reminder. So whoever wishes should take the path leading to Allah, and you do not wish [O People!] until Allah so wishes [according to His law]. Indeed, Allah is All-Knowing and wise. He admits into His mercy whomever He wishes [based on this knowledge and wisdom]. And for the wrongdoers, He has prepared a grievous punishment. (Surah Insaan:29-31)

3 – Beyond-capacity directives

- God never gives directives to human beings in the *Shariah* that are beyond their capacity to act upon.
- God made sure, in every aspect of the religion, that we are not asked to bear more than we can.
- Actions committed in forgetfulness, as a result of misunderstanding, or done inadvertently, are not held against us.
- We are asked to sincerely make an effort to understand a directive and then act upon it in both form and spirit with complete veracity and honesty.
- When people and nations are punished, they are burdened beyond their capacity, but such situations are rare and specific to individuals, revealing God's power and their helplessness.
- When God said in the Quran:

God does not burden a soul more than what it can bear (in *Shariah*)
(Surah Baqarah, 286)

- He meant that He does not burden people with laws and practices in Shariah that they cannot implement or practice.
- Generally, this verse is mistakenly attributed to tests and trials that we go through in our lives. However, this is only related to the teachings of *Shariah*.
- Placing oneself in hardship during worship rituals is not encouraged by the Prophet Muhammad.
- That's why God has given all the rules for relaxation in worship rituals when dealing with abnormal situations.

> God has given us alternative forms of worship rituals when things become difficult.
> Examples:
> - Ablution with dust instead of water
> - Feed the poor when they cannot fast
> - Pray sitting when you cannot stand

In **prohibitions**, He allowed us to consume haram if it is a matter of life and death: Eat prohibited food if it's a matter of life and death.

4 – Rise and Fall of Nations

- Like the law of trials for individuals, God selects nations for similar trials.
- God decided to give every nation on earth a chance to come onto the stage of this universe and play a leading role.
- That nation remains in this leading position if it upholds two things: General **moral character** that distinguishes one nation from another, and the **superiority in various sciences of knowledge**.
- God usually does not interfere with this universal law, as it happens naturally unless it concerns one of the chosen nations of God.
- Nations are destroyed because of one of two reasons:
    - They plunge themselves into lowliness in matters of moral character and knowledge, and their affluent people become corrupt.
    - They reject the messengers sent to them after it is clear to them that he is the true messenger of God.
- Sometimes destroyed means they become insignificant in the geopolitical power hierarchy.
- God describes the law in the following verses:

وَإِن مِّن قَرْيَةٍ إِلَّا نَحْنُ مُهْلِكُوهَا قَبْلَ يَوْمِ الْقِيَامَةِ أَوْ مُعَذِّبُوهَا عَذَابًا شَدِيدًا ۚ كَانَ ذَٰلِكَ فِي الْكِتَابِ مَسْطُورًا

And there is no nation that We shall not destroy or sternly punish before the Day of Judgement. That is decreed in the Book of God. (Surah Bani Israel:58)

إِنَّ اللَّهَ لَا يُغَيِّرُ مَا بِقَوْمٍ حَتَّىٰ يُغَيِّرُوا مَا بِأَنفُسِهِمْ ۗ وَإِذَا أَرَادَ اللَّهُ بِقَوْمٍ سُوءًا فَلَا مَرَدَّ لَهُ ۚ وَمَا لَهُم مِّن دُونِهِ مِن وَالٍ

God does not change His dealings with a people unless they themselves change their national characteristics, and when God decides to afflict them with a misfortune, none can ward it off. And for such people, there is none who can help them against God. (Surah Raad:11)

- Scholars of Abrahamic traditions usually divide human life on earth in this way, as described in divine scriptures.

Note: The progeny of Gog/Magog is everybody else who is not African or Arab.

5 – Divine help

- When God entrusts a person or a group with His mission, He provides His help for their success.
- This includes the propagation of God's message or Jihad.
- However, God's help comes with its own rules and principles.
- What makes a person or a group worthy of God's help is a strong belief in Him, patience, perseverance, and piety.
- There are many details about how God's help comes in the chapter on The Shariah of Jihad in Level 8.
- It is important to note that when God entrusts a group of people during the Messengers' time, and they meet the requirements for help, the help is guaranteed.
- This happens because God promises victory to the Messengers and their companions who agree to help him.
- At other times, when Messengers are not present, God's help is not guaranteed, as certain conditions must be met for it to come; it is important that Muslims understand those conditions and fulfill them.
- It is a common observation that Muslims expect God's help to come without fulfilling the major requirements of it and then complain why God's help is not there.

بَلَىٰ ۚ إِن تَصْبِرُوا وَتَتَّقُوا وَيَأْتُوكُم مِّن فَوْرِهِمْ هَٰذَا يُمْدِدْكُمْ رَبُّكُم بِخَمْسَةِ آلَافٍ مِّنَ الْمَلَائِكَةِ مُسَوِّمِينَ

Definitely! If you persevere and fear God, and your enemies launch an attack on you at this very moment, God will help you with five thousand angels who will be marked with specific signs. (Surah Aal e Imran:125)

وَكَانَ حَقًّا عَلَيْنَا نَصْرُ الْمُؤْمِنِينَ

Helping the believers is incumbent upon Us (Surah Rum:47)

يَا أَيُّهَا الَّذِينَ آمَنُوا إِن تَنصُرُوا اللَّهَ يَنصُرْكُمْ وَيُثَبِّتْ أَقْدَامَكُمْ

O who you believe, If you help God, God will help you and strengthen you (Surah Muhammad:7)

6 – Remorse and Repentance

- When a person commits a sin, as long as the person repents and mends his ways, God **never** punishes him.
- However, repentance is required immediately after sinning.
- God does not guarantee that a person will be forgiven if he continues to indulge in sinning all his life and then repents when death approaches.
- It's our attitude towards life and God that plays a critical role in receiving God's forgiveness. We will always err, but remembering God through daily prayers and reflection on the verses of the Quran, we can always turn back.
- Sincere repentance (*Tawbah*) means feeling deep remorse, immediately abstaining from the sin, and having a firm resolution never to return to it.
- For sins committed solely against God, sincere repentance is generally sufficient for forgiveness.
- In matters where the rights of another person have been violated (e.g., theft, murder, financial dues, emotional harm like breaking a promise of marriage), forgiveness from Allah is contingent upon the aggrieved party also forgiving the wrongdoer or the wrongdoer making amends for the loss/harm caused.
- God said in the Quran in Surah 6, Verse 54, "Your Lord has decreed Mercy for Himself".

اِنَّمَا التَّوْبَةُ عَلَى اللهِ لِلَّذِيْنَ يَعْمَلُوْنَ السُّوْٓءَ بِجَهَالَةٍ ثُمَّ يَتُوْبُوْنَ مِنْ قَرِيْبٍ فَاُولٰٓئِكَ يَتُوْبُ اللهُ عَلَيْهِمْ ۗ وَكَانَ اللهُ عَلِيْمًا حَكِيْمًا وَ لَيْسَتِ التَّوْبَةُ لِلَّذِيْنَ يَعْمَلُوْنَ السَّيِّاٰتِ ۚ حَتّٰٓى اِذَا حَضَرَ اَحَدَهُمُ الْمَوْتُ قَالَ اِنِّيْ تُبْتُ الْـٰٔنَ وَ لَا الَّذِيْنَ يَمُوْتُوْنَ وَ هُمْ كُفَّارٌ ۚ اُولٰٓئِكَ اَعْتَدْنَا لَهُمْ عَذَابًا اَلِيْمًا

God has taken upon Himself to forgive only those who commit a sin while overwhelmed by emotions and then quickly repent. It is they who are forgiven by God. God is all-knowing and wise. But He will not forgive those who sin all their lives and, when death comes to them, say: "Now I repent!" nor those who die as disbelievers. It is for these people that we have prepared a grievous punishment. (Surah Nisaa:17-18)

7 – Reward and Punishment

- Rewards and punishment in the Hereafter are an inevitable reality; it is in our nature that we demand good results for good acts, and we want criminals to be punished.

- At times, this takes place in this world in the form of a lesser judgment – a prelude to the greater judgment.

- For example, after rejecting a messenger (*Rasool*) who has proven his Messengerhood beyond doubt, people are punished in this world as a sign of the Hereafter. This punishment acts as a reminder for others.

- People who accept the message of God and help messengers are rewarded immediately in this life, in the form of safety given to them by God against punishment or through leadership and rulership given on earth.

- All other people at different times who are not the direct addressees of the Messengers will be rewarded and punished for their deeds in the Hereafter. Here in this world, they are being tested. They may or may not face the consequences of their deeds, good or bad.

- The Quran mentions a specific case involving a group of people. People who neglect God/religion completely in their lives and are only behind the provisions of this world will get their account settled in this world – rewards for good and punishment for evil. For example, a person who does not believe in God but regularly performs good deeds. They will be rewarded well in this world.

We recompense in this world the deeds of those who desire the life of this world with all its finery, and they are not given less in it in any way. (Surah Hud:15)

Progeny of Prophet Ibrahim

- God has decreed a special law for the progeny of Prophet Ibrahim, with rewards and punishments in this world.

- If they adhere to the message of God and represent it well in front of other nations, they will lead the nations of the world.

- If they deviate from the message of God, they will be deposed from leadership positions and will face humiliation and subjugation.

- They are like a sign of God to other nations.

- The Quran describes the law of reward and punishment, and special law for the progeny of Prophet Ibrahim in details.

وَلِكُلِّ أُمَّةٍ رَّسُولٌ ۖ فَإِذَا جَاءَ رَسُولُهُمْ قُضِيَ بَيْنَهُم بِالْقِسْطِ وَهُمْ لَا يُظْلَمُونَ

And for each nation, there is a Messenger. Then, when a Messenger comes to a nation, their matter is decided with justice, and they are not wronged. (Surah Yunus:47)

وَعَدَ اللَّهُ الَّذِينَ آمَنُوا مِنكُمْ وَ عَمِلُوا الصَّالِحَاتِ لَيَسْتَخْلِفَنَّهُمْ فِي الْأَرْضِ كَمَا اسْتَخْلَفَ الَّذِينَ مِن قَبْلِهِمْ وَ لَيُمَكِّنَنَّ لَهُمْ دِينَهُمُ الَّذِي ارْتَضَى لَهُمْ وَ لَيُبَدِّلَنَّهُم مِّن بَعْدِ خَوْفِهِمْ أَمْنًا ۚ يَعْبُدُونَنِي لَا يُشْرِكُونَ بِي شَيْئًا ۚ وَ مَن كَفَرَ بَعْدَ ذَٰلِكَ فَأُولَٰئِكَ هُمُ الْفَاسِقُونَ

God's promise with those among you who have professed faith and done righteous deeds is that He shall definitely grant them authority in this land, the way He had granted it to those before them, and He shall fully establish for them their religion which He has chosen for them, and after this state of their fear, He shall certainly transform it into peace. They shall worship Me; associate none with Me. And those who reject even after this are the disobedient. (Surah Nur:55)

أَوْفُوا بِعَهْدِي أُوفِ بِعَهْدِكُمْ

(O Children of Israel) Keep my covenant and I will keep yours (Surah Baqarah:40)

وَإِذِ ابْتَلَىٰ إِبْرَاهِيمَ رَبُّهُ بِكَلِمَاتٍ فَأَتَمَّهُنَّ ۖ قَالَ إِنِّي جَاعِلُكَ لِلنَّاسِ إِمَامًا ۖ قَالَ وَمِن ذُرِّيَّتِي ۖ قَالَ لَا يَنَالُ عَهْدِي الظَّالِمِينَ

And recall when Abraham was tested by his Lord in a few matters, and he fulfilled them. He said, "I have decided to appoint you the leader of mankind." "And what of my descendants?" asked Abraham. He replied: "My covenant does not apply to the evil-doers." (Surah Baqarah:124)

Belief in Angels

- A creation of God made from light, who brings down and implements the directives and Will of God.
- Knowledge about them is only coming through the Scriptures.
- They are the channel for communication between God and human beings.
- God runs His affairs through them.
- They are an embodiment of obedience to God.
- They praise Him all the time.
- Belief in them is directly related to faith in the Books and Prophets – they are the channels of communication.
- That channel of communication is called 'revelation' or *Wahi*.
- Gabriel (*Jibrael*) is the most exalted, noblest, and superior among all angels
- Pagans used to consider them the daughters of God, which the Quran vehemently rejected.

What do Angels do?

- They acquire instructions directly from God.
- They implement directives, among other things.
- They take matters from Earth to the presence of God.
- They reveal God's message to His prophets.
- They write down and preserve the words and deeds of human beings.
- They bring glad tidings and punishment for people.
- They constantly glorify their Lord and even pray to Him for the forgiveness of those who inhabit the earth.
- They retract the souls of the people and give glad tidings of paradise to the believers.
- They are companions of the faithful in this world and the next.
- In the Hereafter, they shall be in the presence of God and shall carry His throne.
- They shall be in charge of Hell and Heaven.

Belief in Prophets & Messengers

- God, through His all-encompassing knowledge and wisdom, selects human beings to guide mankind.
- Prophethood is God-given and cannot be acquired.
- God reveals His guidance to the prophets in one of three ways, and He spoke only to Moses.
- Every prophet is given some preference in certain aspects of prophethood over others, but in the eyes of God, all prophets are the same in their rank and dignity.
- Since Adam, God has sent prophets to every community.
- God told Adam that his progeny would always receive guidance through prophets, giving glad tidings to those who follow it, and news of dreadful fate to the unbelievers.
- Prophethood <u>cannot</u> be acquired through personal efforts, reclusiveness, or any form of mystic experiences.

وَمَا كَانَ لِبَشَرٍ أَن يُكَلِّمَهُ اللَّهُ إِلَّا وَحْيًا أَوْ مِن وَرَاءِ حِجَابٍ أَوْ يُرْسِلَ رَسُولًا فَيُوحِيَ بِإِذْنِهِ مَا يَشَاءُ ۚ إِنَّهُ عَلِيٌّ حَكِيمٌ

And it is not the status of any mortal that God should speak to him except by revelation or from behind a veil, or He sends a messenger, and through His permission, he sends revelation to him of what He wills. Exalted is He, and Wise. (Surah Ash-Shura:51)

إِنَّا أَوْحَيْنَا إِلَيْكَ كَمَا أَوْحَيْنَا إِلَى نُوحٍ وَّ النَّبِيِّنَ مِنْ بَعْدِهِ ۚ وَ أَوْحَيْنَا إِلَى إِبْرَاهِيمَ وَ إِسْمَاعِيلَ وَ إِسْحَاقَ وَ يَعْقُوبَ وَ الْأَسْبَاطِ وَ عِيسَى وَ أَيُّوبَ وَ يُونُسَ وَ هَارُونَ وَ سُلَيْمَانَ ۚ وَ أَتَيْنَا دَاوُدَ زَبُورًا وَ رُسُلًا قَدْ قَصَصْنَاهُمْ عَلَيْكَ مِن قَبْلُ وَ رُسُلًا لَّمْ نَقْصُصْهُمْ عَلَيْكَ ۚ وَ كَلَّمَ اللهُ مُوسَى تَكْلِيمًا رُسُلًا مُّبَشِّرِينَ وَ مُنْذِرِينَ لِئَلَّا يَكُونَ لِلنَّاسِ عَلَى اللهِ حُجَّةٌ بَعْدَ الرُّسُلِ ۚ وَ كَانَ اللهُ عَزِيزًا حَكِيمًا

[O Prophet!] We sent our revelations to you the way We sent them to Noah And to the prophets who came after him, and We revealed it to Abraham, Ishmael, Isaac, Jacob, the progeny of Jacob, Jesus, Job, Jonah, Aaron, Solomon, and We gave the Psalms to David. We have sent revelations to messengers whom we have mentioned to you earlier and to some messengers whom We have not mentioned to you and with Moses God had spoken, the way one speaks: these messengers who were sent as bearers of glad tidings and of admonishment so that after them people are left with no excuse which they can present before God, and God is Mighty and Wise. (Surah Nisaa:163-165)

Belief in Divine Books

- Many prophets are given guidance in the form of a written Book – some of the earlier books are mentioned in the Quran.
- It appears from the Quran and the Bible's anthology of books that some form of written guidance is given to every prophet.
- Naturally, people will differ in their understanding of God's message, and Divine Books are given to judge between them and serve as authority.
- Even prophets are not allowed to make any changes to the text.
- Quran, Gospel/Bible, Torah, Psalms, etc.

يَا أَيُّهَا الَّذِينَ آمَنُوا آمِنُوا بِاللهِ وَ رَسُولِهِ وَ الْكِتْبِ الَّذِي نَزَّلَ عَلَى رَسُولِهِ وَ الْكِتْبِ الَّذِي أَنْزَلَ مِنْ قَبْلُ ۚ وَ مَنْ يَّكْفُرْ بِاللهِ وَ مَلَئِكَتِهِ وَ كُتُبِهِ وَ رُسُلِهِ وَ الْيَوْمِ الْأَخِرِ فَقَدْ ضَلَّ ضَلَلًا بَعِيْدًا

Believers! Have faith in God and His Messenger, in the Book He has revealed to His Messenger, and also in the Book He has previously revealed, and [remember that] he who denies God, His Angels, His Books and His Prophets and the Last Day has strayed far. (Surah Nisaa:136)

وَأَنْزَلَ مَعَهُمُ الْكِتَابَ بِالْحَقِّ لِيَحْكُمَ بَيْنَ النَّاسِ فِيمَا اخْتَلَفُوا فِيهِ

And with these prophets, He sent down His Book as the decisive truth so that it may settle these differences between people. (Surah Baqarah:213)

وَأَنْزَلْنَا مَعَهُمُ الْكِتَابَ وَالْمِيزَانَ لِيَقُومَ النَّاسُ بِالْقِسْطِ

And with these [messengers], We sent down Our Book, which is the Judge [between the right and the wrong], so that [through it] people are able to adhere to justice [regarding religion]. (Surah Hadeed:25)

> Books are given so people/groups can resolve their differences through them and judge between right and wrong.

Belief in the Hereafter

- One of the most foundational beliefs in Islam.
- Central position in the preaching mission of all prophets and messengers, and guidance given in the Books.
- Pillars of the law and moral teachings stand on this belief.
- The Quran is nothing but the bearer of glad tidings and warnings for the next life.
- The Day of Judgement is the start of this life.
- The nature of our lives in the Hereafter (full of bliss, punishment, or otherwise) depends on the outcome of our accountability on the Day of Judgment.
- Man's conscience is the biggest evidence of the Day of Judgment and life in the Hereafter.
- No one except God knows when the Day will occur or when the new life will begin – not even the prophets.
- Some signs are given in the Quran and Sunnah about the proximity of that Day.

وَوُضِعَ الْكِتَابُ فَتَرَى الْمُجْرِمِينَ مُشْفِقِينَ مِمَّا فِيهِ وَيَقُولُونَ يَا وَيْلَتَنَا مَالِ هَذَا الْكِتَابِ لَا يُغَادِرُ صَغِيرَةً وَلَا كَبِيرَةً إِلَّا أَحْصَاهَا ۚ وَوَجَدُوا مَا عَمِلُوا حَاضِرًا ۗ وَلَا يَظْلِمُ رَبُّكَ أَحَدًا

And the record [of deeds] will be placed [open], and you will see the criminals fearful of that within it, and they will say, "Oh, woe to us! What is this book that leaves nothing small or great except that it has enumerated it?" And they will find what they presented [before them]. And your Lord does injustice to no one. (Surah Kahf:49)

Note: Prophets and Messengers, Divine books, especially the Quran, and the Hereafter will be discussed later in their respective chapters in the course.

Who will be successful?

Quran's minimum criteria

Belief in one true God + belief in accountability and righteous deeds (result of belief in accountability)

إِنَّ الَّذِينَ آمَنُوا وَالَّذِينَ هَادُوا وَالنَّصَارَىٰ وَالصَّابِئِينَ مَنْ آمَنَ بِاللَّهِ وَالْيَوْمِ الْآخِرِ
وَعَمِلَ صَالِحًا فَلَهُمْ أَجْرُهُمْ عِندَ رَبِّهِمْ وَلَا خَوْفٌ عَلَيْهِمْ وَلَا هُمْ يَحْزَنُونَ

Surely those who are Muslims, and those who are Jews, and the Christians, and the Sabians, whoever believes in God and the Last Day and does good, they shall have their reward from their Lord, and there is no fear for them, nor shall they grieve. (2:62)

The success criteria

Extent of information received	Criteria for success
1 People who have never heard of revelation, messengers, & books	**Human nature:** Belief in one true God and good deeds based on the sense of accountability
2 People who have received the news of revelation, messengers, & books from the past	Their **sincere efforts** in searching for the truth and unbiased response when they are convinced
3 People who have received a Messenger from God among them in their lifetime	Their **acceptance of the message** and the messenger after receiving undeniable evidence

In which category do the people living around us fall under? And what should be our responsibility and their responsibility in that situation?

Chapter 6

Prophets and Messengers

This chapter introduces the concept of Prophets and Messengers and their role in religion.

The concept of Prophethood

Who are the prophets?

- The envoys of God who have brought this religion to mankind are called "Prophets."

- The Arabic word for Prophet is "*Nabi,*" which means "one who brings news of the unseen" – human beings have no other way to gain this knowledge.

- They were human beings of higher moral and intellectual qualities, selected by God based on His all-embracing knowledge and wisdom.

- Prophethood is God-given and cannot be acquired through efforts, spiritual training, asceticism, etc.

- Moses' narration in Surah Taha is an excellent example of the above statement.

- Some prophets are given unique merits over others, but in the sight of God, they are all equal.

- Prophets are sent to every community, as God promised to Adam when He made him the first prophet.

- After receiving revelations from God, they tell the truth to people, give glad tidings to those who believe in Him, and warn those who do not believe in Him of a dreadful fate.

Prophets	Unique Merits
Prophet Adam	God talked to him directly, the first human being with a human soul/self.
Prophet Ibrahim	God chose him as the leader/father of the nations/prophets after him.
Prophet Musa	God spoke to him and he was given some unique miracles.
Prophet Jesus	God raised him and given unique miracle of giving life to dead.
Prophet Yusuf	God gave him the capability to interpret dreams.
Prophet Dawud	God gave him a beautiful voice, and mountains and birds used to sing hymns with him; he also knew the art of making armor using iron.
Prophet Suleiman	God gave him control over Jinns, birds and animals (ability to understand their languages).
Prophet Muhammad	God sent him for entire humanity and gave him Quran which is a living miracle until the day of judgment.

How does God communicate?

- For guidance, communication from God happens **ONLY in THREE** ways:
  - Communication from behind a veil in which a person hears a voice but cannot see who is speaking – Moses had this experience.
  - Through Wahi, which can occur in two forms:
    1. God directly reveals in the heart with no channel in between.
    2. God sends an angel who reveals something in the prophet's heart on God's behalf.

اللَّهُ يَصْطَفِي مِنَ الْمَلَائِكَةِ رُسُلًا وَمِنَ النَّاسِ ۚ إِنَّ اللَّهَ سَمِيعٌ بَصِيرٌ

Allah chooses from the angels, messengers, and from the people (also). Indeed, Allah is All-Hearing and All-Seeing. (22:75)

إِنَّ اللَّهَ اصْطَفَىٰ آدَمَ وَنُوحًا وَآلَ إِبْرَاهِيمَ وَآلَ عِمْرَانَ عَلَى الْعَالَمِينَ

Indeed, Allah chose Adam and Noah and the family of Abraham and the family of 'Imran over the worlds (3:33)

فَلَمَّا أَتَاهَا نُودِيَ يَا مُوسَىٰ إِنِّي أَنَا رَبُّكَ فَاخْلَعْ نَعْلَيْكَ ۖ إِنَّكَ بِالْوَادِ الْمُقَدَّسِ طُوًى

وَأَنَا اخْتَرْتُكَ فَاسْتَمِعْ لِمَا يُوحَىٰ إِنَّنِي أَنَا اللَّهُ لَا إِلَٰهَ إِلَّا أَنَا فَاعْبُدْنِي وَأَقِمِ الصَّلَاةَ لِذِكْرِي

And when he came to it (near the mountain), he was called, "O Moses, Indeed, I am your Lord, so remove your shoes. Indeed, you are in the sacred valley of Tuwa. And I have chosen you, so listen to what is revealed [to you]. Indeed, I am Allah. There is no deity except Me, so worship Me and establish prayer for My remembrance. (20:11-14)

تِلْكَ الرُّسُلُ فَضَّلْنَا بَعْضَهُمْ عَلَىٰ بَعْضٍ ۘ مِّنْهُم مَّن كَلَّمَ اللَّهُ ۖ وَرَفَعَ بَعْضَهُمْ دَرَجَاتٍ

And those Messengers, some We have preferred above others; some there are to whom God spoke, and some He raised in rank. (2:253)

Wahi (Revelation)
The general definition of Wahi is the act of revealing words or inspirations from the heart. It is a physical experience.

The reality of Prophethood

- Prophethood is the selection of an individual by God to communicate with humans and deliver guidance.
- Direct Wahi can occur when the prophet is awake or in the form of a vision while asleep.
- The experience of receiving Wahi was very intense, and the intensity of the sweating would inundate Prophet Muhammad even in the coldest weather.
- Human beings can't understand or grasp the actual nature of this experience. After Wahi was delivered, Prophet Muhammad would remember it as if he had memorized it.
- Wahi is not a thought or idea – it is in the form of words that the Prophet hears, understands, and preserves in their original form.

وَمَا كَانَ لِبَشَرٍ أَن يُكَلِّمَهُ اللَّهُ إِلَّا وَحْيًا أَوْ مِن وَرَاءِ حِجَابٍ أَوْ يُرْسِلَ رَسُولًا
فَيُوحِيَ بِإِذْنِهِ مَا يَشَاءُ ۚ إِنَّهُ عَلِيٌّ حَكِيمٌ

And it is not the status of any mortal that God should speak to him except by revelation or from behind a veil, or He sends a messenger, and through His permission, he sends revelation to him of what He wills. Exalted is He and Wise. (42:51)

وَلَقَدْ رَآهُ نَزْلَةً أُخْرَىٰ عِندَ سِدْرَةِ الْمُنتَهَىٰ عِندَهَا جَنَّةُ الْمَأْوَىٰ إِذْ يَغْشَى السِّدْرَةَ مَا يَغْشَىٰ
مَا زَاغَ الْبَصَرُ وَمَا طَغَىٰ لَقَدْ رَأَىٰ مِنْ آيَاتِ رَبِّهِ الْكُبْرَىٰ

And he saw him descending once again at the *Sidrah* tree, beyond which no one can pass, near which is the Garden of Repose. At that time, the *Sidrah* tree was covered with that which covered it. [His] sight did not wander or exceed the limit. [In such a manner], he saw some of his Lord's greatest signs. (53:13-18)

Surety of Wahi

Since the experience of Wahi occurs without any desire on the Prophets' part, God makes the experience of Wahi in such a way that the Prophets are sure of the authenticity of this experience and message. Besides Wahi, God shows Prophets extraordinary sights and experiences beyond this world to bring their faith to a certain level. Prophet Muhammad was shown similar experiences during his famous journey of *Isra and Meraj* (a vision he had).

Why does God send Prophets?

- Humans have enormous capabilities for inductive reasoning based on evidence and examples, for deductive reasoning from one or more premises to reach a logical conclusion, and for inferring unseen facts from seen ones.
- Similarly, humans can distinguish between good and evil and even relate these concepts to comprehend their Creator and His justice.
- God endowed humans with these capabilities, and there is no need for prophets to tell them what to do.
- Prophets do not come to tell people how to conduct medical research, develop cities, form governments, manage the economy and financial matters, etc.
- Prophets are sent for a specific reason, which must be considered when looking at a prophet's life.

Reason for Prophets and Messengers

1. **Completion of guidance** – on top of what humans are already endowed with, delivering reminders, necessary details, and recipes for various aspects of religion

2. **Completion of Arguments** – Nations and people who are heedless of the inner guidance and testimony of their intellect are given the proofs for God and His meeting on the Day of Judgment in an undeniable way, such that those who reject clear truth are punished and serve as a lesson for people after them.

وَجَعَلْنَاهُمْ أَئِمَّةً يَهْدُونَ بِأَمْرِنَا وَأَوْحَيْنَا إِلَيْهِمْ فِعْلَ الْخَيْرَاتِ وَإِقَامَ الصَّلَاةِ وَإِيتَاءَ الزَّكَاةِ ۖ وَكَانُوا لَنَا عَابِدِينَ

And We made these [prophets] leaders to give guidance at Our behest and revealed to them to do pious deeds, show diligence in the prayer, and give Zakah. And they devoted their worship to Us (their Lord) (21:73)

يَا مَعْشَرَ الْجِنِّ وَالْإِنسِ أَلَمْ يَأْتِكُمْ رُسُلٌ مِّنكُمْ يَقُصُّونَ عَلَيْكُمْ آيَاتِي وَيُنذِرُونَكُمْ لِقَاءَ يَوْمِكُمْ هَٰذَا ۚ قَالُوا شَهِدْنَا عَلَىٰ أَنفُسِنَا ۖ وَغَرَّتْهُمُ الْحَيَاةُ الدُّنْيَا وَشَهِدُوا عَلَىٰ أَنفُسِهِمْ أَنَّهُمْ كَانُوا كَافِرِينَ ذَٰلِكَ أَن لَّمْ يَكُن رَّبُّكَ مُهْلِكَ الْقُرَىٰ بِظُلْمٍ وَأَهْلُهَا غَافِلُونَ

O groups of Jinn and men! Did there not come to you prophets from among you who proclaimed to you My revelations and warned you about the meeting on this day?" They will reply: "We bear witness against ourselves." – And indeed, the life of this world deceived them, and they testified against themselves that they rejected the truth – We have sent prophets because your Lord does not destroy people because of their oppression if their inhabitants are not aware of the Truth (and they have not been warned).(6:130-131)

Prophets are humans

- All prophets are humans; they eat, drink, walk about, sleep, marry, are born, and die. The Quran emphasizes that there is no difference between prophets and ordinary human beings in their nature of creation.

- There is a tendency among human beings, due to their relationship with and excessive reverence for the prophet, to elevate him to the status of a Godly or God-like being.

- The addressees of Prophet Muhammad demanded from him houses made of gold, flowing canals and rivers, an all-time spring season, orchards full of grapes and dates, pieces of heaven fallen on them, seeing God and angels, bringing a written book from the heavens, etc.

- Their human nature is highly relevant to us, as it shows that the directives are closest to human nature and that people can relate very easily to the Prophet.

- Despite the above facts, they are special in their knowledge of human behavior, intellect, personal character, spirituality, inclination towards virtuous deeds, God-given wisdom, and decision-making ability.

- On top of this, because they keep the flame of their inner guidance fully alight, God helps them in situations where ordinary human beings might falter.

- Because they will receive the divine revelation, their hearts and minds are pure, and the truth is always evident.

قُلْ سُبْحَانَ رَبِّي هَلْ كُنتُ إِلَّا بَشَرًا رَّسُولًا

وَمَا مَنَعَ النَّاسَ أَن يُؤْمِنُوا إِذْ جَاءَهُمُ الْهُدَىٰ إِلَّا أَن قَالُوا أَبَعَثَ اللَّهُ بَشَرًا رَّسُولًا

قُل لَّوْ كَانَ فِي الْأَرْضِ مَلَائِكَةٌ يَمْشُونَ مُطْمَئِنِّينَ لَنَزَّلْنَا عَلَيْهِم مِّنَ السَّمَاءِ مَلَكًا رَّسُولًا

Say: "Glory be to my Lord! Am I not but a Messenger who is just a human being?" And nothing prevents men from professing faith when guidance is revealed to them but the excuse: "Can it be that God has sent a human being as a messenger?" Tell [them]: "Had the angels been walking about comfortably on the earth, We would have sent down to them an angel from heavens as a messenger." (17:93-95)

وَلَمَّا بَلَغَ أَشُدَّهُ وَاسْتَوَىٰ آتَيْنَاهُ حُكْمًا وَعِلْمًا ۚ وَكَذَٰلِكَ نَجْزِي الْمُحْسِنِينَ

And when he had reached maturity and grown to manhood, We bestowed on him knowledge and the ability to make judgments. [This was a reward for his qualities]; thus, do We reward the righteous? (28:14)

Why aren't women chosen as prophets?

- Men and women are the same in their creation as the current human species. However, their nature and capabilities differ according to the roles they play in society.
- God gives responsibilities according to the nature of men and women, the capabilities they have, and the role they can play
- It is not trivial to go out in public one day and start announcing that God is talking to you.
- Prophethood demands extreme efforts, sacrifices, the ability to handle persecution, courage to fight a war with your own family, tribesmen, and countrymen, migration from your land, and going out of the way to ascertain that the message is delivered to each addressee of the prophet.

Prophethood is a grave responsibility

- Prophethood is a grave responsibility and not a privilege.
- God mentioned the nature of this responsibility on many occasions, and the Prophet Muhammad always considered it to be so.

Soon, we are going to **burden you with the responsibility** of a heavy word (73:5)

Abdullah Bin Masud said: The Prophet said to me once, 'Recite the Quran to me." I said, "O Allah's Messenger, shall I recite to you while it has been revealed to you?" He said, "Yes." So, I recited Surat-An-Nisa, but when I recited the Verse: 'How (will it be) then when We bring from each nation a witness and We bring you (O Muhammad) as a witness against these people.' (4.41) He said, "Enough for now." I looked at him, and behold! His eyes were overflowing with tears. (Hadith)

Difference between Prophet and Messenger

- The Quran distinguishes between a Prophet (Nabi) and a Messenger (Rasul), as they deliver the same message but with different outcomes.
- Some Prophets are assigned the additional position of "Messengerhood" called *Risalah*.
- The Prophet's responsibility is to deliver the message in the best possible way, give glad tidings to the believers, and warn the people who reject the message.
- "Risalah" means that a messenger is assigned to his people with the authority to decide their fate through divine sanction if they reject him and his message.

Messengers (*Rusul, plural of Rasool*)

- Messenger practically enforces the sovereignty of the truth upon their people by implementing God's Judgment in this very world on them—the righteous will be rewarded, and the wicked will be punished.
- God gives him and his companions 'victory' over their enemies, no matter what
- God's dealings with messengers and his people are in black and white – if they honor the covenant of God, they will be rewarded; otherwise, they will be punished in this world.
- Messengers are given such signs to prove their truth and are asked to propagate them so that people cannot deny that they are from God – they become Shahadah for them.

What is Shahadah?

- The very existence of the messengers among their nations becomes a sign of God, as if their people can observe God walking on earth with them and delivering His verdicts.
- Based on the signs of truth that they have directly observed, they are directed to propagate the truth and present to the people with full certainty the very guidance of God, the way they have received it from Him. In the Quran, this is called Shahadah (direct witness). Once this is established, it becomes a basis of the judgement of the Almighty both in this world and in that to come.
- The same status of Shahadah that Messengers had was also given to the progeny of Ibrahim.

Fate of Prophet Muhammad's nation

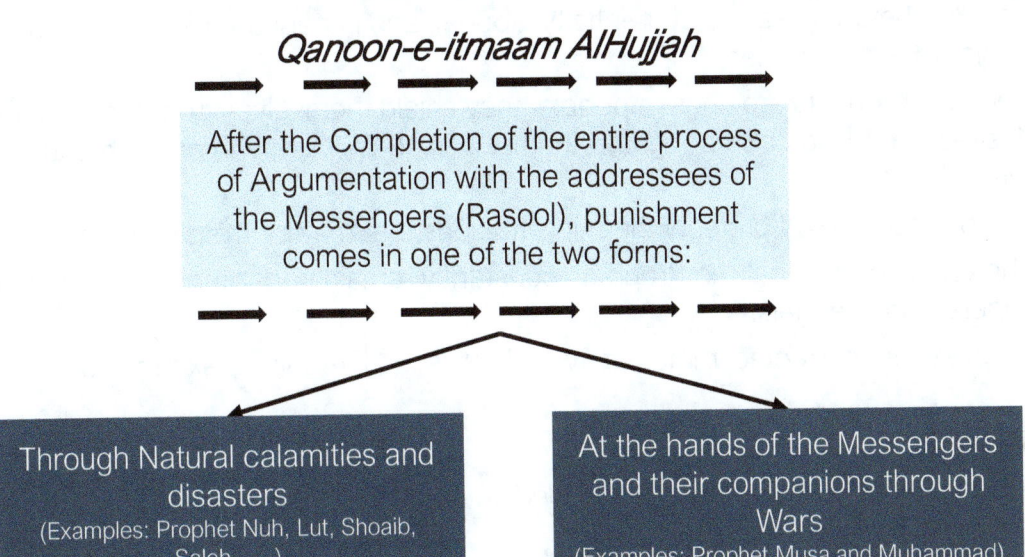

Qanoon-e-itmaam AlHujjah

After the Completion of the entire process of Argumentation with the addressees of the Messengers (Rasool), punishment comes in one of the two forms:

Through Natural calamities and disasters
(Examples: Prophet Nuh, Lut, Shoaib, Saleh .....)

At the hands of the Messengers and their companions through Wars
(Examples: Prophet Musa and Muhammad)

- Most nations where Messengers were sent were punished through natural calamities and disasters like earthquakes, cyclones, floods, etc.
- The Messenger and his companions punished the addressees of the Prophet Muhammad and the Prophet Musa through war.
- Most of the verses in the Quran talking about Prophet Muhammad waging war against his direct addressees are related to the law of Risalah, also called the "Law of Completion of Proof (*Qanoon-e-itmaam AlHujjah*).
- Unfortunately, these verses have been taken out of context and 'hijacked' by various groups in Islam and applied to non-Muslim leaders and nations today.

و هُوَ الَّذِي أَرْسَلَ رَسُولَهُ بِالْهُدَىٰ وَدِينِ الْحَقِّ لِيُظْهِرَهُ عَلَى الدِّينِ كُلِّهِ وَلَوْ كَرِهَ الْمُشْرِكُونَ

It is He Who has sent His Rasul with guidance and the religion of truth that he may make it sovereign over all religions [of Arabia], even though these Idolaters [of Arabia] may detest this. (61:9)

إِنَّ الَّذِينَ يُحَادُّونَ اللَّهَ وَرَسُولَهُ أُولَٰئِكَ فِي الْأَذَلِّينَ

Indeed, those who oppose Allah and His Messenger shall be humiliated. The Almighty has ordained: "My messengers and I shall always prevail. Indeed Allah is Mighty and Powerful." (58:20)

إِنَّا أَرْسَلْنَا إِلَيْكُمْ رَسُولًا شَاهِدًا عَلَيْكُمْ كَمَا أَرْسَلْنَا إِلَىٰ فِرْعَوْنَ رَسُولً

[O Quraysh of Makkah!] We have sent forth a Messenger to you to bear witness before you, just as We sent a Messenger to the Pharaoh. (73:15)

Innocence/Infallibility of Prophets

- The Prophets' Message's authenticity, appeal, and impact are closely tied to their unblemished character.
- Because prophets are chosen people, they shield themselves from the lures of inner desires and those of Satan, guard themselves against sin, and are righteous among their people.
- On top of that, God protects them in situations that may blemish their character.
- The Quran claims that the Prophets constantly remain under the protection and supervision of angels.
- Prophets are corrected immediately and punished if required (example of Yunus).

Examples

- God protected Yusuf when ordinary people couldn't save themselves under the circumstances he faced.
- Imagine if Prophet Yusuf had committed the sin of Zina. What credibility would he have had later, when he was preaching goodness?
- Satan lured Adam many times, acting as a well-wisher and leading him to believe that he would become eternal by eating the forbidden fruit. Adam lamented the act and repented immediately before God
- Musa did not kill the arrogant Coptic deliberately, but accidentally hit him in a brawl that the Coptic started.

وَاذْكُرْ عِبَادَنَا إِبْرَاهِيمَ وَإِسْحَاقَ وَيَعْقُوبَ أُولِي الْأَيْدِي وَالْأَبْصَارِ ۞ إِنَّا أَخْلَصْنَاهُم بِخَالِصَةٍ ذِكْرَى الدَّارِ

وَإِنَّهُمْ عِندَنَا لَمِنَ الْمُصْطَفَيْنَ الْأَخْيَارِ

And remember Our servants Abraham, Isaac, and Jacob: men of might and vision. We chose them for a special mission – reminding [people] about the Hereafter – and with Us they are counted among the best and the most righteous of men. And also remember Ishmael, Elisha, and Dhu al-Kifl. [We chose all of them], and all of these were the best of men. (38:45-47)

إِلَّا مَنِ ارْتَضَىٰ مِن رَّسُولٍ فَإِنَّهُ يَسْلُكُ مِن بَيْنِ يَدَيْهِ وَمِنْ خَلْفِهِ رَصَدًا

لِيَعْلَمَ أَن قَدْ أَبْلَغُوا رِسَالَاتِ رَبِّهِمْ وَأَحَاطَ بِمَا لَدَيْهِمْ وَأَحْصَىٰ كُلَّ شَيْءٍ عَدَدًا

As for those whom He chooses as His Prophets [they can say nothing of their own] because He guards them from behind and from the front that He may know if they have delivered the messages of their Lord; and He surrounds whatever is around them and keeps count of all their things. (72-27-28)

Obeying the Prophet

- Professing faith in a prophet means obeying him because his commands are at God's behest.
- Recognizing a prophet and then not obeying him is like rejecting him.
- He is not a counselor or advisor, but rather someone who should be listened to and followed.
- His followers must seek his guidance in all their affairs while he is among them.
- Obeying him is like obeying God, and that's why the reward for the followers is immense.
- Obeying a prophet is not like a ritual (e.g., praying), but his followers are required to help him and support him with full sincerity and devotion.

Obeying the Prophet is like obeying God

- When the Prophet is among a people, obeying him is actually obeying God, because he is simply implementing God's will, especially in matters of religion.
- However, the Quran demands that when Prophet Muhammad decides a matter among believers (religious or otherwise), they should not feel bad in their hearts, and that is a sign of belief in him and God.

وَمَا أَرْسَلْنَا مِن رَّسُولٍ إِلَّا لِيُطَاعَ بِإِذْنِ اللَّهِ

And whichever messenger We sent forth, was sent so that he be obeyed by God's directive (4:64)

قُلْ إِن كُنتُمْ تُحِبُّونَ اللَّهَ فَاتَّبِعُونِي يُحْبِبْكُمُ اللَّهُ

Tell them: "If you love God, follow me; God will love you" (3:31)

مَّن يُطِعِ الرَّسُولَ فَقَدْ أَطَاعَ اللَّهَ

He who obeys the messenger, in fact, obeys God (4:80)

فَلَا وَرَبِّكَ لَا يُؤْمِنُونَ حَتَّىٰ يُحَكِّمُوكَ فِيمَا شَجَرَ بَيْنَهُمْ ثُمَّ لَا يَجِدُوا فِي أَنفُسِهِمْ حَرَجًا مِّمَّا قَضَيْتَ وَيُسَلِّمُوا تَسْلِيمًا

I swear by your Lord that they cannot be believers until they accept your decision in their disputes, and whatever you decide, they submit to without any unwillingness of their hearts. (4:65)

Recognizing a Prophet of God

- Every prophet displays two virtues that serve as the source of many other human virtues: Remembering God and sympathizing with and supporting the less fortunate in their societies.
- Their personality and intellectual growth do not undergo any visible developmental process that could serve as evidence of the quality of the message they preach when they receive prophethood – they receive prophethood without any training or preparation.
- Besides this, every prophet is blessed with potent signs in his life that even his adversaries cannot deny his veracity and are left with no excuse.
- The nature of the signs given is dependent on society, time, culture, and circumstances.

Signs of a Prophet

1 Every prophet is predicted or prophesied by the previous prophet.

4 Every prophet makes some predictions about the future which cannot be done otherwise.

2 Revelation contains no internal contradictions or inconsistencies.

5 Messengers demonstrate the divine justice in this world for the nation to which they are sent.

3 Every prophet is given miracles according to the time and circumstances he is in.

6 The revelation presented is a literary masterpiece with no effort from the presenter.

- For example, as evidence that the Quran is not a made-up book by Prophet Muhammad, God presented his earlier life before the revelation.
- The people of Quraish did not see any sign in him that he was working towards producing such a beautiful piece of literature as the Quran.

قُل لَّوْ شَاءَ اللَّهُ مَا تَلَوْتُهُ عَلَيْكُمْ وَلَا أَدْرَاكُم بِهِ ۖ فَقَدْ لَبِثْتُ فِيكُمْ عُمُرًا مِّن قَبْلِهِ ۚ أَفَلَا تَعْقِلُونَ

Tell them: "Had God pleased, I would never have recited this Quran to you, nor would He have made you aware of it. [It is His decision] because I have spent a lifetime among you. Do you not use your senses?" (10:16)

Predictions

- Most prophets are predicted by the previous prophets. The Quran mentioned this fact about Prophet Muhammad:

وَإِنَّهُ لَفِي زُبُرِ الْأَوَّلِينَ ۚ أَوَلَمْ يَكُن لَّهُمْ آيَةً أَن يَعْلَمَهُ عُلَمَاءُ بَنِي إِسْرَائِيلَ

And he is already mentioned in previous scriptures. Is it not a sign for them that the scholars of the Children of Israel already know him (from their scriptures)? (26:196-197)

وَإِذْ قَالَ عِيسَى ابْنُ مَرْيَمَ يَا بَنِي إِسْرَائِيلَ إِنِّي رَسُولُ اللَّهِ إِلَيْكُم مُّصَدِّقًا لِّمَا بَيْنَ يَدَيَّ مِنَ التَّوْرَاةِ وَمُبَشِّرًا بِرَسُولٍ يَأْتِي مِن بَعْدِي اسْمُهُ أَحْمَدُ ۖ فَلَمَّا جَاءَهُم بِالْبَيِّنَاتِ قَالُوا هَٰذَا سِحْرٌ مُّبِينٌ

Remember, when Jesus said: O children of Israel, I am the messenger sent to you from God, fulfilling the prophecies written in Torah, and I am prophesying for a messenger after me whose name will be Ahmed. But when he brought clear signs (miracles) to them, they said, "This is open magic" (61:6)

- Also, the Prophet made a few predictions about the future, which are recorded in the Quran. Those are actually God's predictions through him.

غُلِبَتِ الرُّومُ ۝ فِي أَدْنَى الْأَرْضِ وَهُم مِّن بَعْدِ غَلَبِهِمْ سَيَغْلِبُونَ

فِي بِضْعِ سِنِينَ ۗ لِلَّهِ الْأَمْرُ مِن قَبْلُ وَمِن بَعْدُ ۚ وَيَوْمَئِذٍ يَفْرَحُ الْمُؤْمِنُونَ

بِنَصْرِ اللَّهِ ۚ يَنصُرُ مَن يَشَاءُ ۖ وَهُوَ الْعَزِيزُ الرَّحِيمُ

وَعْدَ اللَّهِ ۖ لَا يُخْلِفُ اللَّهُ وَعْدَهُ وَلَٰكِنَّ أَكْثَرَ النَّاسِ لَا يَعْلَمُونَ

The Romans have been defeated in a nearby land. But in a few years after this defeat, they shall become victorious. Whatever happened earlier happened because of God's directive, and whatever happens later will happen because of His directive. And on that day, the believers will rejoice because of God's help. He helps whomsoever He wants, and He is the Mighty and Ever-Merciful. This is God's promise, and God never goes back on His promise, yet most men do not know it. (30:2-6)

Prophet Muhammad – The Last Prophet

- The chain of prophethood started with Adam and ended with Prophet Muhammad.
- The purpose of prophethood was to 'present the Truth from the Lord in the most undeniable way.'
- The Quran will now serve this purpose until the day of judgment – the Quran is the living speech of God with us.
- The Quran declared that Prophet Muhammad is the **SEAL OF THE PROPHETS** and it uses a specific word for his finality (*Khaatam*).
- In Arabic, the word خَاتَم means "a seal." It means that the institution of prophethood has been closed and sealed.
- A seal is also used to testify or attest to something. So if someone claims prophethood today, he must be attested by Prophet Muhammad, and Prophet Muhammad clearly said, "There is no prophet after me."
- The Quran and Prophet Muhammad categorically said that prophethood has been seized in all forms.

مَّا كَانَ مُحَمَّدٌ أَبَا أَحَدٍ مِّن رِّجَالِكُمْ وَلَكِن رَّسُولَ اللَّهِ وَخَاتَمَ النَّبِيِّينَ ۗ وَكَانَ اللَّهُ بِكُلِّ شَيْءٍ عَلِيمًا

Muhammad is the father of no man among you, but he is the Prophet of God and the seal of the prophets, and God has knowledge of all things. (33:40)

لم يَبْقَ من النُّبُوَّةِ إلا الْمُبَشِّرَاتُ قالوا وما الْمُبَشِّرَاتُ قال الرُّؤْيَا الصَّالِحَةُ

"Nothing remains of prophethood except for things which give glad tidings." They asked: "What are these?" He replied: "Good dreams." Al-Bukhari, Al-Jami' al-sahih, 1206, (no. 6990).

The leaders of the Israelites were their prophets. When one prophet would pass away, another would succeed him. But there will be no prophet after me; there will only be successors. Al-Bukhari, Al-Jami' al-sahih, 581-582, (no. 3455)

I and the prophets before me can be likened to a person who constructed a beautiful building, but in a corner, there was a gap for a brick. People would roam around this building, express their wonder at it, and ask: "Why was this brick not placed in its place?" He said: "I am that brick and I am the seal of the prophets." Al-Bukhari, Al-Jami' al-sahih, 595, (no. 3535).

Why did God seize the prophethood?

- Previous scriptures were not protected or preserved, but the message of God, now in the form of the Quran, has been protected and preserved until the Day of Judgment.
- The Quran is the verbatim word of God (Kalam), and human beings have a single place to find what their Lord wants from them.
- All the past events of the Messengers, including the most recent event of Prophet Muhammad in Arabia, when God's justice was demonstrated on earth, are now narrated in detail and saved in the Quran.
- The Children of Ismail are handed over the responsibility for spreading the message of God to the rest of humanity until the day of judgment.
- God wants to make sure that at any given time and place, His message is known to humanity directly from Him through Messengers and Books.

The Role of Children of Ibrahim

- Until Prophet Ibrahim, God maintained 'Risalah' (Messengerhood) within nations through individual prophets – these messengers held the position of *Shahadah* (evidence for or against them) within their nations.
- From Ibrahim's time, God bestowed the same *Shahadah* upon the progeny of Ibrahim – they had the responsibility as a nation to deliver the message, and they were evidence for or against the nations they were among

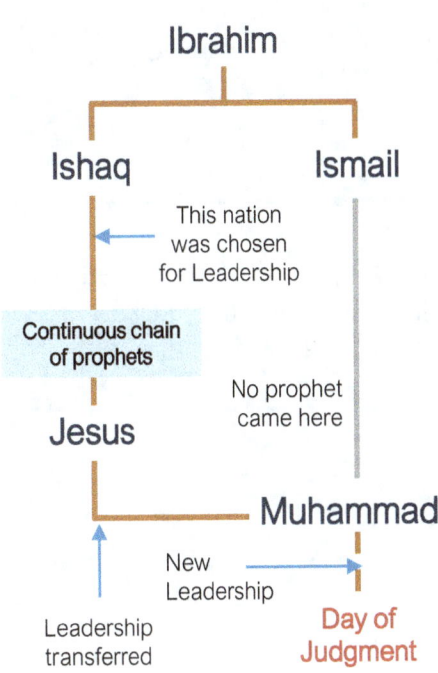

- Almighty has promised the progeny of Ibrahim that if they adhere to the truth, they will lead all the world's nations. If they deviate from it, they will be deposed from this position. They will have to face the punishment of humiliation and subjugation – another aspect of how they become the evidence for God's judgment that He will display on the DoJ.
- A major leadership shift occurred between Prophet Jesus and Prophet Muhammad when the responsibility of Shahadah until the day of judgment was given to the progeny of Prophet Ismail.

- God promised this special relationship with them in various verses of the Quran.

وَإِذِ ابْتَلَىٰ إِبْرَاهِيمَ رَبُّهُ بِكَلِمَاتٍ فَأَتَمَّهُنَّ ۖ قَالَ إِنِّي جَاعِلُكَ لِلنَّاسِ إِمَامًا ۖ قَالَ وَمِن ذُرِّيَّتِي ۖ قَالَ لَا يَنَالُ عَهْدِي الظَّالِمِينَ

And recall when Ibrahim was tried by His Lord on a few matters, and he fulfilled them. He said, "I have decided to appoint you the leader of mankind." "And what of my progeny?" asked Ibrahim. He replied: "My covenant does not reach to the unjust. (2:124)

وَأَوْفُوا بِعَهْدِي أُوفِ بِعَهْدِكُمْ

Keep my covenant, and I will keep yours (2:40)

A group of Muslims, called Sufis, claims that their Sheikhs still receive Wahi from God and they still communicate with Him. Investigate why they say that after categorical statements from the Quran and Sunnah.

The Quran – A Miracle

This chapter introduces the most miraculous book on the face of the earth, the Quran, its importance in Islam, and how we can prove that it is divine.

The purpose of Divine Books

- Many prophets receive Divine Books in various forms.
- God gave Books, so prophets (when they were present) and scholars (after prophets were gone) have documentary evidence of what God actually wanted from them.
- The purpose of revealing these books is to judge between right and wrong, so people can resolve their differences in matters of religious guidance through them. It becomes the ultimate authority on that matter.
- The content depends on who they are sent to and what they are sent for – the Gospel is mostly wisdom behind the religion and religious laws, and the Torah is mostly laws.

وَأَنزَلَ مَعَهُمُ الْكِتَابَ بِالْحَقِّ لِيَحْكُمَ بَيْنَ النَّاسِ فِيمَا اخْتَلَفُوا فِيهِ

And with these [prophets], He sent down His Book as the decisive truth so that it may **settle these differences** between people. (2:213)

وَأَنزَلْنَا مَعَهُمُ الْكِتَابَ وَالْمِيزَانَ لِيَقُومَ النَّاسُ بِالْقِسْطِ

And with these [messengers], We sent down Our Book, which is the Scale, so that [through it] people are able to **adhere to truth with justice**. (57:25)

- The guidance for which Books are used as a Scale is **always religious**.
- Once a Book is considered divine, all religious dogmas, concepts, and interpretations presented by humans must be examined in light of that Book.
- The protection, preservation, originality, and authenticity of the Book require divine intervention; otherwise, the Book is lost over time.
- Matters of faith (which drive our actions) are often corrupted over time, and one of the main areas the Books focus on is restoring them to the correct beliefs.
- God's attributes, His dealings, and His awareness must be known only through these Books.
- All other religious texts outside of the Divine Books must be looked at in the light of these Books.

The Quran – A Miracle

This chapter introduces the most miraculous book on the face of the earth, the Quran, its importance in Islam, and how we can prove that it is divine.

The purpose of Divine Books

- Many prophets receive Divine Books in various forms.
- God gave Books, so prophets (when they were present) and scholars (after prophets were gone) have documentary evidence of what God actually wanted from them.
- The purpose of revealing these books is to judge between right and wrong, so people can resolve their differences in matters of religious guidance through them. It becomes the ultimate authority on that matter.
- The content depends on who they are sent to and what they are sent for – the Gospel is mostly wisdom behind the religion and religious laws, and the Torah is mostly laws.

وَأَنزَلَ مَعَهُمُ الْكِتَابَ بِالْحَقِّ لِيَحْكُمَ بَيْنَ النَّاسِ فِيمَا اخْتَلَفُوا فِيهِ

And with these [prophets], He sent down His Book as the decisive truth so that it may **settle these differences** between people. (2:213)

وَأَنزَلْنَا مَعَهُمُ الْكِتَابَ وَالْمِيزَانَ لِيَقُومَ النَّاسُ بِالْقِسْطِ

And with these [messengers], We sent down Our Book, which is the Scale, so that [through it] people are able to **adhere to truth with justice**. (57:25)

- The guidance for which Books are used as a Scale is **always religious**.
- Once a Book is considered divine, all religious dogmas, concepts, and interpretations presented by humans must be examined in light of that Book.
- The protection, preservation, originality, and authenticity of the Book require divine intervention; otherwise, the Book is lost over time.
- Matters of faith (which drive our actions) are often corrupted over time, and one of the main areas the Books focus on is restoring them to the correct beliefs.
- God's attributes, His dealings, and His awareness must be known only through these Books.
- All other religious texts outside of the Divine Books must be looked at in the light of these Books.

Last Divine Book – The Quran

- Revealed to the last prophet of God, Prophet Muhammad (peace be upon him).
- It's the verbatim speech of God in which not a single dot was added by Prophet Muhammad.
- The revelations occurred incrementally over approximately 23 years, beginning in 610 CE, when Prophet Muhammad was 40, and concluding in 632 CE, the year of his death.
- The Quran is organized into 114 chapters, known as Surahs, which consist of individual verses, called Ayahs. Please note that Surah does not correspond directly to a chapter in other books. A Surah may have a unique theme, and the verses within the Surah may cover many topics, but remain closer to the overall theme. Sometimes, more than one Surah adopts a theme.
- The Surahs are arranged in a different final order than the chronological order.
- Every chapter, except for the ninth (at-Tawbah), begins with the invocation "*Bismi-llahir-Rahmanir-Rahim*" ("In the name of Allah, the Most Gracious, the Most Merciful")
- For reading and memorization purposes, the text is also divided into 30 equal parts, called Juz. This structure allows the entire Quran to be completed in 30 days during the month of Ramadan.
- It calls itself "*Al-Mizan*" – the Scale and "*Al-Furqan*" - The Distinguisher.
- It is in Arabic, revealed to the Prophet's heart by God.
- The Prophet presented it to his people, and from them it was transmitted by consensus and through the oral and written perpetuation of the Muslims.
- The Quran is the only original, authentic, unadulterated, and trustworthy Book of God on earth now.
- In matters of religion, the decision of what's accepted and what's rejected shall be made in light of the Quran – it rules over every other scripture and religious text now.
- Scholars of the Quran do use external sources of knowledge (e.g., history, the Bible, and the Hadith) when explaining its verses, but when those sources contradict the Quran, the Quran is considered the final authority over other religious texts. The external text must be understood in the light of the Quran.

The protection & preservation of the Quran

At the time of revelation

- At the time of revelation, God made sure that **devils (Jinns) were unable to interfere** in the process of divine revelation in any way possible. Devils (Jinns) were barred, through special arrangements, from meddling in revelations in any way, so that they are delivered in their pure form from God to the Prophet Muhammad through the Angel Gabriel (Jibrael).

وَأَنَّا كُنَّا نَقْعُدُ مِنْهَا مَقَاعِدَ لِلسَّمْعِ ۖ فَمَن يَسْتَمِعِ الْآنَ يَجِدْ لَهُ شِهَابًا رَّصَدًا

And indeed, we used to sit there in nearby stations to steal a hearing, but anyone who tries to listen now finds a flaming fire watching him in ambush (72:9)

- The **angel chosen to deliver the Quran** is called by the Quran "the one endued with power, held in honor before the Lord of the Throne, obeyed in Heavens, moreover trustworthy." Archangel Jibrael is so powerful that evil spirits and devils cannot overpower him – when he is entrusted with something, he fully protects and never falls short in his responsibilities

إِنَّهُ لَقَوْلُ رَسُولٍ كَرِيمٍ   ذِي قُوَّةٍ عِندَ ذِي الْعَرْشِ مَكِينٍ   مُّطَاعٍ ثَمَّ أَمِينٍ

Indeed, this is the Word brought by an honorable messenger, very powerful with a high place in the presence of God. His instructions are followed, and he is trustworthy (81:19-21)

- **Revealed to the heart of the person** who was entrusted with the Quran was the best human being on the face of the earth at that time, famously called the Truthful (Al-Sadiq) and the Trustworthy (Al-Amin) among his people. On top of that, God took responsibility for the initial and final arrangements of revelation, its memorization, and its safeguarding by the prophet.

لَا تُحَرِّكْ بِهِ لِسَانَكَ لِتَعْجَلَ بِهِ   إِنَّ عَلَيْنَا جَمْعَهُ وَقُرْآنَهُ

فَإِذَا قَرَأْنَاهُ فَاتَّبِعْ قُرْآنَهُ   ثُمَّ إِنَّ عَلَيْنَا بَيَانَهُ

[To acquire] this [Qur'an] swiftly [O Prophet!] do not move your tongue hastily over it. Indeed, upon Us is its collection and recital. So, when We have (finally) recited it, follow that recital [of Ours]. Then upon Us is to explain it [wherever need be]. (75:16-19)

Protection after the revelation

The All-Powerful God ensured that His Final Book was preserved as it was delivered to the prophet. The Quran is <u>unlike any other book, where a single copy is produced and then replicated</u> to preserve it. The prophet adopts unusual means of memorization and verbal transmission to his companions, and generations after them, to preserve it

- From a purely historical point of view, the Quran is the ONLY religious text that is preserved in its original language, and it has stayed with the Muslim world exactly as Prophet Muhammad gave it.
- The Quran is transferred through verbal and written perpetuation (Tawatur) and consensus (Ijma') of the Muslims, and there has been no gap in any generation for the last 1400+ years.
- God guaranteed its protection in the Quran itself. This guarantee was not given to any other religious test before.

إِنَّا نَحْنُ نَزَّلْنَا الذِّكْرَ وَإِنَّا لَهُ لَحَافِظُونَ

It is Us who revealed this Reminder, and We shall preserve it (15:9)

Primary Method

Memorizers
(Huffaz)

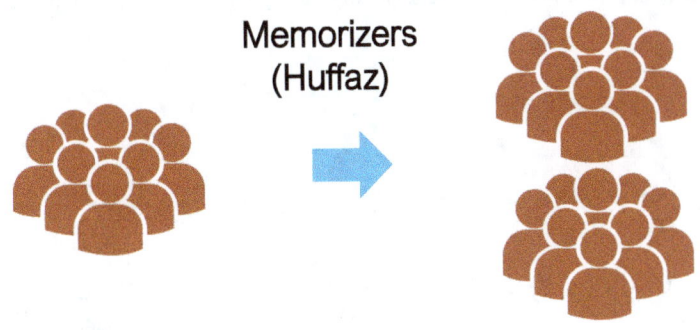

Secondary Method

Written

How God preserved His Last Book

- The Quran was recited 5 times a day in daily prayers. Prophet Muhammad recited it to the people, and people recited it in their Tahajjud prayers, which involved long recitations.

- In every Ramadan, the Prophet Muhammad would recite it to Jibrael, and Jibrael would recite it to him. In his last Ramadan, this review happened twice between them.

- At the time of the passing of the Prophet Muhammad, there were thousands of Quran memorizers who not only memorized it but also created their own copies.

- Muslim Caliphs made sure that the original text of the Quran was reproduced and verified (by memorizers). Copies were sent to far lands where people had newly accepted Islam.

- Since that time, there have been millions of memorizers alive at any given moment in time in this world.

- The Quran is a literary masterpiece – the choice of words, arrangement, and eloquence were so unmatched that any addition to the text would be easily noticed by the people at that time.

The language of the Quran

The original language of the Quran, Arabic, is a living language spoken and written throughout the world. Since the time of the Prophet, thousands of Islamic scholars have studied, practiced, and mastered it. Due to all these arrangements to protect and preserve the Quran, there is no possibility of interpolation in the Quran till the Day of Judgment.

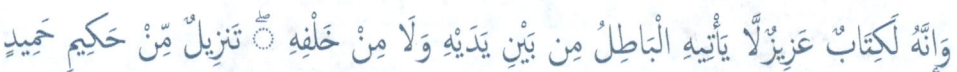

And there is no doubt that it is a powerful scripture. Falsehood cannot reach it from either the front or behind. It is a revelation from a Wise and Glorious God. (41:41-42)

Other Divine Books

- Today, the Bible comprises all previous scriptures associated with the Abrahamic tradition outside the Quran.
- It can be said:

Bible = Torah + Psalms + Gospels

Torah

- It was revealed to Musa and is also called "The Old Testament."
- Composed of the first five books of the Bible, called the Pentateuch.
- The majority of the text contains the Law.
- The Quran calls it light and directs Jews to get guidance from it.

Psalms

- Revealed to Dawud and is also called "Psalms of David".
- Collection of Hymns. It has five books and 150 Psalms.
- It is mostly the praises of God and the wisdom behind the religion.

Gospels

- Revealed to Jesus and are part of "The New Testament".
- The Gospels could not be compiled, so the disciples of Jesus narrated it – 4 of them were selected (Matthew, Mark, Luke, and John).
- Originally written in Greek, but Jesus' language is known to be Aramaic.
- Contains the wisdom of religion.

Quran is the Guardian

- God called the Quran *Muhaymin,* meaning the Guardian or Protector, above other divine books. That's why the Quran skips many historical details in the stories of the prophets, knowing that its addressees know them from their own scriptures.

$$\text{وَأَنزَلْنَا إِلَيْكَ الْكِتَابَ بِالْحَقِّ مُصَدِّقًا لِّمَا بَيْنَ يَدَيْهِ مِنَ الْكِتَابِ وَمُهَيْمِنًا عَلَيْهِ ۖ فَاحْكُم بَيْنَهُم}$$

$$\text{بِمَا أَنزَلَ اللَّهُ ۚ وَلَا تَتَّبِعْ أَهْوَاءَهُمْ عَمَّا جَاءَكَ مِنَ الْحَقِّ}$$

And [O Prophet!] We have revealed the Book with the truth, confirming it before it and standing as **a guardian over it**. Therefore, give judgment among them according to the guidance revealed by God and do not yield to their whims by swerving from the truth revealed to you. (5:48)

Quran and Science

- Some non-Muslims try to create a conflict between religion and science, and the main reason behind it is the interpretation of the Quran by some Muslim scholars who were or are influenced by the science of that time when they interpreted the verses of the Quran.
- When scientific knowledge evolves, they see a conflict because the earlier interpretation is no longer valid.
- The Quran is a literary masterpiece revealed to the Prophet to provide guidance on religious matters and to convey news about the unseen.
- The Quran is **NOT** a book of science.

The Question	Science's Answers
What is God's scheme for this universe?	✖
What is the purpose of our lives in this world?	✖
I have a unique personality; where does it come from, and where does it go when I die?	✖
What is death and what is life after death?	✖
Which deeds are we accountable for, and when will we stand in front of God?	✖
How should one prepare for that day to be successful?	✖

The Question	Quran's Answers
Why is the sky blue?	✖
What is the universe made of?	✖
How do we get energy from the sun?	✖
How do we treat bacterial infection?	✖
How to improve the speed of a computer?	✖

The relationship between Quran and Science

- Science is the intellectual and practical activity encompassing the systematic study of the structure and behavior of the physical and natural world through observation and experiment.
- However, scientists' (not science's) attempts to answer some questions about our existence have so far failed to address the most fundamental existential questions, those related to the metaphysical world.
- People who deny God need an anchor for their position, and science is that anchor. Atheism advocates will always try to provide an 'alternate' response to every question, regardless of whether it is their 'domain' or not.

- As can be seen from the previous slides, the Quran and Science address two distinct domains of our lives and this universe.
- The aim of religion (or the Quran) is the moral purification of human beings so they can achieve success in the Hereafter.
- Science studies matter, the universe, and the laws within it—it gives answers to HOW, not WHY.
- The Quran alludes to various aspects of human nature, natural science, and history ONLY to substantiate its arguments.
- However, when the Quran mentions a scientific fact to substantiate an argument, it cannot conflict with the latest scientific facts (not theories), because the knowledge comes directly from God.
- Verses related to scientific phenomena must be interpreted literally.

> It is not recommended to read science into the Quran or to interpret it in light of scientific discoveries. Science is a progressive subject, and new research makes the older research obsolete. The scholars must translate the Quranic verses within the bounds of the language and in a way that linguistically delivers the message.

- Scientific research has established that the brain is the center of human thought. Similarly, it has been established that the heart is not related to the thought process.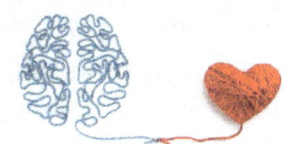
- The Quran uses literary metaphors and addresses the hearts.

- It uses the word "heart" as a seat of thought and the center of all our emotions and thoughts. This metaphor is common in many languages. We usually say, "My heart is not in it." When we are emotionally down, we say, "It breaks my heart."
- Can we say that the Quran is scientifically wrong?

Note: https://www.sciencenews.org/article/new-3-d-map-illuminates-little-brain-nerve-cells-within-heart

Understanding the Quran

Quran's Law of Completion of Argument

- The Quran is the story of Prophet Muhammad's warning mission (Indhar) to his people and those around him, which occurred in accordance with the Law of Completion of Argument.

- When reading and interpreting the Quran, this law, which is very visible in the Quran, must be taken into consideration. This law defines the different stages of Prophet Muhammad's mission.

- A summary of this law is described here:

Warning (Indhar)
Announcement of Messengerhood and initial warning to specific people around the Prophet

→

General Warning (Indhar-e-Aam)
General warning to the people in that area and around that area

↓

Migration and Disassociation
If possible, Messenger and his people migrate to another land and completely disassociate themselves from the people who rejected the message

←

Completion of Arguments (Itmam-al-Hujjah)
Arguments are completed, and evidence is presented in its concrete and undeniable form

↓

Punishment (Azaab)
Punishment at the hands of Messenger and his companions and/or Angels

→ Through Natural calamities and disasters (Examples: Prophet Nuh, Lut, Shoaib, Saleh ....)

→ At the hands of Messengers and their companions through Wars (Examples: Prophet Musa (after Firaun), and Muhammad)

- In most cases of Messengers, such as Noah or Lot, God separated non-believers from believers at the time of punishment, as per His Law. The Quran states that all associations must be severed before a punishment is meted out.

- In the case of Prophet Muhammad, the Polytheists were killed, and the People of the Book were overpowered and forced to pay tax (Jizyah).

- This law is clearly evident in the Quran when addressing the Prophet Muhammad and his nation.

The subject matter of Quran

- Verses in the Quran were revealed according to the circumstances, situations, needs of the time, place, addressees, questions asked, etc.
- Even though the Quran describes laws, matters of faith, and stories of previous nations, they appear in the middle of that time's story, as needed.
- The Quran has documented all the phases of his preaching mission as outlined in the previous page. A couple of examples are shown here:

Disassociation and Migration

قُلْ يَآ أَيُّهَا الْكَفِرُونَ ۝ لَآ أَعْبُدُ مَا تَعْبُدُونَ ۝ وَلَآ أَنْتُمْ عَبِدُونَ مَآ أَعْبُدُ ۝ وَلَآ أَنَا عَابِدٌ مَّا عَبَدْتُّمْ

وَلَآ أَنْتُمْ عَبِدُونَ مَآ أَعْبُدُ ۝ لَكُمْ دِينُكُمْ وَلِيَ دِينِ

Declare you [O Prophet!]: "O Disbelievers! I shall not worship those you worship. And you will never worship [alone] He whom I worship. And [before this] never was I prepared to worship those you have worshipped. And neither were you ever prepared to worship [alone] whom I have been worshipping. [So, now] to you, your religion, and mine. (109)

General Warning

O, you enwrapped in the shawl! Arise and heighten the warning. (74:1-2)

يَآ أَيُّهَا الْمُدَّثِّرُ ۝ قُمْ فَأَنْذِرْ

The Style and Genre of Quran

- The Quran is the verbatim speech of God – its style is like a series of thematically arranged sermons.
- When it comes to literary style, the Quran has a unique style, and its genre does not resemble anything that human beings are aware of.
- It has simplicity and flow of prose, but it cannot be called prose. It has the music, rhythm, and composure of poetry, yet it is not poetry.
- While maintaining the simplicity and flow of prose and the music/rhythm/rhyme of poetry, the Quran provides sound reasoning for its arguments, subtly harmonizes and connects topics with each other, shifts its stresses, cites stories and anecdotes, swings back and forth from its main theme, intimidates, encourages, and emotionally attaches with its readers in a unique way.
- In its genre, the closest we can resemble it is Oration.

Considerations for understanding the Quran

- The Quran is **not a regular book**, so its students must keep certain considerations in mind when studying it.

- It's the **life story of a prophet** who came to warn his people and nations around him, and that's its main theme and subject matter – everything else is amalgamated within this main subject.

- After careful deliberation on the content of a Surah, the exact phase of the Prophet's preaching mission in which the Surah/verses are revealed must be determined correctly.

- The **addressees of each surah and its verses** must be determined from among the people present at the time of the revelation of the Quran. They could be the idolaters, the People of the Book, the hypocrites, the Prophet, the companions, and/or a specific sub-group/people within these major groups.

- Depending on the **primary and secondary addressees** of the surah and its verses, the preceding pronoun, the referred-to entity of every definite article (alif lam), and the connotation of every term and expression must be determined in the light of its addressees.

- In case of directives given in relation to the **punishment associated with messengers**, or supremacy of political authority, or supremacy of true religion of God, it must be determined carefully if the directives are permanent or specifically related to the addressees of the prophet's time and cannot be extended beyond that.

- Each **surah's ambiance** must be carefully examined – situation, background, and requisites. It should be determined within the surah, not from outside.

- The **direction of its address shifts** very quickly - it shifts multiple times in Surah and sometimes even within a verse. When delivering direct statements, the speaker may also shift very quickly. The orator shifts from one addressee to another, changing his tone, facial expressions, and the grandeur of his words.

- **General and specific verses** should be differentiated.

Examples from Quran

Example 1:

مَثَلُهُمْ كَمَثَلِ الَّذِي اسْتَوْقَدَ نَارًا فَلَمَّا أَضَاءَتْ مَا حَوْلَهُ ذَهَبَ اللَّهُ بِنُورِهِمْ وَتَرَكَهُمْ فِي ظُلُمَاتٍ لَّا يُبْصِرُونَ

صُمٌّ بُكْمٌ عُمْيٌ فَهُمْ لَا يَرْجِعُونَ أَوْ كَصَيِّبٍ مِّنَ السَّمَاءِ فِيهِ ظُلُمَاتٌ وَرَعْدٌ وَبَرْقٌ يَجْعَلُونَ أَصَابِعَهُمْ فِي آذَانِهِم

مِّنَ الصَّوَاعِقِ حَذَرَ الْمَوْتِ ۚ وَاللَّهُ مُحِيطٌ بِالْكَافِرِينَ يَكَادُ الْبَرْقُ يَخْطَفُ أَبْصَارَهُمْ ۖ كُلَّمَا أَضَاءَ لَهُم مَّشَوْا فِيهِ وَإِذَا

أَظْلَمَ عَلَيْهِمْ قَامُوا ۚ وَلَوْ شَاءَ اللَّهُ لَذَهَبَ بِسَمْعِهِمْ وَأَبْصَارِهِمْ ۚ إِنَّ اللَّهَ عَلَىٰ كُلِّ شَيْءٍ قَدِيرٌ

Their parable is like the **parable of one who kindled a fire**, but when it had illumined all around him, Allah took away their light and left them in utter darkness -- they do not see. Deaf, dumb (and) blind, so they will not turn back (**disbelievers**). Or like abundant rain from the cloud in which is utter darkness and thunder and lightning, they put their fingers into their ears because of the thunder peal, for fear of death, and Allah encompasses the unbelievers. The lightning almost takes away their sight; whenever it shines on them, they walk in it, and when it becomes dark to them, they stand still; and if Allah had pleased, He would certainly have taken away their hearing and their sight; surely Allah has power over all things (**hypocrites**) (2:17-20)

- Before these verses, God talked about two distinct groups of disbelievers:
  - Disbelievers who outrightly rejected the message and became open enemies.
  - Hypocrites who wanted to have a compromise between the new message and what the people of the book were preaching. They did not come out openly against Islam, but played a negative role against Islam in the garb of being mediators between Muslims and other religious groups.
- The two parables given after their mention must be related to their mention. Upon closer examination, the first example clearly refers to disbelievers, and the second pertains to hypocrites.

Example 2:

يَا أَيُّهَا الَّذِينَ آمَنُوا لَا تَتَّخِذُوا الْيَهُودَ وَالنَّصَارَىٰ أَوْلِيَاءَ ۘ بَعْضُهُمْ أَوْلِيَاءُ بَعْضٍ ۚ وَمَن يَتَوَلَّهُم مِّنكُمْ فَإِنَّهُ

مِنْهُمْ ۗ إِنَّ اللَّهَ لَا يَهْدِي الْقَوْمَ الظَّالِمِينَ

O Believers, do not take **these Jews and Christians** as your friends, they are friends of each other. And whoever of you befriended them (after this warning), then he/she will be regarded among them. Indeed, Allah does not guide such transgressors. (5:51)

- These instructions are given specifically for the Jews and Christians of the time towards the end of the mission of Prophet Muhammad in order to cut all ties with them before the pronouncement of the punishment for all disbelieving groups.
- The Alif-Lam at the beginning of Yahud and Nasara must be interpreted in the time when the verse was revealed and cannot be extended to all times.

Is the Quran divine?

- This section is very important, and it evaluates the methodology and the facts that make any piece of content divine. We will use the same methodology to prove that the Quran is divine.

Our sources of knowledge

- Three sources or mediums of knowledge shape how we understand the world, develop concepts, acquire skills, and make decisions. This is true in every field.

    - **Sensory perception** - source of knowledge rooted in empiricism, the philosophical theory that all knowledge is derived from direct sensory experience. It involves using the five senses to gather information about the external world. Perception is considered the most direct and reliable source of knowledge because it provides immediate evidence of what is happening around us. However, sometimes, it can be deceptive.

    - **Inference** - the process of using existing evidence and reasoning to draw a conclusion or an educated guess about something that is not directly observed. It combines what is currently known with background knowledge to "read between the lines".

    - **History** - History is a source of knowledge because it provides an extensive evidential base for understanding how people and societies behave over time. The study of history is essential for understanding how the present came to be, as past events shape our current social, political, and cultural landscape.

Universal Truth

- A universal truth is a fact or a principle that is always true for all people, in all places, and at all times, until someone challenges it. They don't depend on someone's opinion, culture, or feelings – they remain true no matter what and are accepted by all.

- Some examples of universal truths are:

 The sun rises in the East
 All living things need water to survive
 Kindness makes life better for everyone
 Every action has a reaction

The process of deriving universal truths

- The picture below shows how we come to derive universal truths.

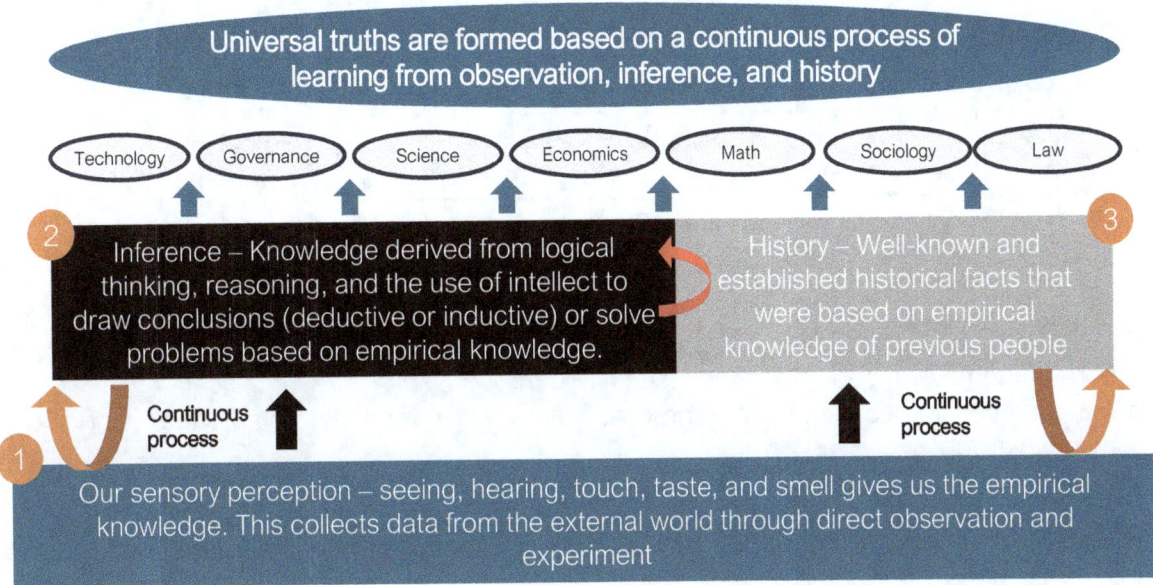

General Examples

Universal Truths	Source
Water maintains its level	Empirical
World War II occurred	Established history
Earth revolves around the sun	Empirical, Inference
A baby takes 6-9 months in a mother's womb to be born	Empirical
The universe is expanding	Empirical, Inference
The universe started at some point in time	Inference
All matter is formed of atoms and atoms are made of sub-atomic particles	Empirical, Inference
All crows are black	Empirical, Inference
Greece was the center of Western Philosophy	Established history
Socrates is the father of Western Philosophy	Established history

Some specific examples of universal truths

- Some specific examples of universal truths are shown here to make the case for Prophet Muhammad and the Quran. Let's review them.

Universal Truths	Source
An author who claims to write or present a high-quality scholarly work or book develops their thoughts and ideas from a young age.	Empirical, established history
Every book or writing has an age. After 100 or so years, it loses its relevance because human civilization, thoughts, ideas, various types of science, and discoveries progress, and it becomes only a great piece of historical work.	Empirical, established history
A book written over a couple of decades must go through a development, correction, and editing process before a final version is made available.	Empirical, established history
A book written over more than two decades without any development or editing will contain internal conflicts in its thoughts, ideas, and events.	Empirical, Inference
A person who challenges a powerful existing system with the support of only a few hundred people behind him never claims early on that in a few years, he and his supporters will be ruling the entire region over all the powerful nations around him.	Established history
A person who has never written an academic work cannot suddenly produce a high-quality scholarly work.	Empirical, inference, established history
A large book claims it will be protected forever, become easy to memorize, and be memorized by millions of people, cover to cover.	Empirical, established history

Now, let's look at some of the facts about the Quran and Prophet Muhammad in the light of the universal truths we just learned

Fact #1: No development in thoughts and ideas

- There is no sign in Prophet Muhammad's life that he **ever** went through the development of any of the thoughts and ideas presented in the Quran.

قُل لَّوْ شَاءَ اللَّهُ مَا تَلَوْتُهُ عَلَيْكُمْ وَلَا أَدْرَاكُم بِهِ ۖ فَقَدْ لَبِثْتُ فِيكُمْ عُمُرًا مِّن قَبْلِهِ ۚ أَفَلَا تَعْقِلُونَ

Tell them: "Had God pleased, I would never have recited this Quran to you, nor would He have made you aware of it. [It is His decision] because I have spent a lifetime among you (have you ever seen me writing or saying such a thing before). Do you not use your senses?" (10:16)

- The Quran is an ageless book. After 1455 years, it hasn't lost its relevance, even as human civilization, ideas, various sciences, and discoveries have made significant progress. Muslims still benefit from it to this day. It is still considered the center and focus of Islam.

Fact #2: No Contradictions in the Quran

- The Quran was revealed over a period of more than 23 years. Prophet Muhammad and his companions memorized it as it was revealed, without any editing. Even when it was written, it never underwent any editing. Still, it is free of internal contradictions in its thoughts, ideas, and events.

أَفَلَا يَتَدَبَّرُونَ الْقُرْآنَ ۚ وَلَوْ كَانَ مِنْ عِنْدِ غَيْرِ اللهِ لَوَجَدُوا فِيهِ اخْتِلَافًا كَثِيرًا

Do these people not ponder the Quran? Had it been from someone other than God, they would have found many (internal) contradictions in it. (Nisa: 82)

- The Quran was completed and written in 632 AD. Nothing in the Quran contradicts or conflicts with any facts associated with other sciences from that time until today.

وَ إِنَّهُ لَكِتَابٌ عَزِيزٌ لَّا يَأْتِيهِ الْبَاطِلُ مِن بَيْنِ يَدَيْهِ وَلَا مِنْ خَلْفِهِ ۖ تَنزِيلٌ مِّنْ حَكِيمٍ حَمِيدٍ

In reality, this is a lofty Book. Wrong cannot enter it from the front (in the future) nor from the back (in history). It is revealed comprehensively from the Being, Who is an embodiment of wisdom and has praiseworthy attributes. (Fussilat: 42)

Fact #3: He was not a writer or author

• Prophet Muhammad did not know how to read or write academically before he presented the Quran. There were many poets and writers at that time, but he never uttered a single word before the Quran.

وَمَا كُنتَ تَتْلُو مِن قَبْلِهِ مِن كِتَابٍ وَلَا تَخُطُّهُ بِيَمِينِكَ ۖ إِذًا لَّارْتَابَ الْمُبْطِلُونَ

And, O Muhammad, you did not recite any book before this or write one with your right hand. Had this been the case, these disbelievers may get into doubts (Ankabut:48)

Fact #4: God protected the Quran

• The Quran states that God will protect this book until the Day of Judgment. The Quran, a 600+ page book, is the most memorized book in the world since the time of Prophet Muhammad. Kids as young as five (5) years old have memorized it cover-to-cover.

إِنَّا نَحْنُ نَزَّلْنَا الذِّكْرَ وَإِنَّا لَهُ لَحَافِظُونَ

Indeed, We have revealed this Reminder (Quran), and We shall preserve it (Raad:9)

Fact #5: Quran predicted his dominance early on

• Prophet Muhammad challenged the most powerful religious systems (Makkah was the hub of idol worship, and other neighboring powers were Christians and Fire Worshipers) with the support of only 10-20 people behind him.

• The Quran announced very early on that, in a few years, Islam would rule the entire region, subjugate all powerful nations around it, and dominate all other religions in that area.

هُوَ الَّذِيٓ أَرْسَلَ رَسُولَهُ بِالْهُدَىٰ وَ دِينِ الْحَقِّ لِيُظْهِرَهُ عَلَى الدِّينِ كُلِّهِ ۗ وَ كَفَىٰ بِاللهِ شَهِيدًا

He has sent His Messenger with guidance and the true religion so that it will prevail over all other religions. God is a Sufficient witness to this Truth. (Fath:28)

In less than 100 years, Muslims were ruling pretty much in the entire civilized world

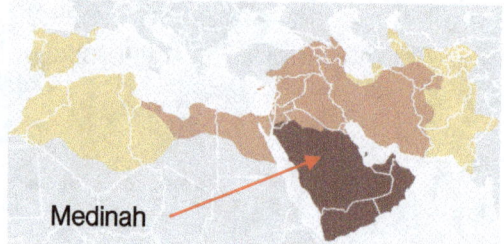

Medinah

Fact#6: Its relevance is eternal

- Its language and style are unique yet eloquent, making it a source of wisdom for us.
- As a great reminder, it brings us back to our real purpose in this life.
- Keep us focused on the Hereafter in everything we do.
- Explain matters that are necessary for the spiritual upbringing of mankind.
- Provides moral guidance that led to the development of figures such as Muhammad, Umar, and Abu Bakr.
- A discourse that intuition bears witness to, corroborated by the established facts derived from knowledge and reason.
- Describes human psychology and emotions closest to the reality that we can witness.
- Touches billions of lives every day.
- Brings dead hearts to life.

Quran's challenge

وَإِن كُنتُمْ فِي رَيْبٍ مِّمَّا نَزَّلْنَا عَلَىٰ عَبْدِنَا فَأْتُوا بِسُورَةٍ مِّن مِّثْلِهِ وَادْعُوا شُهَدَاءَكُم مِّن دُونِ اللَّهِ إِن كُنتُمْ صَادِقِينَ ۝ فَإِن لَّمْ تَفْعَلُوا وَلَن تَفْعَلُوا فَاتَّقُوا النَّارَ الَّتِي وَقُودُهَا النَّاسُ وَالْحِجَارَةُ ۖ أُعِدَّتْ لِلْكَافِرِينَ

And if you are in doubt about what We have revealed to Our servant, then [go and] produce a single surah like it. And [for this purpose] also call your leaders besides Allah if you are truthful [in your claim]. But if you cannot – and surely you cannot – then fear the Fire whose fuel is these men [who do not believe] and these stones also [whom they worship]. It has been prepared for these rejecters. (2:23-24)

أَمْ يَقُولُونَ افْتَرَاهُ ۖ قُلْ فَأْتُوا بِعَشْرِ سُوَرٍ مِّثْلِهِ مُفْتَرَيَاتٍ وَادْعُوا مَنِ اسْتَطَعْتُم مِّن دُونِ اللَّهِ إِن كُنتُمْ صَادِقِينَ

Do they say he has made it up for himself? Then, O Prophet, tell them to bring ten Surahs like these, fabricated, and call anyone who can help you besides God, in case you are truthful (11:13)

Answer these questions and submit:

1. If the Quran is the word of God, why should we not present its verses related to science as evidence for its truth from God?

2. If the central matter the Quran addresses concerns the unseen, how does it then establish its evidence?

3. What if science, one day, is able to answer all the questions that only religion can answer today?

Chapter 8

The Day of Judgment

This chapter goes into detail about the most important belief in Islam after believing in Allah: the belief in the Day of Judgement from the Quran and authentic narrations of Prophet Muhammad.

The Day of Judgment and the Hereafter

Note: The details of the Day of Judgment fall under the "*Mutashabihaat*," which means we can understand the meaning of the verses related to that, but we can not comprehend its true nature. The Day of Judgment is in the *Ghaib*, which we cannot see. Only the Prophet Muhammad and the Quran can speak about this Day. No other source can claim the news associated with it.

- Human life is created for eternity.
- Humans' eternal life is divided into two spans:
  - Life on Earth
  - Life in the Hereafter
- We spend a very small portion of this on Earth.
- We will spend most of it in the Hereafter.
- These two lifespans are separated by the Day of Judgment.
- On the Day of Judgment, results will decide where we will spend our lives in the Hereafter.

كَيْفَ تَكْفُرُونَ بِاللَّهِ وَكُنتُمْ أَمْوَاتًا فَأَحْيَاكُمْ ۖ ثُمَّ يُمِيتُكُمْ ثُمَّ يُحْيِيكُمْ ثُمَّ إِلَيْهِ تُرْجَعُونَ

How can you disbelieve in Allah when you were dead, and He gave you life, and He will give you death again and resurrect you, and then you will be returned to Him (2:28)

Life and death

- The concept of life and death in Islam is very different from how humans understand it, as the Quran explains in verse 2:28 (above).
- Our soul was created way before we came to this world.
- The soul is the focus of this life and the next. The body is just the carrier. We will be given physical bodies twice when we become alive.

Significance of the Day of Judgment

- The Day of Judgment has a central position in the mission of the prophets.
- This is the central theme of the Abrahamic religions, which is also preached by Christianity and Judaism.
- The Quran's entire message revolves around this important day.
- The Quran presented arguments for it from our lives:
  - We are in the state of 'minor death' when we sleep (Surah 39:42)
  - Rain enlivens a dead and barren terrain
    (Surah 7:57, 35:9, 50:9-11)
  - We originally sprang from a mere drop of water
    (Surah 75:36-40)
- Quran's addressees expressed their wonder, just like what we hear today about the life given to the dead bones.
- The Day of Judgment is also called the Hour in the Quran.
- For Allah, it is as easy as speaking a word.

فَوَرَبِّ السَّمَاءِ وَالْأَرْضِ إِنَّهُ لَحَقٌّ مِّثْلَ مَا أَنَّكُمْ تَنطِقُونَ

Thus, I swear by the Lord of heavens and the earth that this (the Day of Resurrection) shall definitely come [with the same ease] as you speak (51:23)

إِذَا زُلْزِلَتِ الْأَرْضُ زِلْزَالَهَا ۞ وَأَخْرَجَتِ الْأَرْضُ أَثْقَالَهَا ۞ وَقَالَ الْإِنسَانُ مَا لَهَا ۞ يَوْمَئِذٍ تُحَدِّثُ أَخْبَارَهَا ۞ بِأَنَّ رَبَّكَ أَوْحَىٰ لَهَا ۞ يَوْمَئِذٍ يَصْدُرُ النَّاسُ أَشْتَاتًا لِّيُرَوْا أَعْمَالَهُمْ ۞ فَمَن يَعْمَلْ مِثْقَالَ ذَرَّةٍ خَيْرًا يَرَهُ ۞ وَمَن يَعْمَلْ مِثْقَالَ ذَرَّةٍ شَرًّا يَرَهُ

[They should remember the Day] when the earth is shaken the way it should be shaken, and it throws out its burdens. And man cries out: "What is the matter with her?" On that Day, she will narrate her story at the inspiration of your Lord. On that Day, men shall come forth individually so that their deeds can be shown to them. Then, whoever has done the smallest bit of good shall see it, and whoever has done the smallest bit of evil shall also see it. (99:1-8)

> Without the Day of Judgment, the universe has no purpose and can only be regarded as the playground of divine forces. The concepts of virtue, piety, justice, reward, and punishment have no meaning.

Evidence of the Day of Judgment

The Quran and the narrations of Prophet Muhammad provide extensive evidence for the Day of Judgment from both scriptural and rational perspectives. In this section, we will go through those arguments:

Human Conscience

- We are, by design, aware of good and evil.
- Our conscience chides us when we commit evil.
- We feel 'good' when we do good – our heart is more content.
- A mini court of justice is already within us, delivering unbiased verdicts all the time.
- Deeply involved in evil lulls that 'inner voice'.
- This lesser abode of judgment testifies that there should be a greater abode of judgment for the entire world. Denying this universal judgment is like denying the self. Our inner self is a constant reminder of it.
- The two terms commonly used in Islam for universal good and evil are *Maruf* and *Munkir*.

Maruf	Maruf
Universal ethics and morals that are considered good and praiseworthy by human nature and intellect	Acts considered universally immoral, unethical, or evil by human nature and intellect

- According to the Quran, humans know them very well.

بَلِ الْإِنسَانُ عَلَىٰ نَفْسِهِ بَصِيرَةٌ وَلَوْ أَلْقَىٰ مَعَاذِيرَهُ

In fact, he (the person) is a witness to himself, no matter how much he may put up excuses for that. (51:23)

قَالَ رَسُولُ اللَّهِ صَلَّى اللَّهُ عَلَيْهِ وَسَلَّمَ الْبِرُّ حُسْنُ الْخُلُقِ وَالإِثْمُ مَا حَاكَ فِي صَدْرِكَ وَكَرِهْتَ
أَنْ يَطَّلِعَ عَلَيْهِ النَّاسُ

The Messenger of Allah said, "Righteousness is good character, and sin is what pricks your heart and you hate for people to find out about it." (Sahih Muslim #2553)

Concept of Justice

- Humans possess an innate sense of right and wrong and a deep desire to see justice prevail. This universal moral instinct (which Islam attributes to a divine design) requires a mechanism for its fulfillment. This concept underpins the belief that a perfect and just Creator would not create a world in which ultimate justice remains unrealized.

- Humans like justice and dislike injustice. We don't like the injustice committed against us. For example, no one goes to a marketplace and asks sellers to cheat them. We may commit injustice to others because we are overwhelmed by our desires and emotions, but if we have not corrupted our character, we soon realize that we have done wrong.

- Justice is our need; if we fight for justice in this world, why must there not be a day when justice will be served in its ultimate form?

- In Islam, the inherent human need for justice is considered a primary rational argument for the Day of Judgment. This concept underpins the belief that a perfect and just Creator would not create a world in which ultimate justice remains unrealized.

- Life on Earth clearly demonstrates that justice is often incomplete. The wicked sometimes prosper and escape the consequences of their actions, while the righteous and the oppressed often suffer without full retribution or compensation.

أَفَنَجْعَلُ الْمُسْلِمِينَ كَالْمُجْرِمِينَ ۚ مَا لَكُمْ كَيْفَ تَحْكُمُونَ

Should we deal with the one who submits (to Allah) the same way as the one who rejects? What is the matter with you? How do you judge? (68:35-36)

وَ نَضَعُ الْمَوَازِينَ الْقِسْطَ لِيَوْمِ الْقِيَامَةِ فَلَا تُظْلَمُ نَفْسٌ شَيْئًا ۚ وَ اِنْ كَانَ مِثْقَالَ حَبَّةٍ مِّنْ خَرْدَلٍ اَتَيْنَا بِهَا ۗ وَ كَفَى بِنَا حَاسِبِينَ

On the Day of Judgement, We shall place the balance of justice. Then not the slightest injustice shall any soul suffer, and if a person has a deed of the size of even a mustard seed, We shall bring it forth. And We are sufficient to take account [of people]. (21:47)

عَنْ اللَّهِ تَبَارَكَ وَتَعَالَى أَنَّهُ قَالَ يَا عِبَادِي إِنِّي حَرَّمْتُ الظُّلْمَ عَلَى نَفْسِي وَجَعَلْتُهُ بَيْنَكُمْ مُحَرَّمًا فَلَا تَظَالَمُوا

Allah the Exalted said: O my servants, I have forbidden oppression for myself and have made it forbidden among you, so do not oppress (commit injustice) one another. Sahih Muslim #2577

Incompleteness

- We observe extraordinary thoroughness and creativity in ourselves and in this universe, which show complete harmony. However, without the concept of an ultimate life to come, there is incompleteness and a lack of purpose.

- For the sake of argument, if this universe and everything in it is designed, including life, then a 'design' with no purpose is meaningless. We don't do this in this world.

- The entire universe is designed to serve humanity, providing both physical and spiritual sustenance, and we are given a place of honor. However, if everything is serving us, then who should we serve?

- We want people to adhere to justice and truth, but we don't see any real motivation for that desire.

- People are committing injustice and leaving the world without paying any price.

- Nature is full of stark dualities: night and day, light and darkness, heaven and earth, life and death, sun and moon, land and sea. These oppositions create balance and function through their interplay. The existence of things in distinct kinds or classifications (*azwaj*) means they are dependent on each other or complementary parts of a greater system.

- So, if everything is in pairs, then what does this life or universe pair with?

وَمَا خَلَقْنَا السَّمَاءَ وَالْأَرْضَ وَمَا بَيْنَهُمَا لَاعِبِينَ ۝ لَوْ أَرَدْنَا أَن نَّتَّخِذَ لَهْوًا لَّاتَّخَذْنَاهُ مِن لَّدُنَّا إِن كُنَّا فَاعِلِينَ

And it was not for gaming and sport that We created the heavens, earth, and everything between them. Had it been Our will to create a game, We could have found one near at hand if We wanted to do this. (21:16-17)

- We desire a lot, but can hardly fulfill any of them. For example, we want to see God, but this is not possible here.

- We have creativity and imagination, but we can't realize their full potential.

- Nobody wants sorrow, grief, and hardship, but rather a life of happiness and contentment, but where is it?

أَفَحَسِبْتُمْ أَنَّمَا خَلَقْنَاكُمْ عَبَثًا وَأَنَّكُمْ إِلَيْنَا لَا تُرْجَعُونَ

So, do you think that We have created you in vain and that to Us you will never be returned? (21:16-17)

- We barely have answers to the above questions, which show that this life and the universe are incomplete.
- As soon as the concept of the Day of Judgment and life in the Hereafter is presented:
  - All of these questions get an answer
  - All voids are filled
  - All known phenomena are explained
  - Everything fits in place
  - The picture of life and this universe is complete
- This world and the next, and this life and the next, become perfect pairs and present a meaningful whole.

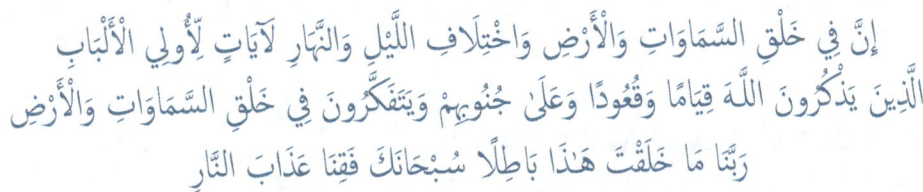

In the creation of the heavens and the earth, and in the alternation of night and day, there are many signs for men of understanding: those who remember God while standing, sitting, and lying down, and reflect on the creation of the heavens and the earth. [They admit] "Lord! You have not created this without a purpose. Glory be to You for you do not do anything in vain! Save us from the punishment of the Fire." (3:190-191)

God's Attributes

- God's most recounted attributes in the Quran are Providence and Mercy.
- God declared that the Day of Judgment is the direct consequence of His Mercy, Power, and Wisdom.
- God has made extraordinary arrangements in this world to nurture and nourish. man. The big question is, why would He leave them unaccountable after taking such great care of their welfare?
- His Mercy also demands that He should deal with the criminals with heavy hands, so the affected can be compensated.

He has made mercy mandatory on Himself. He will definitely gather you to take you to the Day of Judgement, about which there is no doubt. (6:12)

Empirical evidence

- Many Messengers were sent to nations, and God brought justice to the earth through them, as He will on the Day of Judgment.
- People had been presented the truth, given time and freedom to think and respond, shown miracles that no human being can demonstrate, and given a final ultimatum to accept and serve justice according to their faith and deeds.
- Those who accepted the message and helped the messengers were given salvation in this world and the hereafter.
- Those who rejected were punished by death or through humiliating subjugation.
- These predictions about salvation and punishment were made during periods when the Messenger and his followers were oppressed by their own people.
- This empirical evidence has been presented to the world many times.
- The first time, it was given through the nation of Nuh, and the last time, it was given through the nation of Prophet Muhammad.

Judgment through Prophet Muhammad

- According to historical records, the last time this judgment occurred was in the 7th century AD.
- Prophet Muhammad, who was known for his honesty and trustworthiness even among his enemies, gave the same message of God to the people of Arabia.
- He declared from day 1 that he is the messenger of God sent to his people, and God will punish those who deny him and reward those who accept and help him.
- He made those statements at the lowest point in his life (with no power, no help, and no army of supporters).
- He declared that Baytullah (which was a sign of leadership) would be taken and given to him, and the reign of the surrounding nations would be given to Muslims.
- On the night of Isra, he was told that he would be given the ownership of both the Kabaah and the Bait-al-Maqdas in Palestine.
- He wrote letters to the heads of the surrounding nations that they should accept Islam, or their leadership would be taken away.
- History shows that all the mission-related predictions he made came true.

Prophet Ibrahim's Progeny

From the time of Prophet Ibrahim, this responsibility of messengers was delegated collectively to the entire nations of his children.

- This law of Messengers is called the Law of Conclusive Argument (*Qanoon e Itmam al Hujjah*).
- The Quran has explained this law in detail.

وَعَدَ اللَّهُ الَّذِينَ آمَنُوا مِنكُمْ وَعَمِلُوا الصَّالِحَاتِ لَيَسْتَخْلِفَنَّهُمْ فِي الْأَرْضِ كَمَا اسْتَخْلَفَ الَّذِينَ مِن قَبْلِهِمْ وَلَيُمَكِّنَنَّ لَهُمْ دِينَهُمُ الَّذِي ارْتَضَىٰ لَهُمْ وَلَيُبَدِّلَنَّهُم مِّن بَعْدِ خَوْفِهِمْ أَمْنًا ۚ يَعْبُدُونَنِي لَا يُشْرِكُونَ بِي شَيْئًا ۚ وَمَن كَفَرَ بَعْدَ ذَٰلِكَ فَأُولَٰئِكَ هُمُ الْفَاسِقُونَ

God has promised those of you who professed belief and did good deeds that He would grant them political authority in the land, the way He granted political authority to those who were before them, and He would strongly establish [here] the religion He chose for them, and replace their fear with peace. They will worship Me and serve none besides Me, and he who rejects even after this will indeed be among the disobedient. (24:55)

يُرِيدُونَ لِيُطْفِئُوا نُورَ اللَّهِ بِأَفْوَاهِهِمْ وَاللَّهُ مُتِمُّ نُورِهِ وَلَوْ كَرِهَ الْكَافِرُونَ
هُوَ الَّذِي أَرْسَلَ رَسُولَهُ بِالْهُدَىٰ وَدِينِ الْحَقِّ لِيُظْهِرَهُ عَلَى الدِّينِ كُلِّهِ وَلَوْ كَرِهَ الْمُشْرِكُونَ

They seek to extinguish the light of God with their mouths, and God has decided that He will perfect His light, much as the disbelievers may dislike it. He has sent forth His messenger with guidance, which is the religion of truth, so that he may have it prevail over all religions [of Arabia], much as the idolaters may dislike it. (61:8-9)

إِذَا جَاءَ نَصْرُ اللَّهِ وَالْفَتْحُ   وَرَأَيْتَ النَّاسَ يَدْخُلُونَ فِي دِينِ اللَّهِ أَفْوَاجًا
فَسَبِّحْ بِحَمْدِ رَبِّكَ وَاسْتَغْفِرْهُ ۚ إِنَّهُ كَانَ تَوَّابًا

When comes the help of God and that victory [which We have promised you O Prophet!] and you see men embrace the religion of God in multitudes, exalt His glory while being thankful to Him and seek His forgiveness. For, indeed, He is always ready to forgive. (110:1-3)

How should it impact our lives

- The fleeting nature of this world and death are undisputable facts of life. Death is imminent, but its time and place are unknown.
- We get 'absorbed' in this life, but suddenly face the inevitable when we hear about someone's death or when a loved one is afflicted with a terminal disease. This is the time when we reevaluate our priorities and lifestyles.
- Life does not end on earth. However, our actions in this span will decide our fate in the next. Adopt a 'lifestyle' that constantly reminds us of this inevitable truth. The certainty of accountability and the Day of Judgment creates patience and contentment within us.
- We did not choose many things in this life, but the next life is entirely based on merit. If we focus on this immediate life, we will miss out on the bigger life. We should cherish this life and 'prepare' for the next.
- Live your life with a sense of accountability, and your focus will shift to the next.
- We should practice this consciously.

وَمَا هَٰذِهِ الْحَيَاةُ الدُّنْيَا إِلَّا لَهْوٌ وَلَعِبٌ ۚ وَإِنَّ الدَّارَ الْآخِرَةَ لَهِيَ الْحَيَوَانُ ۚ لَوْ كَانُوا يَعْلَمُونَ

The life of this world is merely an amusement and a play; the true life is in the Hereafter, if only they knew. (29:64)

كُلُّ نَفْسٍ ذَائِقَةُ الْمَوْتِ ۗ وَإِنَّمَا تُوَفَّوْنَ أُجُورَكُمْ يَوْمَ الْقِيَامَةِ ۖ فَمَن زُحْزِحَ عَنِ النَّارِ وَأُدْخِلَ الْجَنَّةَ فَقَدْ فَازَ ۗ وَمَا الْحَيَاةُ الدُّنْيَا إِلَّا مَتَاعُ الْغُرُورِ

Every soul shall taste death, and you will be fully recompensed on the Day of Judgment. Then whosoever will be saved from hellfire and admitted to paradise is truly a successful one. The life of this world is merely a comfort of deception (illusion) (3:185)

فَمِنَ النَّاسِ مَن يَقُولُ رَبَّنَا آتِنَا فِي الدُّنْيَا وَمَا لَهُ فِي الْآخِرَةِ مِنْ خَلَاقٍ

وَمِنْهُم مَّن يَقُولُ رَبَّنَا آتِنَا فِي الدُّنْيَا حَسَنَةً وَفِي الْآخِرَةِ حَسَنَةً وَقِنَا عَذَابَ النَّارِ

أُولَٰئِكَ لَهُمْ نَصِيبٌ مِّمَّا كَسَبُوا ۚ وَاللَّهُ سَرِيعُ الْحِسَابِ

And there are some among the people who say, O Lord, give us our portion in this world, but then in the Hereafter they will get no portion of it, and there are some among them who say, O Lord, give us the best in this world and best in the Hereafter, and save us from the Hellfire. They are the ones who will get the portion of their reward, and Allah is swift in reckoning (2:200-202)

When will be the Day of Judgment?

Only GOD Knows

Not even the messengers, prophets, and angels know

The Events of the Day of Judgment

- The Quran presented the events of the DoJ in the most graphic terms to deliver the message to its audience in the best possible way.

First phase

- The first 'trumpet' (called Al-Sur) will be blown at a time when people will be doing their regular routines – it will be sudden.
- The sound of the trumpet would strike panic and fear among the creatures of the earth – the intensity of the fear would be evident on their faces, making them forget their dearest belongings, even their relationships.
- The event of the DOJ on Earth will be similar to earthquake jolts.

وَيَوْمَ يُنفَخُ فِي الصُّورِ فَفَزِعَ مَن فِي السَّمَاوَاتِ وَمَن فِي الْأَرْضِ إِلَّا مَن شَاءَ اللَّهُ

Watch for the day when the Trumpet will be blown in such a way that whatever is between the earth and the heavens will be terrorized except for those whom God wants to save (from that feeling of terror) (27:87)

يَا أَيُّهَا النَّاسُ اتَّقُوا رَبَّكُمْ ۚ إِنَّ زَلْزَلَةَ السَّاعَةِ شَيْءٌ عَظِيمٌ

يَوْمَ تَرَوْنَهَا تَذْهَلُ كُلُّ مُرْضِعَةٍ عَمَّا أَرْضَعَتْ وَتَضَعُ كُلُّ ذَاتِ حَمْلٍ حَمْلَهَا وَتَرَى

النَّاسَ سُكَارَىٰ وَمَا هُم بِسُكَارَىٰ وَلَٰكِنَّ عَذَابَ اللَّهِ شَدِيدٌ

O People! Fear your Lord. The cataclysm of the Day of Judgement is very dreadful indeed. On that day, you will see that every suckling mother shall forget her infant and every pregnant female shall cast her burden, and you shall see people in a state of intoxication though they are not intoxicated, it would be because (of the fear of) God's punishment, that would be so grave. (22:1-2)

- The current physical form of the entire universe will be disrupted to the extent that mountains will be crushed to grains, oceans will burst forth with fire, and all planets and galaxies will collapse into one another – no mind can imagine, and no words can describe it.
- Only God knows how long this turmoil will last.

Second phase

- In the second phase, God will recreate everything the way He created it for the very first time. A new physical world will re-emerge, and new earths and heavens will be formed, which will be different from the one that we see today.

- The Quran painted the picture for that:

يَوْمَ نَطْوِي السَّمَاءَ كَطَيِّ السِّجِلِّ لِلْكُتُبِ ۚ كَمَا بَدَأْنَا أَوَّلَ خَلْقٍ نُّعِيدُهُ ۚ وَعْدًا عَلَيْنَا ۚ إِنَّا كُنَّا فَاعِلِينَ

Remember the day when We shall roll up the heavens like a scroll wrapped in parchment. Just as We brought about the first creation, so will We do it again. This is a promise liable to us, and We shall assuredly fulfill it. (21:104)

يَوْمَ تُبَدَّلُ الْأَرْضُ غَيْرَ الْأَرْضِ وَ السَّمٰوٰتُ وَ بَرَزُوا لِلّٰهِ الْوَاحِدِ الْقَهَّارِ

Remember the day when this **earth will be replaced by another** and this sky too, and everyone [alone and helpless] will set off towards God, the One and Mighty.(Ibrahim:48)

Third phase

- In the third phase, the Trumpet will be blown a second time, after which mankind will rise from their graves (symbolizing that people will receive a different body and their souls will be returned to them).

- Everyone will appear in the court of justice of their Lord.

- People will be presented with their deeds record.

وَنُفِخَ فِي الصُّورِ فَإِذَا هُم مِّنَ الْأَجْدَاثِ إِلَىٰ رَبِّهِمْ يَنسِلُونَ

And the trumpet will be blown, and all of a sudden, they will rise up from their graves and hasten to their Lord. (36:51)

Details of the Phases and Abodes

Death

- Death starts the journey towards our Lord.
- There is no escape from death.
- It 'meets' you at the exact place where it is written.
- Its time and place are only known to God.
- We are made up of our mortal body and our 'personality' (the soul).
- This personality (or soul) is given to us in our mother's womb about 120 days after conception.
- At the time of death, our real 'personality' (the soul) is separated from this physical body.
- A specific angel (team) is dedicated to this task.
- They 'collect' the soul in a safe place.

قُلْ يَتَوَفَّاكُم مَّلَكُ الْمَوْتِ الَّذِي وُكِّلَ بِكُمْ ثُمَّ إِلَىٰ رَبِّكُمْ تُرْجَعُونَ

Tell them: "The angel of death deputed over you shall claim your souls. Then to your Lord you shall be returned." (32:11)

إِنَّ اللهَ عِنْدَهُ عِلْمُ السَّاعَةِ وَ يُنَزِّلُ الْغَيْثَ وَ يَعْلَمُ مَا فِي الْأَرْحَامِ وَ مَا تَدْرِى نَفْسٌ مَّاذَا تَكْسِبُ غَدًا وَ مَا تَدْرِى نَفْسٌ بِأَيِّ أَرْضٍ تَمُوتُ إِنَّ اللهَ عَلِيمٌ خَبِيرٌ

Only God knows that Hour. [Do you not see that] He sends down the rain and knows what is in the wombs. No one knows what he will earn tomorrow, nor where he will die. In reality, God alone is aware of all and has knowledge of everything.(Luqman:34)

Barzakh. (Barrier)

- It means a curtain, but actually a boundary or barrier beyond which the souls of the people are kept (apparently without bodies).
- No soul can cross that barrier into the world.
- Since we bury our dead in the grave, we usually term this 'life in Barzakh' as 'the life in the grave'.
- Souls are 'alive' here, but apparently without a physical body.

- The nature of awareness, emotions, observations, and experiences is similar to that of our dreams.
- Souls are rewarded, punished, or put to sleep in Barzakh (which we refer to as the grave).
- The Quran presented pictures of only two extreme situations (rewarded or punished).

وَلَا تَحْسَبَنَّ الَّذِينَ قُتِلُوا فِي سَبِيلِ اللَّهِ أَمْوَاتًا ۚ بَلْ أَحْيَاءٌ عِندَ رَبِّهِمْ يُرْزَقُونَ

فَرِحِينَ بِمَا آتَاهُمُ اللَّهُ مِن فَضْلِهِ

And do not consider those who were killed in the path of Allah as dead. They are definitely not dead; they are alive with the Lord, receiving their provisions. They are happy with what God has provided for them (3:169)

وَحَاقَ بِآلِ فِرْعَوْنَ سُوءُ الْعَذَابِ

النَّارُ يُعْرَضُونَ عَلَيْهَا غُدُوًّا وَعَشِيًّا ۖ وَيَوْمَ تَقُومُ السَّاعَةُ أَدْخِلُوا آلَ فِرْعَوْنَ أَشَدَّ الْعَذَابِ

But Pharaoh and his people are surrounded by a dreadful punishment. They are presented to the fire of hell day and night, and the day when that Hour will come, it will be ordered to throw them into a more severe punishment (40:45-46)

Place of Gathering (Mahshar)

- Before the judgment starts, all mankind, from Adam to the last person, will be raised to life again (called *Hashr*).
- With the same personality and soul, everyone will be recreated and given a "second life" in a new body.
- A person's abilities and powers would be greatly enhanced.
- This new earth (must be much larger than today's) will be lit up with the light of God.
- Everyone, including the criminals, will declare God's praises and exaltedness due to His Majesty on that day.
- This is the main event that all disbelievers in the Quran denied.

وَقَالُوا أَإِذَا كُنَّا عِظَامًا وَرُفَاتًا أَإِنَّا لَمَبْعُوثُونَ خَلْقًا جَدِيدًا ۞ قُلْ كُونُوا حِجَارَةً أَوْ حَدِيدًا

And they say: "When we are turned to bones and bits of dust, shall we be raised to life again?" Tell them: "Whether you turn into stone or iron, or any other substance which in your opinion is even harder than these [even then you shall still be gathered to Us]." (17:49-50)

ثُمَّ نُفِخَ فِيهِ أُخْرَىٰ فَإِذَا هُمْ قِيَامٌ يَنْظُرُونَ ۞ وَأَشْرَقَتِ الْأَرْضُ بِنُورِ رَبِّهَا

Then the trumpet will be blown again, and they will suddenly rise whilst looking around, and the earth on that Day will be lit up with the light of her Lord. (39:68-69)

وَتَرَى الْمَلَائِكَةَ حَافِّينَ مِنْ حَوْلِ الْعَرْشِ يُسَبِّحُونَ بِحَمْدِ رَبِّهِمْ ۖ وَقُضِيَ بَيْنَهُمْ بِالْحَقِّ وَقِيلَ الْحَمْدُ لِلَّهِ رَبِّ الْعَالَمِينَ

And you will see the angels encircling the Throne, glorifying their Lord and declaring His praises, and judgment will be passed with fairness between people, and it will be declared: "Gratitude is for God, Lord of the Universe!" (39:75)

- It will be a severe day for people who have committed crimes against people and God.
- Due to the panic and severity of that day, people will only be thinking about themselves.
- Wrongdoers will be treated like criminals, will be easily recognized, and will be together with their leaders.

فَإِذَا جَاءَتِ الصَّاخَّةُ ۞ يَوْمَ يَفِرُّ الْمَرْءُ مِنْ أَخِيهِ ۞ وَأُمِّهِ وَأَبِيهِ ۞ وَصَاحِبَتِهِ وَبَنِيهِ لِكُلِّ امْرِئٍ مِّنْهُمْ يَوْمَئِذٍ شَأْنٌ يُغْنِيهِ

So when the deafening blast comes [ask them: where will they go] , on that day, the man will flee from his brother, mother, father, wife, and children. Everyone will be concerned with their own self. (80:33-37)

يُعْرَفُ الْمُجْرِمُونَ بِسِيمَاهُمْ فَيُؤْخَذُ بِالنَّوَاصِي وَالْأَقْدَامِ

The wrongdoers will be recognized through their looks; then they shall be seized by their forelocks and their feet [and thrown into Hell]. (55:41)

يَوْمَ يُكْشَفُ عَن سَاقٍ وَيُدْعَوْنَ إِلَى السُّجُودِ فَلَا يَسْتَطِيعُونَ

خَاشِعَةً أَبْصَارُهُمْ تَرْهَقُهُمْ ذِلَّةٌ ۖ وَقَدْ كَانُوا يُدْعَوْنَ إِلَى السُّجُودِ وَهُمْ سَالِمُونَ

They must remember the day when a great tumult will take place, and they will be called to prostrate, and they will not be able to do so. Dismayed will be their looks; disgrace will cover them. They also used to be called to prostrate when they were capable of doing it. (68: 42-43)

Grouping of mankind

- Mankind will be divided into **three** groups
  - **Foremost in faith and righteous deeds** – these are those righteous souls who are always ahead in every good deed; they were the foremost in accepting the call of Prophet Muhammad, and even today do not allow their egos or biases to come in the way of accepting the truth when they hear it. Some of these people will not have any accountability
  - **Faithful and Righteous** – these are the people whose results on the Day of Judgment will be handed over in their right hand. That is a sign of success on that day. They are usually the ones who follow the first group (foremost).
  - **Wrongdoers / Criminals** – these are the people whose results on the Day of Judgment will be handed over in their left hand. That is a sign of failure on that day. They are usually the ones who corrupt their souls through their desires and whims.

وَكُنتُمْ أَزْوَاجًا ثَلَاثَةً ۚ فَأَصْحَابُ الْمَيْمَنَةِ مَا أَصْحَابُ الْمَيْمَنَةِ

وَأَصْحَابُ الْمَشْأَمَةِ مَا أَصْحَابُ الْمَشْأَمَةِ ۚ وَالسَّابِقُونَ السَّابِقُونَ

And on that Day, you will be divided into three groups: the companions of the right hand, so what to speak of the [good fortune] of the companions of the right hand, and the companions of the left hand so what to speak of the [misfortune] of the companions of the left hand and the foremost are after all the foremost. (56:7-10)

فَأَمَّا مَنْ أُوتِيَ كِتَابَهُ بِيَمِينِهِ ۚ فَسَوْفَ يُحَاسَبُ حِسَابًا يَسِيرًا

وَأَمَّا مَنْ أُوتِيَ كِتَابَهُ وَرَاءَ ظَهْرِهِ ۚ وَيَصْلَىٰ سَعِيرًا ۚ فَسَوْفَ يَدْعُو ثُبُورًا

Then whose book of accounting is given in the right hand, then his accountability is done lightly (because of overwhelming good deeds), and whose book of accounting is given from the back in his left hand, then soon he will be crying for death, and he will be thrown in the hellfire (84:7-8,10-12)

- The reality behind people's differences will be revealed. All religious groups will be informed about their interpretations of religious texts. That way, all religious differences will be settled.
- Every deed and its weight will be accounted for, no matter how small it is.
- No one will be wronged.
- No friendship, sale/purchase, ransom, or intercession will be of any use.

إِلَى اللَّهِ مَرْجِعُكُمْ جَمِيعًا فَيُنَبِّئُكُم بِمَا كُنتُمْ فِيهِ تَخْتَلِفُونَ

To God shall you all return, and then He shall inform you about that in which you were differing. (5:48)

وَنَضَعُ الْمَوَازِينَ الْقِسْطَ لِيَوْمِ الْقِيَامَةِ فَلَا تُظْلَمُ نَفْسٌ شَيْئًا ۖ وَإِن كَانَ مِثْقَالَ حَبَّةٍ مِّنْ خَرْدَلٍ أَتَيْنَا بِهَا ۗ وَكَفَىٰ بِنَا حَاسِبِينَ

And on the Day of Judgement, We shall set up the scales of justice so that no man shall in the least be wronged. And if a person has done a deed as small as a grain of mustard seed, We shall bring it forward, and sufficient are We for taking account. (21:47)

وَاتَّقُوا يَوْمًا لَّا تَجْزِي نَفْسٌ عَن نَّفْسٍ شَيْئًا وَلَا يُقْبَلُ مِنْهَا شَفَاعَةٌ وَلَا يُؤْخَذُ مِنْهَا عَدْلٌ وَلَا هُمْ يُنصَرُونَ

And guard yourselves against the day when no soul shall be of use to another in any way, no intercession shall be accepted, no compensation will be taken from it, and no people will be helped. (2:48)

- Witnesses will be presented so that wrongdoers cannot deny their actions.
- Prophets, angels, and even our own hands, feet, ears, eyes, and skin will bear witness.

وَوُضِعَ الْكِتَابُ وَجِيءَ بِالنَّبِيِّينَ وَالشُّهَدَاءِ وَقُضِيَ بَيْنَهُم بِالْحَقِّ وَهُمْ لَا يُظْلَمُونَ

And the register of accounts shall be laid open, and all the prophets shall be called, and those who were given the responsibility of bearing witness, and people shall be judged with fairness so that none shall be wronged. (39:69)

حَتَّىٰ إِذَا مَا جَاءُوهَا شَهِدَ عَلَيْهِمْ سَمْعُهُمْ وَأَبْصَارُهُمْ وَجُلُودُهُم بِمَا كَانُوا يَعْمَلُونَ

وَقَالُوا لِجُلُودِهِمْ لِمَ شَهِدتُّمْ عَلَيْنَا قَالُوا أَنطَقَنَا اللَّهُ الَّذِي أَنطَقَ كُلَّ شَيْءٍ وَهُوَ خَلَقَكُمْ أَوَّلَ مَرَّةٍ وَإِلَيْهِ تُرْجَعُونَ

Until they come near it, their ears, eyes, and very skin will be a witness to what they had been doing in the previous world. "Why did you bear witness against us?" they will ask their skins, and their skins will reply: "God, who gives speech to all things, has given us speech." And He created you the first time, and now you are being returned to Him. (41:20-21)

- Most people do not accept the truth because they follow someone as their leader, and they become a hindrance in the acceptance. On that day, Satan and the corrupt leaders who acted as the agents of Satan will disown their followers and even renounce them.

وَقَالَ الشَّيْطَانُ لَمَّا قُضِيَ الْأَمْرُ إِنَّ اللَّهَ وَعَدَكُمْ وَعْدَ الْحَقِّ وَوَعَدتُّكُمْ فَأَخْلَفْتُكُمْ ۖ وَمَا كَانَ لِيَ عَلَيْكُم مِّن سُلْطَانٍ إِلَّا أَن دَعَوْتُكُمْ فَاسْتَجَبْتُمْ لِي ۖ فَلَا تَلُومُونِي وَلُومُوا أَنفُسَكُم ۖ مَّا أَنَا بِمُصْرِخِكُمْ وَمَا أَنتُم بِمُصْرِخِيَّ ۖ إِنِّي كَفَرْتُ بِمَا أَشْرَكْتُمُونِ مِن قَبْلُ ۗ إِنَّ الظَّالِمِينَ لَهُمْ عَذَابٌ أَلِيمٌ

And after the judgment has been passed, Satan will say to them: "Indeed, true was the promise which God made with you, and I never fulfilled the promises I made with you. And I had no power over you. I only called you, and you answered. Do not now blame me, but blame yourselves. I cannot address your grievances, nor can you address mine. I have already denied your making me a partner [with God, by listening to me]. Indeed, it is for such wrong-doers that there is a grievous penalty." (14:22)

Intercession of the Prophets

- Prophets will be allowed to intercede for their people before God.
- In this world, it applies to the people living with the Prophets: if they commit sins and ask for forgiveness from God, the Prophets also add their voices to their requests.
- The law of repentance in the Quran is that God always forgives people who, while overcome by emotion, commit a sin and then repent immediately.
- He does not forgive people who, after spending all their lives in sins, finally come to terms with God when death approaches.
- There will be people who, though they did not repent immediately, did not delay it till their death, either.
- It is for these people that the Prophet's intercession will be accepted on the day of judgment, only when permitted by God, when their good deeds would require some push to be forgiven by God.
- This is very similar to how we intercede for someone in this life when they are deserving but need a small push to be successful.

أَمِ اتَّخَذُوا مِن دُونِ اللَّهِ شُفَعَاءَ ۚ قُلْ أَوَلَوْ كَانُوا لَا يَمْلِكُونَ شَيْئًا وَلَا يَعْقِلُونَ
قُل لِّلَّهِ الشَّفَاعَةُ جَمِيعًا ۖ لَّهُ مُلْكُ السَّمَاوَاتِ وَالْأَرْضِ ۖ ثُمَّ إِلَيْهِ تُرْجَعُونَ

Have they chosen others besides God to intercede for them? Tell them: "Can they intercede even if they have no power or understanding?" Tell them: "Only God has authority over intercession. His rule extends over the heavens and the earth. Then to Him shall you be returned." (39:43-44)

يَعْلَمُ مَا بَيْنَ أَيْدِيهِمْ وَمَا خَلْفَهُمْ وَلَا يَشْفَعُونَ إِلَّا لِمَنِ ارْتَضَىٰ وَهُم مِّنْ خَشْيَتِهِ مُشْفِقُونَ

He knows what is before them and behind them. And they intercede for none except those whom He permits and tremble in awe of Him. (21:28)

يَوْمَئِذٍ لَّا تَنفَعُ الشَّفَاعَةُ إِلَّا مَنْ أَذِنَ لَهُ الرَّحْمَٰنُ وَرَضِيَ لَهُ قَوْلًا
يَعْلَمُ مَا بَيْنَ أَيْدِيهِمْ وَمَا خَلْفَهُمْ وَلَا يُحِيطُونَ بِهِ عِلْمًا

On that Day, no intercession will avail except for him who is allowed by the Merciful, and words about that person are acceptable to Him. He knows what is before them and behind them, and their knowledge cannot truly embrace Him. (20:109-110)

A Quick Summary of the Chapter

- Human life is created for eternity. It is divided into two spans: life on earth and life in the hereafter. DoJ divides the two spans.

- On the Day of Judgment, results will decide where we will spend our lives in the Hereafter.

- Without the Day of Judgment, the universe has no purpose and can only be regarded as the playground of divine forces. The concepts of virtue, piety, justice, reward, and punishment have no meaning.

- There is ample evidence around us and in the Quran for the DoJ.

- The last time this judgment occurred was witnessed by the world and is recorded in history, in the 7th century AD.

- If we focus on this immediate life, we will miss out on the bigger life.

- Live your life with a sense of accountability, and your focus will shift to the next.

Chapter 9

Signs near the Day of Judgment

This chapter discusses various signs near the Day of Judgment mentioned in the Quran and the Sunnah.

Who can tell the signs?

- No one except God alone knows when the Day of Judgement will come.
- Some of the signs and portents that will signal its closeness are mentioned in the Quran, Hadith, and previous Scriptures.
- This is the knowledge of the unseen, and we have no way of knowing it.
- Even the Prophets were unaware of these signs; God told them to give us some sense of the DoJ.
- These signs are also presented as evidence of the truth that the Messengers brought from God.
- Although it is good to know the signs, our focus should always be on our faith and actions.
- Many Muslims and Christians tend to focus on the details of the signs leading up to the Day of Judgment. We should remember that our DoJ will start as soon as we die.

Sahl Bin Sa'ad narrated:
I saw Allah's Messenger pointing with his index and middle fingers, saying. "The time of my Advent and the Hour are like these two fingers." (Sahih al-Bukhari #4936)

Aisha narrated:
Some men among the Bedouins came to the Prophet and said, "When is the Hour?" The Prophet looked to the youngest of them and said, "If this boy lives, he will not reach old age before your Hour is already established." (Sahih al-Bukhari #6146, Sahih Muslim #2952)

Type of Signs

- There is too much literature on this topic, and various minor and major signs are mentioned in different categories of Ahadith.
- We should restrict ourselves to some major and authentic signs mentioned in the Quran and Sahih Ahadith.
- Some signs have already appeared, and some will manifest later (if the ascription towards the Prophet is correct).
- There are two types of signs:

General signs about the overall situation of the world	Specific events and incidents of great significance

Major signs of the Day of Judgment

1 Destitute Arab Shepherds walking barefoot, barely clothed, will compete with one another in making tall buildings [Source: Hadith e Jibrael]

2 The slave lady will give birth to her mistress. [Source: Hadith e Jibrael]

Note: Scholars have interpreted it in different ways. However, the most plausible explanation is that slavery will end.

Note:
These two signs are unique because they are not told in any other hadith except Hadith-e-Jibrael. This is a famous hadith that we have discussed earlier. It is one of the most authentic hadith in the books of Ahadith. Both of these signs have already occurred.

3 The onslaught of Gog and Magog after almost 1000 years from Prophet Muhammad. Gog and Magog are the descendants of Nuh's son Jafet (Japhet), who inhabited the northern areas of Asia. Later, some tribes reached Europe and finally settled in America and Australia. They also migrated to India, as we know them, as Aryans. They also got settled in Russia. They will outnumber other major nations (Arabs and Africans) on earth and will control the affairs of the world at the end of time [Source: Quran (21:96-97) and Previous Scriptures (Ezekiel, 38:1-2, Ezekiel, 39:1-2, Revelation, 20:7-9]

4 Moral degradation in societies - lack of true knowledge, proliferation of ignorance, fornication, drinking, killings without a purpose, looting, and embezzlement of money, women will outnumber men, non-religious people will outnumber people who would take God's name, and children misbehaving with their parents [Source: Various Ahadith]

5 Sinking of the earth in the East, in the West, and in the Arabian Peninsula [Source: Ahadith]

6 A large Smoke (could be an atomic explosion) will come out from one part of the earth [Source: Ahadith]

7 Appearance of Dajjal. Dajjal is an adjective meaning "a great deceiver." He is also called 'Al-Masih al-Dajjal. An imposter who will falsely claim to be Jesus and will 'show' the miracles (magical) attributed to Jesus, taking advantage of the notion of the return of Jesus found in Muslims, Christians, and Jews. He would be blind in one eye. [Source: Ahadith]

8 A land animal will appear, which will probably be born directly from the earth, the way all creatures used to be born at the beginning of life on earth [Source: Ahadith]

9 The rise of the sun from the West [Source: Ahadith]

Note: Scholars have interpreted it both ways. This can be physical or, allegorically speaking.

10 A fire that will rise from a pit of the Yemenite city of Eden and drive people away from behind [Source: Ahadith]

11 A wind that will blow people away into the sea [Source: Ahadith]

Note: Scholars have interpreted it for a specific group of people in a specific part of the world.

Minor signs

- In the books of Ahadith, many minor signs are mentioned.
- It is recommended to give them a cursory look.
- There are some lecture series worth watching.
- **Reminder:** Let's pay attention to the major signs to learn what the Quran and authentic Sunnah have to say about them.

https://www.iium.edu.my/deed/hadith/muslim/content41.html

https://www.youtube.com/watch?v=WOf_kDWA_KM&list=PL82zpK9Gj7_hZM4m-7lnMlCkK-b7m1HfQ

Second coming of Jesus

- This is regarded as one of the major signs near the end times in Islam. The majority of scholars think that Jesus will physically descend near the end of time and will lead Muslims to victory against Dajjal.
- A very small minority of scholars raise concerns about this interpretation, citing several Quranic passages that contradict the view.
- Some verses are interpreted to indicate Jesus' second coming (43:61, 4:159), but carefully looking at those verses clarifies that they are not talking about his second coming (in other words, it is not in clear terms).
- The concept of the second coming is well presented in many Ahadith, and there are many authentic Ahadith about it, so it cannot be just ignored.
- However, the understanding of the small minority group about these Ahadith is that these are the dreams of Prophet Muhammad and require some interpretation, as other dreams of Prophet Muhammad do.
- Knowing both sides of the argument is good for a student of knowledge. Arguments about the Second Coming are presented in many places; here, we will restrict ourselves to the arguments against it.

Note: Some scholars have considered the second coming of Jesus part of the beliefs or creed of Islam, but this is not true, as the creed is clearly stated in the Quran and well explained in Ahadith.

Arguments against Second Coming (minority opinion)

- Even though Jesus is discussed in the Quran from many aspects and some major signs of the DoJ are also discussed, the Quran is completely quiet on his second coming.
- In verse 3:55, God speaks of the punishment He announced for the Children of Israel (the nation to whom Jesus was sent), and that announcement remains in effect until the Day of Judgment. This goes against the concept that He is coming back physically and fighting wars with Dajjal and the Jews.
- Finally, there is one verse (next slide) in the Quran that raises many questions, leading those scholars to wonder whether this concept of the second coming is properly understood in light of the Quran and Ahadith.
- The scholars who do not hold the view that Jesus will return in the end time in person interpret the Ahadith about Jesus's return as symbolic, allegorical visions or dreams, rather than literal occurrences. This is similar to how other events in religious texts, such as the *Isra* (Night Journey), are described as visions that need interpretation.

Dialogue between God and Jesus on the DoJ

وَإِذْ قَالَ اللَّهُ يَا عِيسَى ابْنَ مَرْيَمَ أَأَنتَ قُلْتَ لِلنَّاسِ اتَّخِذُونِي وَأُمِّيَ إِلَهَيْنِ مِن دُونِ اللَّهِ ۖ قَالَ سُبْحَانَكَ مَا يَكُونُ لِي أَنْ أَقُولَ مَا لَيْسَ لِي بِحَقٍّ ۚ إِن كُنتُ قُلْتُهُ فَقَدْ عَلِمْتَهُ ۚ تَعْلَمُ مَا فِي نَفْسِي وَلَا أَعْلَمُ مَا فِي نَفْسِكَ ۚ إِنَّكَ أَنتَ عَلَّامُ الْغُيُوبِ مَا قُلْتُ لَهُمْ إِلَّا مَا أَمَرْتَنِي بِهِ أَنِ اعْبُدُوا اللَّهَ رَبِّي وَرَبَّكُمْ ۚ وَكُنتُ عَلَيْهِمْ شَهِيدًا مَّا دُمْتُ فِيهِمْ ۖ فَلَمَّا تَوَفَّيْتَنِي كُنتَ أَنتَ الرَّقِيبَ عَلَيْهِمْ ۚ وَأَنتَ عَلَىٰ كُلِّ شَيْءٍ شَهِيدٌ

And when God said to Jesus, O Jesus, did you tell people to worship you and your mother besides Allah? He would say, Glory be to You, Why would I say something I do not have any right to say? If I said that, you would have known about it. You know what's inside my heart, while I do not know what's in yours. Indeed, You are the knower of the unseen. Never did I say to them except what You commanded me to do: "Worship Allah my Lord and your Lord," and I was a witness over them while I dwelt among them. When You gave death to me, You were the guardian/watcher over them, and You are a witness over all things. (5:116-117)

- After reading many passages discussing Jesus' birth and death, it is clear that, if the concept of Jesus' second coming is true, as most scholars understand it, the concept must have arisen in the Quran.

- For example, verses 5:116-117 could be the **best place in the Quran** where God addresses the second coming of Jesus.

- However, in these verses, Jesus even denies that he was aware of the deviation they had developed after he was gone. This suggests that he never returned to learn of their situation.

- This dialogue is recorded in the Quran and took place on the Day of Judgment, and it completely rejects the idea that Jesus will come before that day.

How do the signs relate to me?

- They are a prelude to the most important day that humanity will face.
- The Quran mentioned them, and Jibrael taught Prophet Muhammad about them, so they have significance in our faith.
- Fulfillment of these signs in front of our eyes should reinforce:
  - Our faith in the Day of Judgment itself
  - Our faith in the sources of Islam (through revelations) and its teachings
- Most of the signs of the DoJ are described as the 'tribulations'; knowing them helps us relate them to the world's situation around us.
- Knowing them from authentic sources like the Quran and authentic Ahadith helps us avoid misguided beliefs in this day and age of social media.
- In many Ahadith, the Prophet provided guidance on how to react in times of tribulation.

Example: Prophet's guidance on how to react

- For example, one of the tribulations that Prophet Muhammad warned us about is the division among Muslims. His instructions were that we should avoid associating ourselves with different sects and stick to the majority and the leadership running the affairs.

Hudhaifa ibn al-Yaman reported: The people used to ask the Messenger of Allah about good, but I would ask about evil for fear it would overtake me. I said, "O Messenger of Allah, we were ignorant and evil, and Allah sent us this good. Will there be evil after this good?"

The Prophet said, "Yes." I said, "Will there be good after that evil?" The Prophet said, "Yes, but within it is smoke." I said, "What is its smoke?" The Prophet said, "A people who are not guided by my guidance. You will recognize them and reject them."

I said, "Will there be evil after that good?" The Prophet said, "Yes, callers to the gates of Hellfire. Whoever answers them will taste it from within." I said, "O Messenger of Allah, describe them to us." The Prophet said, "They are from our progeny and speak our language." I said, "What do you command me should that overtake me?" The Prophet said, "Hold fast to the community of Muslims and their leader." I said, "What if there is no community and no leader?" The Prophet said, "Then withdraw from all of the sects, even if you must bite at the root of trees until death overtakes you in that state."

Investigate and write about how many scholarly interpretations exist for the following event reported in the hadith:

The slave lady will give birth to her mistress. [Source: Hadith e Jibrael]

Chapter 10

Heaven and Hell

This chapter talks about the description of Heaven and Hell as depicted in the Quran and authentic Ahadith attributed to Prophet Muhammad.

Note: We should seek God's protection from the punishment of Hellfire.

The concept of Reward and Punishment

- Humans across cultures possess an inherent sense of morality and a desire for justice. The idea that good deeds should be rewarded and evil deeds punished resonates with this deeply ingrained moral intuition.
- That's why the concepts of reward and punishment exist in almost every major religion in some form.
- The actual concept of heaven and hell as places for reward and punishment is more prominent in Abrahamic religions (Although, in Jewish scriptures, it is very vague).
- Heaven and hell represent the culmination or the logical conclusion of that accountability that started with the DoJ.
- The people who received their books of accountability (with results) in their right hands, or who did not go through any accountability (because they were the best of the best), will be entered into heaven or paradise.
- The people who got their books of accountability (with results) in their left hands, or who did not go through any accountability (because they were the worst of the worst), will be sent to hell or hellfire.
- Heaven and hell will be prepared when all creation dies after the first trumpet is blown from the same material that already exists today (billions of stars).
- Both heaven and hell have many grades and levels, like places to live on this earth. The Quran has described both in detail.

إِنَّ الْمُنَافِقِينَ فِي الدَّرْكِ الْأَسْفَلِ مِنَ النَّارِ وَلَن تَجِدَ لَهُمْ نَصِيرًا

Indeed, the hypocrites will be in the lowest depths of the Fire (the Hellfire) - and never will you find for them a helper (4:145)

وَالَّذِينَ آمَنُوا وَاتَّبَعَتْهُمْ ذُرِّيَّتُهُم بِإِيمَانٍ أَلْحَقْنَا بِهِمْ ذُرِّيَّتَهُمْ وَمَا أَلَتْنَاهُم مِّنْ عَمَلِهِم مِّن شَيْءٍ ۚ كُلُّ امْرِئٍ بِمَا كَسَبَ رَهِينٌ

Those who have accepted faith and their children followed them with any level of faith; we shall unite their children with them [at their level] and not even slightly diminish the reward of their deeds. (52:21)

The Hell in the Quran

Description of Hell and its dwellers

- Hell is the abode of punishment for the sinners to cleanse them from their sins. In the Quran, many names are used for Hell: *Jahannum, Saqar, Al-Saeer, Al Nar*, etc.
- Hellfire is the most intense part of Hell, and it has multiple depths.
- There are seven doors to it, and each will get its share of sinners.
- Apparently, it will be huge, but may be much smaller than the paradise, but it will be full of its dwellers. Nineteen angels are in charge of it.
- The Quran called it the worst of abodes in many places (2:126, 206; 3:151; 14:29).

وَإِنَّ جَهَنَّمَ لَمَوْعِدُهُمْ أَجْمَعِينَ ۞ لَهَا سَبْعَةُ أَبْوَابٍ لِّكُلِّ بَابٍ مِّنْهُمْ جُزْءٌ مَّقْسُومٌ

For all of them, there is a promise of hell, which has seven doors, and for every door, a special share of people has been allocated from them (15:44)

سَأُصْلِيهِ سَقَرَ ۞ وَمَا أَدْرَاكَ مَا سَقَرُ ۞ لَا تُبْقِي وَلَا تَذَرُ ۞ لَوَّاحَةٌ لِّلْبَشَرِ ۞ عَلَيْهَا تِسْعَةَ عَشَرَ

And what do you know about this Hell? It will show no mercy and spare no one. It scorches the skin. [Deputed] over it are nineteen. (74:27-30)

- People who are lighter on their scale of good deeds will be entered into Hell.
- The worst criminals will be punished in the deepest depths of Hell.
- There is no distinction between men and women.
- Some people 'may' get punished in Hell for eternity.
- People who deliberately commit shirk, murderers, those who fought against prophets, and people who usurp other people's inheritance/properties.
- Some people will be released after completing their punishment term.
- Hell may cease to exist at some point in time, as it is a threat from God, not a promise, as alluded to in the following verses.

فَأَمَّا الَّذِينَ شَقُوا فَفِي النَّارِ لَهُمْ فِيهَا زَفِيرٌ وَشَهِيقٌ

خَالِدِينَ فِيهَا مَا دَامَتِ السَّمَاوَاتُ وَالْأَرْضُ إِلَّا مَا شَاءَ رَبُّكَ ۚ إِنَّ رَبَّكَ فَعَّالٌ لِّمَا يُرِيدُ

Then the damned shall be cast into the Fire; here they will groan and scream like donkeys and shall abide in it as long as the heavens and the earth [of that world] exist unless your Lord ordains otherwise. Indeed, your Lord can do whatever He wants. (11:106-107)

Types of punishment in Hell

- There will be spiritual and corporal punishments for criminals, according to the severity of their crimes.
- Punishment of burning in fire (22:9, 74:29, 23:104, 70:16, 104:6-7, 77:32, 22:19).
- People will neither die nor receive any comfort in the fire (35:36, 87:12-13).
- Boiling water will be poured on them and given to drink as well (47:15, 22:19).
- Thorny bushes and the tree of Al-Zaqqum will be the food (88:6, 44:43-46), which will neither nourish them nor satisfy their hunger (88:7).
- Their necks will be collared, and their feet will be in chains (40:71, 76:4).
- They and their sufferings will not be paid any attention to by God, and He will not even look at them (83:15, 3:77).

إِنَّ جَهَنَّمَ كَانَتْ مِرْصَادًا ۞ لِلطَّاغِينَ مَآبًا ۞ لَّابِثِينَ فِيهَا أَحْقَابًا ۞ لَّا يَذُوقُونَ فِيهَا بَرْدًا وَلَا شَرَابًا ۞ إِلَّا حَمِيمًا وَغَسَّاقًا ۞ جَزَاءً وِفَاقًا ۞ إِنَّهُمْ كَانُوا لَا يَرْجُونَ حِسَابًا ۞ وَكَذَّبُوا بِآيَاتِنَا كِذَّابًا ۞ وَكُلَّ شَيْءٍ أَحْصَيْنَاهُ كِتَابًا ۞ فَذُوقُوا فَلَن نَّزِيدَكُمْ إِلَّا عَذَابًا

Indeed, Hell lurks in ambush, a place for the transgressors. They will abide therein for ages. Nothing cool will they taste therein, nor will they have anything to drink save hot water and pus. A recompense according to their deeds. These are the people who did not expect any account [of their deeds] and had recklessly denied Our revelations, [whereas] We have recorded all their deeds in writing. So taste [you O people!] We shall only increase torment for you. (78:21-30)

A unique conversation

يَوْمَ نَقُولُ لِجَهَنَّمَ هَلِ امْتَلَأْتِ وَ تَقُولُ هَلْ مِنْ مَّزِيدٍ

> When We will ask Hell: "Are you filled up?" and she will reply: "Are there some more?!"

- This question and answer are an expression of God's self-sufficient nature and also of His intense wrath: seeing the inhabitants of Hell fill it will not be any cause of hesitancy for Him; He will, in fact, have them thrown in it without any concern, because they deserve it and will then ask Hell if she is packed to capacity. The implication is that no one should be deceived by the fact that God will be saddened after throwing such arrogant people into Hell.

The Heaven in the Quran

Description of Heaven and its dwellers

- Heaven has many levels and places, and people qualify for them based on their faith and efforts.
- Jesus called it the Kingdom of Heaven, and the Quran called it the Garden, the Orchard, the Orchard of Blessings, the Orchard of eternal life, the Orchard of eternal abode, etc. It will be VAST, really VAST – as expansive as this universe.
- No concept of death, sorrow, worry, hardship, or torment. Everything it offers is eternal with no ending in sight, without bringing any monotony and boredom in life.
- There will be places like on this earth, but much more beautiful and satisfying, including gardens full of fruits of all types, rivers flowing beneath the gardens, rivers of honey and drinks, etc.

وَأَمَّا الَّذِينَ سُعِدُوا فَفِي الْجَنَّةِ خَالِدِينَ فِيهَا مَا دَامَتِ السَّمَاوَاتُ وَالْأَرْضُ إِلَّا مَا شَاءَ رَبُّكَ ۖ عَطَاءً غَيْرَ مَجْذُوذٍ

And as for the fortunate, they shall abide in Paradise and remain there as long as the heavens and the earth [of that world] endure, unless your Lord ordains otherwise. This is a never-ending favor. (11:108)

- Heaven or Paradise is the abode of the righteous (in simple terms, whoever was saved from Hell). There is no distinction between men and women.
- People who are foremost in their faith and righteousness will get the highest place in Heaven.
- People entering Heaven will receive rewards suited to their gender. Spouses (male or female) will continue their relationship in Heaven if both are there.
- Children who died in this world before adolescence will be serving the people of Paradise.
- The angels will welcome the people of Paradise.

وَسِيقَ الَّذِينَ اتَّقَوْا رَبَّهُمْ إِلَى الْجَنَّةِ زُمَرًا ۖ حَتَّىٰ إِذَا جَاءُوهَا وَفُتِحَتْ أَبْوَابُهَا وَقَالَ لَهُمْ خَزَنَتُهَا سَلَامٌ عَلَيْكُمْ طِبْتُمْ فَادْخُلُوهَا خَالِدِينَ

And those who fear their Lord shall be led in crowds to Paradise. As they draw near, its gates will open for them, and its keepers will say to them, "Peace be to you; rejoice and enter into it to dwell forever." (39:73)

Rewards in Heaven

- The Quran presented a very attractive and unique picture of life in paradise, one that resembles a royal lifestyle. Lush green orchards, flowing streams, luxuriant gardens, towering castles, very expensive utensils, slaves wearing golden waist-bands, thrones made of gold, clothes of satin and brocade, goblets of crystal, blissful gatherings, and beautiful mates.

- Luxuries of heaven are depicted in a way that makes it more suitable for its audience (Arabs). However, in other places, the Quran uses general terms for the rewards: they will receive whatever they desire (41:31, 43:71, 50:35).

- Heart cleansed from envy and malice (7:43, 15:47), and people will always be content and satisfied (15:48, 18:108, 35:34-35). They will not have regrets of the past nor any fear of the future (2:62, 112, 262, 274, 272).

- God will be pleased with them, and they will be pleased with God.

- They will eat and drink but will neither spit nor have any need to urinate or defecate (Hadith). Their sweat will smell like musk; no illness, disease, or death.

- People will always remain young and never age.

فَوَقَاهُمُ اللَّهُ شَرَّ ذَٰلِكَ الْيَوْمِ وَلَقَّاهُمْ نَضْرَةً وَسُرُورًا ۝ وَجَزَاهُم بِمَا صَبَرُوا جَنَّةً وَحَرِيرًا

مُّتَّكِئِينَ فِيهَا عَلَى الْأَرَائِكِ ۖ لَا يَرَوْنَ فِيهَا شَمْسًا وَلَا زَمْهَرِيرًا ۝ وَدَانِيَةً عَلَيْهِمْ ظِلَالُهَا وَذُلِّلَتْ قُطُوفُهَا تَذْلِيلًا

وَيُطَافُ عَلَيْهِم بِآنِيَةٍ مِّن فِضَّةٍ وَأَكْوَابٍ كَانَتْ قَوَارِيرَا ۝ قَوَارِيرَ مِن فِضَّةٍ قَدَّرُوهَا تَقْدِيرًا

وَيُسْقَوْنَ فِيهَا كَأْسًا كَانَ مِزَاجُهَا زَنجَبِيلًا ۝ عَيْنًا فِيهَا تُسَمَّىٰ سَلْسَبِيلًا

وَيَطُوفُ عَلَيْهِمْ وِلْدَانٌ مُّخَلَّدُونَ إِذَا رَأَيْتَهُمْ حَسِبْتَهُمْ لُؤْلُؤًا مَّنثُورًا وَإِذَا رَأَيْتَ ثَمَّ رَأَيْتَ نَعِيمًا وَمُلْكًا كَبِيرًا

عَالِيَهُمْ ثِيَابُ سُندُسٍ خُضْرٌ وَإِسْتَبْرَقٌ ۖ وَحُلُّوا أَسَاوِرَ مِن فِضَّةٍ وَسَقَاهُمْ رَبُّهُمْ شَرَابًا طَهُورًا

So Allah [their Lord] saved them from the affliction of that Day and bestowed them with freshness and joy, and as a reward for being patient [in this world] gave them Paradise [to live in] and robes of silk [to wear]. They will be reclining in it on thrones and will feel neither the heat of the sun nor the cold of winter. The shades of its trees will bow down over them, and the clusters of their fruits will be within their easy reach. And dishes of silver [to eat from] and goblets of crystal [to drink from] will be passed around them. And the crystal will be silver, which they [—their attendants—] will have aptly arranged [for every service]. [Besides this], they will be given to drink a wine flavored with *Zanjabil*. There is also a spring therein called *Salsabil*. And they will be attended by boys graced with eternal youth; they will be running around. When you see them, you will think that they are pearls scattered about. And wherever you look, you will see great bliss and a kingdom glorious [such] that even the outer garments of [the dwellers of paradise] will be of green silk, brocade, and satin. And they were adorned with bracelets of silver [and then they reached the place where] their Lord entertained them with pure wine. (76:11-22)

Rewards in Heaven – Quran's Real Message

- Quran summarized the rewards of Heaven for people of all times in this verse

فَلَا تَعْلَمُ نَفْسٌ مَّا أُخْفِيَ لَهُم مِّن قُرَّةِ أَعْيُنٍ جَزَاءً بِمَا كَانُوا يَعْمَلُونَ

Then, no one knows what bliss has been hidden for him as a reward for his deeds. (32:17)

Is Heaven solely for Muslims?

- Like the Jews, Muslims also claim that Heaven is only for Muslims.
- However, the Quran took a completely different approach. Instead of associating Heaven with any group of people, it declared a criterion for success in the Hereafter.

إِنَّ الَّذِينَ آمَنُوا وَالَّذِينَ هَادُوا وَالنَّصَارَىٰ وَالصَّابِئِينَ مَنْ آمَنَ بِاللَّهِ وَالْيَوْمِ الْآخِرِ وَعَمِلَ صَالِحًا فَلَهُمْ أَجْرُهُمْ عِندَ رَبِّهِمْ وَلَا خَوْفٌ عَلَيْهِمْ وَلَا هُمْ يَحْزَنُونَ

Verily! Those who believe, and those who are Jews, Christians, and Sabians, (among those) whoever believes in Allah and the Last Day and does righteous good deeds shall have their reward with their Lord; on them shall be no fear, nor shall they grieve.

- These 3 requirements are fundamental, and there is no need for any prophet to come.
- Association with any group or any name tag like Muslim, Jew, or Christian is not the criterion for success and will <u>NOT</u> help on the day of Judgment.
- Jews were under the same impression that the Quran rejected: "Hellfire will not touch us, and if it does, then maybe just for a few moments/days."
- Everyone will be held accountable for their efforts to seek true knowledge and for their behavior toward it.
- However, many people wonder how this criterion for success will be applied across different groups, given that people face different circumstances in this world when it comes to their approach to religion and religious knowledge.
- The simple answer to this question is that it depends on the extent of their knowledge about the last prophet/messenger (of their time) and their teachings.

Criteria for success in the Hereafter

Level of Knowledge	Attitude in this life	Expected Result
Human Nature (God, good and evil). No knowledge about a Prophet	Responded to human nature and lived righteously No heed to human nature & lived unrighteously (crime)	Good Bad
Living with the Prophet of the time	Accepted, obeyed and lived righteously Rejected and remained neutral (crime) Rejected and became enemy (crime)	Excellent Bad Worst
Non-Muslim but knows last Prophet in history	Convinced, accepted and lived righteously	Excellent
	Not convinced and lived righteously	Good/Excellent
	Convinced but still rejected, lived righteously	Good/Bad
	Convinced but became enemy (crime)	Worst
Muslim	Practiced Islam and lived righteously	Excellent
	Practiced Islam but had mixed life	Good/Excellent
	Muslim by name and lived an unrighteous life	Bad
	Practiced Islam but killed another Muslim intentionally or committed multiple major sins, disrespecting God's commands	Worst

Deciding people's fate in this world

- People's fate in the hereafter is completely unknown to any human being on earth.
- When Prophets make such declarations for some people in their lifetime, it is because God has informed them. This principle is evident in the Quran.
- People's fate is entirely dependent on how convinced they are of the knowledge required for success, and we have no way to determine this.
- Our job is to convey the message and make dua for guidance.
- Even Prophet Muhammad and previous Prophets were given the same task and nothing more or nothing less (the decision to punish comes directly from God, and the Messenger never makes that decision).

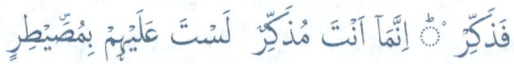

(If they do not believe in spite of this) Then just remind them [O Prophet]! You are only a reminder; you are not made a guardian over them. (88:21-22)

How hard is it to be successful?

- There is a common misunderstanding among people, both Muslims and non-Muslims, that Islam is a very difficult and strict religion, and God wants to send everyone to Hell.
- Looking at the Quran and Hadith on these matters, it is clear that the reality is very different from this misunderstanding.
- Let's look at some of the verses about the reward for evil and righteous deeds.

مَن جَاءَ بِالْحَسَنَةِ فَلَهُ عَشْرُ أَمْثَالِهَا ۖ وَمَن جَاءَ بِالسَّيِّئَةِ فَلَا يُجْزَىٰ إِلَّا مِثْلَهَا وَهُمْ لَا يُظْلَمُونَ

Whoever comes with one good deed will get 10 times its reward, whoever comes with one sin will get its equivalent, and they will not be wronged (6:160)

إِن تَجْتَنِبُوا كَبَائِرَ مَا تُنْهَوْنَ عَنْهُ نُكَفِّرْ عَنكُمْ سَيِّئَاتِكُمْ وَنُدْخِلْكُم مُّدْخَلًا كَرِيمًا

If you save yourselves from greater sins among those which you have been asked to avoid, then we will wipe out completely your minor sins and will make you enter into a respectable dwelling (4:31)

Note: Major sins are discussed later in the course

- Some Quranic verses and Hadith mention that the reward for some deeds can be 700 times, and in a few cases, it can be unlimited (for example, fasting).
- On the other hand, God also guaranteed that there will be no injustice, not even the size of an atom, that will be committed on that day.

يُظْلَمُونَ ثُمَّ تُوَفَّىٰ كُلُّ نَفْسٍ مَّا كَسَبَتْ وَهُمْ لَا

Then every soul will be rewarded for what they have earned and will not be wronged (2:281)

فَلَا نَفْسٌ شَيْئًا تُظْلَمُ وَنَضَعُ الْمَوَازِينَ الْقِسْطَ لِيَوْمِ الْقِيَامَةِ

And the scale of justice will be set for the day of judgment and no injustice will be committed to any soul (21:47)

مِثْقَالَ ذَرَّةٍ يَظْلِمُ إِنَّ اللَّهَ لَا

Allah does not commit injustice even of the size of an atom (4:40)

لِلْعَبِيدِ بِظَلَّامٍ ذَٰلِكَ بِمَا قَدَّمَتْ أَيْدِيكُمْ وَأَنَّ اللَّهَ لَيْسَ

This is what you have sent forward (from your deeds) and Allah is not unjust to his servants (3:182)

- Anyone who gets the full picture from the Quran and Hadith can easily see that God wants us to succeed in the Hereafter, and He has given us plenty of opportunities to do so.

1. Why is there an 'eternal' punishment of Hell for some crimes like Shirk?
2. What are the main reasons for people to be forgetful of the Hereafter?

Chapter 11

Islamic Morals and Morality

This chapter and the next will cover the Islamic guidance on morals and morality. In this chapter, we will first cover the fundamental principles that the Quran has stated about morals.

Fundamental Principles

The significance of good character

- After faith, the second most important requirement of religion is doing righteous/good deeds.
- Purifying morals or building a good character is the source of all righteous deeds.
- In essence, doing righteous deeds means we are required to purify our relationships with God and our fellow human beings.

- The rest of the religious instructions are its corollary.
- Over time, laws change, but the moral demands of Islam remain constant.
- It will help us the most on the day of judgment to be successful.

" Nothing will be heavier on the Day of Judgment in the believer's scale than good character. (Hadith Tirmidhi: 626)"

Prophet Muhammad is our role model

- For us today, the life of Prophet Muhammad offers a powerful blueprint for navigating modern challenges with integrity, emotional intelligence, and purpose. He was not just a leader of a nation, but a person who excelled in the small, everyday moments that define our character.
- The Quran has attested to that character.

وَإِنَّكَ لَعَلَىٰ خُلُقٍ عَظِيمٍ

And indeed, (O Muhammad), you are of a great moral character. (Quran 68:4)

- Building character on moral values is so dear to God that Prophet Muhammad once said that his sole reason for coming to this world is to perfect the good character that every human being has been endowed by God.

بُعِثْتُ لِأُتَمِّمَ حُسْنَ الْأَخْلَاقِ

I have been sent to perfect good moral character. (Hadith Al-Muwatta #1614)

"The religion itself is good character, so whoever surpasses you in good character has surpassed you in religion." *(Ibn Al Qayyam)*

Our knowledge of good and evil is inspired

How are we different from other animals?

- Three things distinguish humans from other animals:

(1) We are intellectual beings. We possess the ability to learn, form concepts, and apply logic and reason, enabling us to solve problems, innovate, plan, make decisions, and use language to communicate.

(2) We have an aesthetic sense. Since time immemorial, we have produced art. We beautify things, including ourselves. This sense creates music, poetry, artwork, cities, houses, dresses, interiors, etc. It impacts us psychologically.

(3) We are moral beings. We can differentiate between right and wrong, good and evil. This is the basis for all our relationships: with God, family, friends, neighbors, society, and the world at large.

Our knowledge of good and evil is inspired

- Like the faculty of seeing and hearing, God has blessed human beings with a faculty that distinguishes between good and evil (or right and wrong).
- Human beings are moral beings.
- Like we enjoy music, appreciate art, beautify houses, we can tell the difference between good and evil.
- We love, respect, and revere what is good.
- We create justice systems to curb evil in society.
- Fundamental morality is innate and universal, but its implementations in society can take different forms.
- For example, being good and kind to parents is a fundamental moral or ethical principle. In Asia, it may mean keeping them in your home and serving them; in North America, it may mean visiting them and doing their grocery shopping.

And by the soul, when We fashioned it, We inspired it with its evil and its good then whoever purified it, will be successful and whoever corrupted it will be failed (91:7-8)

Role of nature

- Nature (*Fitrah*) is the foundational bedrock of all divine teachings and Shariah.
- In other words, religion is not an external imposition but a confirmation and completion of the moral and rational truths already ingrained in human nature.
- Islam is called Deen-al-Fitrah in the Quran. Meaning its laws and teachings are in perfect harmony with natural human inclinations. The prophetic revelation serves to "awaken" and provide formal structure to the intuitive knowledge already present within the human soul.
- There is no conflict between the laws of nature (which humans explore through science) and the laws of religion (revealed through prophets). They complete the picture. While reason and nature can lead one to acknowledge a Creator, revelation is required to confirm the specific details of God's commands and the reality of the afterlife.
- In summary, the religion of Islam and many aspects related to it are completely compatible with human nature.

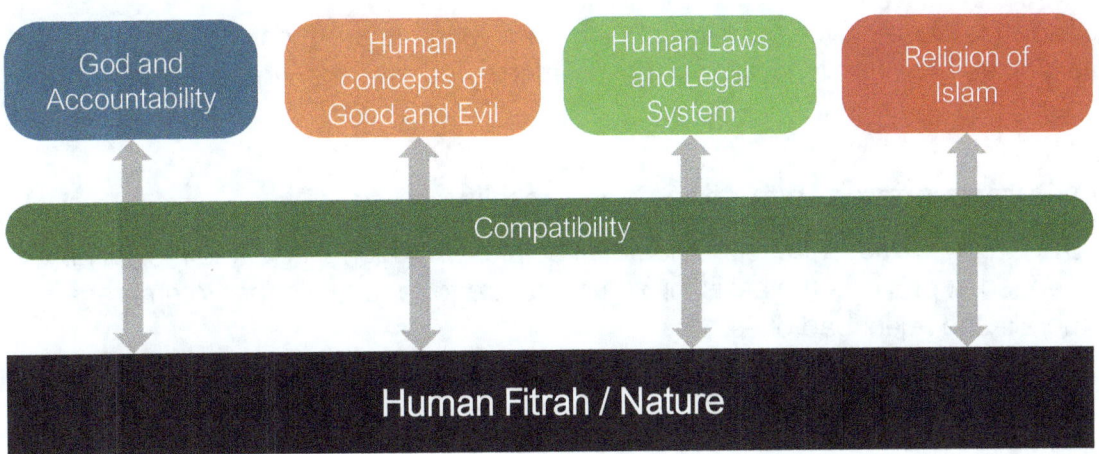

فَأَقِمْ وَجْهَكَ لِلدِّيْنِ حَنِيْفًا ۚ فِطْرَتَ اللّٰهِ الَّتِيْ فَطَرَ النَّاسَ عَلَيْهَا ۚ لَا تَبْدِيْلَ لِخَلْقِ اللّٰهِ ۚ ذٰلِكَ الدِّيْنُ الْقَيِّمُ ۙ وَ لٰكِنَّ اَكْثَرَ النَّاسِ لَا يَعْلَمُوْنَ

So, [now that these facts have become evident,] following one God continues to point your face [like your father Abraham] towards his religion. Follow the nature created by God [O Prophet!] on which He has created people. This nature created by God cannot be changed. This is the only straight path, but most people do not know it. (30:30)

Islam's guidance on moral behavior

Who sets the standards for right and wrong?

- On top of the God-gifted sense, God explained the details of good and evil through His Messengers and Book.
- This guidance is now eternally saved in the Quran.
- This guidance is entirely compatible with what's already inspired inside us and only explains it.
- Human beings have a natural tendency to differ in their interpretations and details of this innate moral sense and in its application across different periods.
- There is a consensus among humans on basic morals/ethics.
- The differences we see across societies are due to preferences for one value over another. That does not negate the value's presence.

Indeed, this Quran gives guidance to the path which is the most upright and gives glad tidings of a great reward to those among its believers who do good deeds. (17:9)

The Quran's approach to ethics and morality

- The Quran provides the fundamental principles on which ethics and morality are founded. It provides the basis for human nature to require him/her to embrace good morals and reject bad ones.
- The Quran offers ethical/moral guidelines that people can adopt in accordance with their culture and practices. The guidelines are universal and fully compatible with human nature.
- For example, the Quran told us to show excellence in our behavior towards our parents. This is a fundamental principle. In different cultures, this principle manifests itself differently.
- In Asia, adult children would keep their parents in their homes and serve them. In the US, people who live nearby might visit them, call them often, and do their grocery shopping when needed. Both behaviors can be good manifestations of the guiding principle in the Quran regarding parents.

Humans tend to justify their deeds (usually bad ones)

- We witness the manifestation of this inspired knowledge when we commit wrong.
- Even the worst people don't want to expose their evil deeds (at least at first).
- Instead of rejecting the gravity of evil, we tend to create excuses for it.
- If we are faced with the same evil, we call it wrong with full conviction.
- This mini court of justice we have inside is the strongest evidence for the larger court of justice on the Day of Judgment.
- The incident of Able and Cain is a good example.

وَلَوْ أَلْقَىٰ مَعَاذِيرَهُ بَلِ الْإِنسَانُ عَلَىٰ نَفْسِهِ بَصِيرَةٌ

In reality, man himself is a witness to his own self, even though he puts forth his excuses. (75:14-15)

وَكَرِهْتَ أَنْ يَطَّلِعَ عَلَيْهِ اَلنَّاسُ ,مَا حَاكَ فِي صَدْرِكَ :وَالْإِثْمُ ,حُسْنُ اَلْخُلُقِ :اَلْبِرُّ

Righteousness is good morals, and sinful conduct is what pricks in your heart and you hate (Hadith)

What drives us to be good?

- We fully understand and appreciate the consequences of good and evil, and we agree that the results cannot be the same.
- We strongly feel that good should be rewarded with good and evil should be recompensed accordingly.
- This creates a sense of accountability within us, prompting us to do good and making us fearful of the consequences of evil.
- Faith in God relates this natural sense of accountability to the grand scheme of accountability that God has prescribed for this universe.
- Besides natural inclination, for a believer, the love of God, His pleasure, and anger drive him to adhere to good morals and refrain from evil.

فَآتِ ذَا الْقُرْبَىٰ حَقَّهُ وَالْمِسْكِينَ وَابْنَ السَّبِيلِ ۚ ذَٰلِكَ خَيْرٌ لِّلَّذِينَ يُرِيدُونَ وَجْهَ اللَّهِ ۖ وَأُولَٰئِكَ هُمُ الْمُفْلِحُونَ

So, give their due to the next of kin, the destitute, and the traveler. That is best for those who want to please God, and it is those who shall surely prosper. (30:38)

وَيُطْعِمُونَ الطَّعَامَ عَلَىٰ حُبِّهِ مِسْكِينًا وَيَتِيمًا وَأَسِيرًا إِنَّمَا نُطْعِمُكُمْ لِوَجْهِ اللَّهِ لَا نُرِيدُ مِنكُمْ جَزَاءً وَلَا شُكُورًا

And they feed the needy, orphans, and prisoners with the food that they themselves desire for, saying that we feed you for the sake of God and we do not want any reward or thanks from anyone (76:8-9))

Guidance from Hadith

On the Day of Judgment, the foremost among people whose fate shall be decided would be scholars of the Quran, those who had been killed in Jihad, or those who had been blessed with wealth by God. They shall be brought over, and God will remind them of His favors. They will acknowledge these favors. God will then ask them: "What did you do to benefit from them?" The scholar will reply: "I was educated, and then I educated others and recited the Quran before others to call them towards You." The soldier will say: "I fought in Your way and was killed." The rich person will say: "I spent on every occasion you are pleased with spending." God will say: "All of this was done by you so that people should call you a scholar, a brave person, and a generous person [respectively]; so you have been called so in the world." It shall thus be ordered, and they shall be dragged into Hell. (Sahih Muslim: 4923)

The objective of being good

- Some people do good to feel happy about it.
- Some do it to achieve perfection in human virtues.
- God made the purification of the soul (through faith and deeds) the main objective for being bestowed with God's eternal Kingdom.
- It is a constant endeavor.
- Through the purification of faith and deeds, one can aim to achieve perfection and true happiness.

يَا أَيَّتُهَا النَّفْسُ الْمُطْمَئِنَّةُ ارْجِعِي إِلَىٰ رَبِّكِ رَاضِيَةً مَّرْضِيَّةً فَادْخُلِي فِي عِبَادِي وَادْخُلِي جَنَّتِي

O you, the delighted soul! Return unto your Lord, such that He is pleased with you and you are pleased with Him. [Return] and enter among My servants and enter My Paradise. (89:27-30)

The foundation of good deeds is based on good intentions. This drive and objective of earning the pleasure of God make all virtuous deeds free of show and pretense.

The foundation of good and evil

- The beauty of the Quran is that it not only tells us about the individual good and evil that a human can commit, but also provides the foundation for all the good morals one wants to acquire and the evil traits one wants to avoid.

- This not only helps us understand what to acquire and what to avoid in our lives, but also helps us navigate new situations and decide on the behavior we should adopt to please Allah.

- This remarkable verse is in Surah Nahl, which describes three positives to adopt and three negatives to avoid:

God enjoins you to justice, goodness, and spending on the kindred and forbids vulgarity, evil, and rebellious arrogance. He admonishes you so that you may take heed. (16:90)

Positives	Negatives
Justice, goodness and spending on the kindred	Vulgarity, evil and rebellious arrogance

- Let's understand them one by one.

Justice (Adl)

- This means placing things in their rightful place.
- Whatever obligation is imposed on a person concerning other fellow human beings and God, they should discharge it the way it should be in an impartial manner.
- This even includes other creations of Allah around us, like animals and plants, etc.
- It is governed by an unwritten contract that human being has with God and with other creations of God.
- While discharging the obligations written in that unwritten contract, other fellows' weakness or strength, or your liking or disliking, relationships, etc., must not influence it.
- In Islam, the concept of justice starts with you and me before it applies to the court or the ruler, and it is a broader concept.
- Justice is a personal virtue and one of the standards of moral excellence that a believer is encouraged to attain as part of his God-consciousness.
- Justice becomes more critical when it concerns people who are less fortunate, more vulnerable, or under your authority.
- Allah warned us against committing injustice at two levels: personal and national.

يَا أَيُّهَا الَّذِينَ آمَنُوا كُونُوا قَوَّامِينَ بِالْقِسْطِ شُهَدَاءَ لِلَّهِ وَلَوْ عَلَىٰ أَنفُسِكُمْ أَوِ الْوَالِدَيْنِ وَالْأَقْرَبِينَ ۚ إِن يَكُنْ غَنِيًّا أَوْ فَقِيرًا فَاللَّهُ أَوْلَىٰ بِهِمَا ۖ فَلَا تَتَّبِعُوا الْهَوَىٰ أَن تَعْدِلُوا ۚ وَإِن تَلْوُوا أَوْ تُعْرِضُوا فَإِنَّ اللَّهَ كَانَ بِمَا تَعْمَلُونَ خَبِيرًا

Believers! Adhere to justice by bearing witness for God, even though it be against yourselves, your parents, or your kinsfolk. If someone is rich or poor, God is worthy of having His law followed for both. So, by leaving aside the guidance of God, do not be led by base desires, lest you swerve from the truth, and remember that if you distort what is the truth and what is just, or evade it, God is well aware of all your deeds. (4:135)

وَا أَيُّهَا الَّذِينَ آمَنُوا كُونُوا قَوَّامِينَ لِلَّهِ شُهَدَاءَ بِالْقِسْطِ ۖ وَلَا يَجْرِمَنَّكُمْ شَنَآنُ قَوْمٍ عَلَىٰ أَلَّا تَعْدِلُوا ۚ اعْدِلُوا هُوَ أَقْرَبُ لِلتَّقْوَىٰ ۖ وَاتَّقُوا اللَّهَ ۚ إِنَّ اللَّهَ خَبِيرٌ بِمَا تَعْمَلُونَ

Believers! Be those who adhere to justice by bearing witness to it for God. And your animosity for some people/nation should not induce you to turn away from justice. Be just; this is nearer to piety. And have a fear of God; indeed, God is well aware of all your deeds. (Quran 5:8)

Goodness (Ihsan)

- Goodness is beyond justice and is the pinnacle of ethics and morality. It can be termed as "justice plus".
- Rights should be fulfilled in such a way that one would say, "it is fulfilled in the best possible manner".
- Sometimes, it demands sacrifice on our part.
- It is a requirement of our faith and not an 'optional' status that one could achieve as a result of going through certain 'religious practices' (a common misconception about 'Ihsan'.
- Goodness is contagious.
- Values such as love, sympathy, compassion, sacrifice, sincerity, and gratitude are enriched in a society by the prevalence of goodness.

وَ قَضٰى رَبُّكَ اَلَّا تَعْبُدُوْٓا اِلَّآ اِيَّاهُ وَ بِالْوَالِدَيْنِ اِحْسَانًا ؕ اِمَّا يَبْلُغَنَّ عِنْدَكَ الْكِبَرَ اَحَدُهُمَآ اَوْ كِلٰهُمَا فَلَا تَقُلْ لَّهُمَآ اُفٍّ وَّ لَا تَنْهَرْهُمَا وَ قُلْ لَّهُمَا قَوْلًا كَرِيْمًا

Your Lord has enjoined you to worship none but Him, and to treat your parents **very well**. If either or both of them attain old age before you, show them no sign of impatience, nor scold them while answering; speak to them with respect, and with softness. (10:25-26)

وَ اللّٰهُ يَدْعُوْٓا اِلٰى دَارِ السَّلٰمِ ؕ وَ يَهْدِيْ مَنْ يَّشَآءُ اِلٰى صِرَاطٍ مُّسْتَقِيْمٍ لِلَّذِيْنَ اَحْسَنُوا الْحُسْنٰى وَ زِيَادَةٌ ؕ وَ لَا يَرْهَقُ وُجُوْهَهُمْ قَتَرٌ وَّ لَا ذِلَّةٌ ؕ اُولٰئِكَ اَصْحٰبُ الْجَنَّةِ ۚ هُمْ فِيْهَا خٰلِدُوْنَ

And God calls you to the abode of peace, and for this shows the straight path to whomsoever He wants to [in accordance with His law]. [Then] those who showed goodness, for them is goodness and even more. Neither darkness will overspread their faces nor humiliation. It is they who are the people of Paradise. They shall remain in it forever. (17:23)

وَ اَنْفِقُوْا فِيْ سَبِيْلِ اللّٰهِ وَ لَا تُلْقُوْا بِاَيْدِيْكُمْ اِلَى التَّهْلُكَةِ ۚۛ وَ اَحْسِنُوْا ۚۛ اِنَّ اللّٰهَ يُحِبُّ الْمُحْسِنِيْنَ

Spend for the cause of God and [by evading it] do not with your own hands cast yourselves into destruction. And **do [this spending] graciously** because God loves those who are gracious (give more than due). (2:145)

Spending on the Kindred

- This is an extension, but an essential branch of goodness specific to our relatives, which is why God separated it out.
- Our blood relatives do not just deserve justice and goodness from us, but also have a right to our wealth and riches.
- The general principle is that spending starts with your closest ones.
- **Wisdom in this instruction:** God wants people to take care of their immediate family, extended family, friends, neighbors, people they know, and the community in that order.

The upper hand is better than the lower hand (Hadith)

- Spending on our relatives should be without consideration of their religion and race.
- Holding our spending in times of need (with one of your relatives) when we can afford has severe consequences in the hereafter.
- Every larger or extended family has a few rich people in it. If every family is taken care of by their rich (or relatively rich) family members, then no one needs to go and ask strangers for help.

لَيْسَ الْبِرَّ اَنْ تُوَلُّوْا وُجُوْهَكُمْ قِبَلَ الْمَشْرِقِ وَ الْمَغْرِبِ وَ لٰكِنَّ الْبِرَّ مَنْ اٰمَنَ بِاللهِ وَ الْيَوْمِ الْاٰخِرِ وَ الْمَلٰٓئِكَةِ وَ الْكِتٰبِ وَ النَّبِيّٖنَ ۚ وَ اٰتَى الْمَالَ عَلٰى حُبِّهٖ ذَوِى الْقُرْبٰى وَ الْيَتٰمٰى وَ الْمَسٰكِيْنَ وَ ابْنَ السَّبِيْلِ ۙ وَ السَّآئِلِيْنَ وَ فِى الرِّقَابِ ۚ وَ اَقَامَ الصَّلٰوةَ وَ اٰتَى الزَّكٰوةَ ۚ وَ الْمُوْفُوْنَ بِعَهْدِهِمْ اِذَا عٰهَدُوْا ۚ وَ الصّٰبِرِيْنَ فِى الْبَأْسَآءِ وَ الضَّرَّآءِ وَ حِيْنَ الْبَأْسِ ۗ اُولٰٓئِكَ الَّذِيْنَ صَدَقُوْا ۗ وَ اُولٰٓئِكَ هُمُ الْمُتَّقُوْنَ

They think that the duty imposed on them to be loyal to God is fulfilled simply by observing certain rites and rituals (such as facing east or west). They should know that loyalty to God does not merely mean that you face the East or the West [in the prayer,] but loyalty is the loyalty of those who believe in God with all their heart and in the Last Day and in the angels of God and in His Books and in His prophets and who, in spite of their love for wealth, spend it on kinsfolk, the orphans, the destitute, the traveler and on those who ask and for the liberation of necks and who are diligent in the prayer and pay zakah. And loyalty is the loyalty of those who, when they make a promise, fulfil it, and especially of those who are steadfast in scarcity, illness, and in times of war. These are the people who are truthful [to God in fulfilling the promise of loyalty to Him], and these are the ones who are, in fact, God-conscious. (2:177)

Lewdness / Vulgarity (Fahsha)

- The Arabic word 'Fahsha' is very comprehensive.
- It covers everything that comes in the realm of fornication, homosexuality, and other acts of vulgarity, and anything that leads to one of these acts.
- The *Fahsha* includes every act where our private parts are exposed, discussed, or referred to in a way that is allowed by Allah.
- It covers these acts, whether done in public or secret.
- It is at the root of many evils and sins in society.
- Open vulgarity is the worst form of it.
- In the age of the internet, acts of immorality spread more easily than ever.
- Allah forbade every form of *Fahsha* because this is one aspect where human beings are weak and can easily be dragged into what is ultimately forbidden or haram, and that is *Zina*.

يَٰٓأَيُّهَا الَّذِينَ اٰمَنُوا لَا تَتَّبِعُوا خُطُوٰتِ الشَّيْطٰنِ ۚ وَ مَنْ يَّتَّبِعْ خُطُوٰتِ الشَّيْطٰنِ فَاِنَّهٗ يَأْمُرُ بِالْفَحْشَآءِ وَ الْمُنْكَرِ

Believers! Do not follow the footsteps of Satan, and [remember that] he who follows the footsteps of Satan will only ruin himself because he entices people to lewdness and evil. (24:21)

وَ لِلّٰهِ مَا فِي السَّمٰوٰتِ وَ مَا فِي الْاَرْضِ ۙ لِيَجْزِيَ الَّذِينَ اَسَآءُوا بِمَا عَمِلُوا وَ يَجْزِيَ الَّذِينَ اَحْسَنُوا بِالْحُسْنَى

اَلَّذِينَ يَجْتَنِبُونَ كَبٰٓئِرَ الْاِثْمِ وَ الْفَوَاحِشَ اِلَّا اللَّمَمَ ۚ اِنَّ رَبَّكَ وَاسِعُ الْمَغْفِرَةِ ۚ

Whatever is in the heavens and in the earth is in the jurisdiction of God alone. The result of this will only be that He punishes the evil-doers for their deeds and bestows a good reward on those who did good deeds, who abstained from major sins and open indecencies, except if they became a little contaminated for a while. [He will forgive them.] Your Lord surely is vast in mercy. (53:31-32)

اِنَّ الصَّلٰوةَ تَنْهٰى عَنِ الْفَحْشَآءِ وَ الْمُنْكَرِ

Undoubtedly, the prayer fends off lewdness and evil. (29:45)

Evil (Munkar)

- It is a very encompassing word and the exact opposite of universal goodness (attributes that are considered universally good).
- This contains all those evil sins that are universally considered wrong, and you don't have to explain to someone about their evilness.
- In other places in the Quran, the word 'Ithm' (sin) is used for such acts, which usually involve usurping other people's rights.
- Examples: Cheating, deceiving, spreading lies, distorting the truth, sowing discord among people, etc.

وَلْتَكُنْ مِّنكُمْ أُمَّةٌ يَّدْعُوْنَ اِلَى الْخَيْرِ وَ يَأْمُرُوْنَ بِالْمَعْرُوْفِ وَ يَنْهَوْنَ عَنِ الْمُنْكَرِ ۚ وَ اُولٰئِكَ هُمُ الْمُفْلِحُوْنَ

And let there be appointed among you some people who call towards righteousness, urge towards virtue, and forbid evil. [Diligently arrange for this] and [remember that] those who do so shall only attain success. (3:104)

اَلَّذِيْنَ اِنْ مَّكَّنّٰهُمْ فِى الْاَرْضِ اَقَامُوا الصَّلٰوةَ وَ اٰتَوُا الزَّكٰوةَ وَ اَمَرُوْا بِالْمَعْرُوْفِ وَ نَهَوْا عَنِ الْمُنْكَرِ ۚ وَ لِلّٰهِ عَاقِبَةُ الْاُمُوْرِ

Those whom We grant sovereignty in this land shall be diligent in prayer and pay zakah and exhort towards good and forbid evil. [God shall definitely help them], and the fate of all matters is in the hands of God alone. (22:41)

- It is not only the responsibility of an individual to stay away from evil, because it corrupts society, but also the responsibility of a state or government to appoint people who monitor the spread of evil in society and to advise or admonish those committing it for such behavior. They can even arrest and punish them through a legal process.
- Because some evils take the form of crime, the department of law enforcement is often created to tackle societal evils that become crimes.
- Similar to vulgarity, the Quran also provided a recipe for avoiding evil in the same verse.

اِنَّ الصَّلٰوةَ تَنْهٰى عَنِ الْفَحْشَآءِ وَ الْمُنْكَرِ

Undoubtedly, the prayer fends off lewdness and evil. (29:45)

Arrogance/Rebel/Excess (*Baghi*)

- In Islam, arrogance is the worst attitude a person can adopt, especially in front of God.
- *Baghi* is the type of arrogance that manifests rebelliousness, especially towards people.
- This is one step ahead of *Ithm*, where the person not only usurps people's rights but also exceeds their limits and bounds in depriving them of basic human rights through power and influence, and commits excess against them.
- A person who is rebelliously arrogant toward God is often rebellious toward people, but not necessarily.
- Some of the examples of *Baghi* are: murder, rape, armed robbery, torture, extortion, etc.
- If we carefully look at this verse in discussion, it covers a full spectrum of human behavior on both sides (positive and negative).

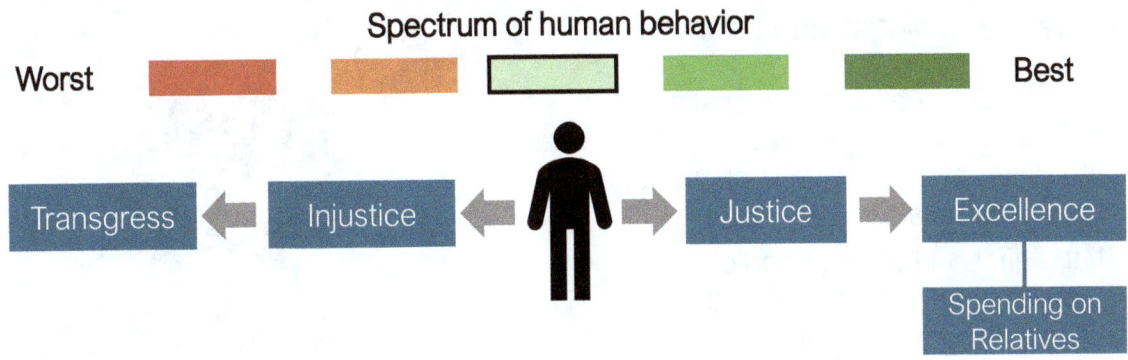

قُلْ إِنَّمَا حَرَّمَ رَبِّيَ الْفَوَاحِشَ مَا ظَهَرَ مِنْهَا وَ مَا بَطَنَ وَ الْإِثْمَ وَ الْبَغْىَ بِغَيْرِ الْحَقِّ

Say: My Lord has only forbidden lewd acts, whether open or hidden, and usurping rights and wrongful oppression. (7:33)

- At the end of verse 16:90, which we are discussing, God told us that He is admonishing us with this guidance so we may take heed and not make excuses before God when we meet Him.
- This verse is the summary of all do's and don'ts of Shariah, and the foundation of all good and evil mentioned in this verse is in full conformity with human nature. Even if you tell this verse to a non-Muslim, they would not disagree with any of the attributes mentioned in this verse.

Character building is a lifelong struggle

Character building is more than a foundation

- In verse 16:90, we learned what to avoid and what to acquire, but that was just the foundation of everything. Acquiring good traits and preserving them is a lifelong struggle because it is more than just the foundation.
- We face different situations every day that test our morals.
- Strengthening our character is a two-step process:
    - Get rid of bad habits and negative traits.
    - Develop and nourish good habits and positive traits.
- Basic principle: No bad deed is SMALL & no good deed is SMALL.
- Get help with prayers and patience, as this is the recipe given in the Quran for people facing challenges.
- Eliminate this concept: "I am doing it for God"; you are actually doing it for yourself, as it is going to benefit you in this world and in the Hereafter.

Faith and building moral character

- Faith in God (*Eeman*) is not just a set of beliefs but a transformative force that builds character by aligning your inner nature with your external actions.
- If the effort of building good character is rooted in strong faith in God, then it builds a much stronger character.
- It is like a deeply rooted tree that can weather the powerful storms of life's challenges.
- Most of the time, our morals are tested in challenging times, and this is where faith helps us make the right decision.

A character deeply rooted in faith in God can weather powerful storms in this life.

Foundation of Prohibitions (*Haraam*)

- In verse 16:90, we learned the foundation of good and evil, which is more related to the moral guidance provided by the Quran.

- The Quran also guided us regarding the foundation of prohibitions (*haraam*) that must be taken into consideration when deriving Shariah laws. Meaning what those elements are in a human act that make it prohibited in *Shariah*, and Allah will ask about them, and we will face the consequences of acting on them.

- Any act related to God is not punishable in this life unless God's Messenger is sent and He may decide to do it through the Messenger.

- Everything else outside this list will be considered acts permitted in religion.

- There are two places in the Quran where, in describing Shariah, God uses the word "*Innama*," which restricts something to what is described. In English, we use the phrase "Nothing but …"

- This principle, in a way, gives us the four corners for what is prohibited in Islam.

Food

اِنَّمَا حَرَّمَ عَلَيْكُمُ الْمَيْتَةَ وَ الدَّمَ وَ لَحْمَ الْخِنْزِيْرِ وَ مَاۤ اُهِلَّ بِهٖ لِغَيْرِ اللّٰهِ ۚ

He has **only** forbidden to you dead animals, blood, the flesh of swine, and that which has been dedicated to other than Allah. (Al-Baqarah:173)

Morality

قُلْ اِنَّمَا حَرَّمَ رَبِّيَ الْفَوَاحِشَ مَا ظَهَرَ مِنْهَا وَ مَا بَطَنَ وَ الْاِثْمَ وَ الْبَغْيَ بِغَيْرِ الْحَقِّ وَ اَنْ تُشْرِكُوْا بِاللّٰهِ مَا لَمْ يُنَزِّلْ بِهٖ سُلْطٰنًا وَّ اَنْ تَقُوْلُوْا عَلَى اللّٰهِ مَا لَا تَعْلَمُوْنَ

Say: My Lord has only prohibited indecencies, those of them that are apparent as well as those that are concealed, and sin and rebellion without justice, and that you associate with Allah that for which He has not sent down any authority, and that you say against Allah what you do not know.

- When it comes to food, God told us that among the foods human beings normally prefer, only a few are prohibited. This is clear from other parts of the Quran: it includes nothing humans generally don't like to eat. For example, there is no reason to add a lion in this list because it's a human consensus that it is not good for eating.

- Similarly, when it comes to prohibitions, rooted in moral behavior, God gave a list of things that fundamentally make an action morally prohibited in Islam. This is the foundation for Muslims to create Shariah laws related to human beings.

What is Prohibited in Islam?

Indecencies (Fawahish)

- Openly exposing your private parts to someone or engaging in any sexual activities with someone other than your wives.
- This includes all forms: speaking, writing, art, poetry, music, relationships, etc.
- Humans are very well aware of what is considered indecency.

Sin (any act that usurps others' rights)

- We are living in a world of responsibilities and rights. We have rights over others, and others have rights over us.
- Usurping someone's rights without any reason is a sin.
- Breaking ties, cheating in business, hiding a testimony, hiding or changing lineage, disrespect, and gossip about others.

Rebellion without Justice (Transgress)

- Going above and beyond the limits set for someone (transgression).
- An act that violates a social, moral, ethical, or relational rule, boundary, or expectation.
- Transgressions can range in severity.
- Fraud, assault, persecution, harassment, discrimination, and many other forms.

Shirk (Associating someone with God)

- Associating someone with the person of God. For example, Jesus, Angels, etc.
- Attributing someone with the abilities to do acts of God. For example, running the affairs of the universe, granting help without means, etc.
- All acts that are dedicated to God, if related to someone, come under Shirk.

Attributing something to God which He never said

- Most Muslims undermine this prohibition. If Allah is quiet on a matter, we should not just use Allah's name to support our assertion as if He said something about a matter. That is a big sin.
- Scholars who issue religious verdicts must be careful of this prohibition.
- Examples: adding a creed to the list of creeds in the Quran, interpreting the Quran without regard for its text and context, issuing a religious verdict without a basis in the Quran or Sunnah.

Quick Recap

The basis of all Virtues	The basis of all Evil
✔ Justice	✔ Vulgarity/Lewdness
✔ Goodness	✔ Evil (universal wrong)
✔ Spending on the kindred	✔ Rebellious arrogance

The Foundation of Haram

✔ Indecencies   ✔ Shirk

✔ Sin   ✔ Attributing something to God that he never said

✔ Rebellious behavior

1. If we are moral beings, why do individuals and societies act otherwise?
2. How can you counter the argument? Morality is not God-given; rather, human beings learn their morality from the environments and societies they live in, and there is an agreed-upon universal code of ethics that we all follow now.

Islamic Moral Standards

Now that we have learned the foundation of moral principles on which Islamic morality is based, it is time to learn what standard Islam provides for morality. In other words, the 10 commandments of the Quran.

Quick Recap

The basis of all Virtues	The basis of all Evil
✔ Justice ✔ Goodness ✔ Spending on the kindred	✔ Vulgarity/Lewdness ✔ Evil (universal wrong) ✔ Rebellious arrogance

The Foundation of Haram

✔ Indecencies   ✔ Shirk

✔ Sin   ✔ Attributing something to God that he
                                 never said

✔ Rebellious behavior

1. If we are moral beings, why do individuals and societies act otherwise?
2. How can you counter the argument? Morality is not God-given; rather, human beings learn their morality from the environments and societies they live in, and there is an agreed-upon universal code of ethics that we all follow now.

Chapter 12

Islamic Moral Standards

Now that we have learned the foundation of moral principles on which Islamic morality is based, it is time to learn what standard Islam provides for morality. In other words, the 10 commandments of the Quran.

Islam's moral guidance

Introduction

- The Quran not only provides the foundation of morality and ethics but also explains them through the virtues one should adopt and the vices one should avoid.
- The Quran provided the guidance above on two occasions: 6:151-153 and 17:23-39. **Verses 17:23-39** explain them in detail.
- They are also referred to as the **Ten Commandments of the Quran**.
- We will discuss 17:23-39 to understand what the Quran considers morally sound and what it considers morally unsound.
- Humans tend to derive different conclusions from the same principle: the Quran's guidance.

Common word

- It is interesting to note that all major religions pretty much preach the same moral standards. The reason is that all man-made religions are deviations from the religion of God, and they are also compatible with human natural inclinations.
- These commandments begin and end with pure monotheism, which is considered the common belief among adherents of the Abrahamic religions.
- Besides monotheism, other commandments are also among the core teachings of Judaism and Christianity (in the Torah).
- These are well-known instructions revealed to Moses, who then passed these on to his nation.
- These commandments can serve as the basis for interfaith dialogue and mutually beneficial cooperation.
- That's exactly what the Quran argues when it invites the People of the Book to join Muslims.

قُلْ يَا أَهْلَ الْكِتَابِ تَعَالَوْا إِلَى كَلِمَةٍ سَوَاءٍ بَيْنَنَا وَبَيْنَكُمْ أَلَّا نَعْبُدَ إِلَّا اللَّهَ وَلَا نُشْرِكَ بِهِ شَيْئًا

Say, O people of the book, let us come to a common word between us, that we will not worship anything other than Allah, we will not associate anything with Him. (3:64)

10 COMMANDMENTS

Verses 17:23-39

Do not associate partners with God

1. Worship God alone
2. Take care of parents and relatives
3. Spending your wealth
4. Be chaste and modest
5. Do not kill a human life
6. Don't waste the orphan's wealth
7. Keep your promises & contracts
8. Be honest in dealings
9. Do not follow speculations
10. Do not be arrogant

Do not associate partners with God

Do not associate partners with God

لَّا تَجْعَلْ مَعَ اللَّهِ إِلَٰهًا آخَرَ فَتَقْعُدَ مَذْمُومًا مَّخْذُولًا

Do not take any deity besides Allah, lest [on the Day of Judgement] you are left blameworthy and disgraceful.

وَلَا تَجْعَلْ مَعَ اللَّهِ إِلَٰهًا آخَرَ فَتُلْقَىٰ فِي جَهَنَّمَ مَلُومًا مَّدْحُورًا

Do not take any deity besides Allah, lest [on the Day of Judgement] you will be cast into Hell condemned and rejected.

- The importance of monotheism, or not worshiping any other deity, is vividly evident in these verses.
- Verses of the Islamic moral framework started and ended with instructions not to take any deity other than the one true God.
- It is our first and foremost moral obligation not to associate any partners with God.
- We usually do not look at it this way, but it is unjust to associate partners with God. It will be utterly unjust and immoral if we worship other gods whom we have no proof that God has given any position of authority in His kingdom.
- It is like we know that our parents have nurtured us throughout our lives and have been taking care of us through thick and thin, but when we grow up, we start giving the respect and care that they deserve to others.
- Any sane person would call it unjust.
- If we know that God alone is the Lord and that He will be King on the Day of Judgment, and that no intermediary will do anything on our behalf, then our moral behavior will not be lax.
- It is like a defensive wall around our morality, which, if breached, will also allow an attack on other morals.
- The Quran called it "the great injustice or darkness."
- The Quran warned us that on the Day of Judgment, when we will see that only God is the authority on that day, we will regret any type of Shirk committed because that won't help.

Note: Please refer to Chapter "Beliefs in Islam" for more details on Monotheism and *Shirk*.

Worshipping God alone

وَقَضَىٰ رَبُّكَ أَلَّا تَعْبُدُوا إِلَّا إِيَّاهُ

And [remember that] your Lord has enjoined you to worship none but Him.

- This is the natural consequence of avoiding Shirk.
- If He is the only God, He should be worshiped alone.
- The essence of worship is humility and servility.
- Humility results in glorification and praises for Him, and praying and supplicating to Him.
- Servility results in submitting to God's directives in practical life.
- In this case, no jurists, saints, or scholars should possess divine authority in matters of worship or directive.
- The authority of declaring something as lawful or unlawful resides with God and His Messengers.

When the last moment of the life of Prophet Muhammad came, while he was feeling very sick, he said, "May Allah curse the Jews and Christians, for they built the places of worship at the graves of their Prophets." (Sahih Bukhari 436)

② Take care of parents and relatives

وَبِالْوَالِدَيْنِ إِحْسَانًا إِمَّا يَبْلُغَنَّ عِندَكَ الْكِبَرَ أَحَدُهُمَا أَوْ كِلَاهُمَا فَلَا تَقُل لَّهُمَا أُفٍّ وَلَا تَنْهَرْهُمَا وَقُل لَّهُمَا قَوْلًا كَرِيمًا

وَاخْفِضْ لَهُمَا جَنَاحَ الذُّلِّ مِنَ الرَّحْمَةِ وَقُل رَّبِّ ارْحَمْهُمَا كَمَا رَبَّيَانِي صَغِيرًا

رَّبُّكُمْ أَعْلَمُ بِمَا فِي نُفُوسِكُمْ إِن تَكُونُوا صَالِحِينَ فَإِنَّهُ كَانَ لِلْأَوَّابِينَ غَفُورًا

And treat your parents with kindness. If either or both of them attain old age in your life before you, show them no sign of impatience, nor scold them while answering; but speak to them with good etiquette and treat them with humility and tenderness, and say: "Lord, be merciful to them the way they nursed me in childhood." Your Lord fully knows what is in your hearts; if you remain obedient [to them, then you should know that] He forgives those who turn to Him.

Respect for parents

- Parents must be treated with RESPECT.
- The respect they deserve outwardly should emanate from the gratitude deep in our hearts.
- The Quran talked about their old age because this is when we are in control of the situation. In their old age, no aversion should be displayed in our attitude.
- Always remember those days when they nurtured us, when we were unable to fulfill our basic needs (food, shelter, and relief).
- Although it can be considered as "repayment" time, what we do for them can never be compared with what they have gone through for us.
- Disagreements are natural due to generational differences, but every disagreement should be handled with respect.

Treat parents with kindness

- This topic is repeated many times in the Quran and Ahadith. (29:8, 31:14-15, 46:15)
- There is no doubt that among human beings, a person's foremost obligation is toward his parents.
- God creates a human being through his/her parents and gives them the responsibility to nourish him/her.
- Both have an equal place, but the mother is regarded more highly in terms of rights because of the hardships she undertakes for her child.
- These rights cannot be fulfilled by just saying "thank you." Kindness encompasses three aspects, as stipulated in the verse: Respect, kindness, and supplications.

Pray for them

- This should be our supplication throughout our life – when they are living and when they have left this world.

"O our Lord, be merciful to them for the way they nurtured me in my childhood."

Prophet said: "Disgrace is for that person. Disgrace is for that person. Disgrace is for that person." People asked: "For whom, O Prophet?" He replied: "A person whose parents or any of them reached old age in his presence, and still he could not enter Paradise. (Sahih Muslim, 6510)

Once, a person asked the Prophet (sws) to participate in jihad. At this, the Prophet (sws) inquired: "Are your parents alive?" The person replied in the affirmative. The Prophet (sws) then remarked: "Keep serving them. This is jihad. (Sahih Bukhari, 3004)

Relatives, orphans, the needy, neighbors ……

• Other human relationships are covered from two aspects: our attitude towards them and our spending on them.

• This includes our other relatives, orphans, the needy, the poor, neighbors, colleagues, friends, travelers, and anyone we know.

• After parents, people who deserve our most attention are our blood relatives.

• This is the knot tied by our Lord, and we have no choice in this – it makes it a test for us.

• It is not befitting for someone to break this tie.

• Breaking ties with blood relatives is considered a grievous sin in Islam.

• If some of them are poor, needy, or orphans, then their rights toward us increase.

• Fulfilling the needs of orphans and the needy, and freeing slaves, is considered the first step toward attaining piety and goodness.

• Among non-blood relations, neighbors have the most rights over us.

• Neighbors can be people who live next to our house or people who accompany us on travel while we are stationed somewhere.

وَاعْبُدُوا اللَّهَ وَلَا تُشْرِكُوا بِهِ شَيْئًا ۖ وَبِالْوَالِدَيْنِ إِحْسَانًا وَبِذِي الْقُرْبَىٰ وَالْيَتَامَىٰ وَالْمَسَاكِينِ وَالْجَارِ ذِي الْقُرْبَىٰ وَالْجَارِ الْجُنُبِ وَالصَّاحِبِ بِالْجَنبِ وَابْنِ السَّبِيلِ وَمَا مَلَكَتْ أَيْمَانُكُمْ ۗ إِنَّ اللَّهَ لَا يُحِبُّ مَن كَانَ مُخْتَالًا فَخُورًا

Worship God and associate with None. And show kindness to parents and to relatives and to orphans and to the destitute, to neighbors who are your relatives and those you do not know, and to those that keep company with you, and to the traveler, and to the slaves also, because God does not like the arrogant and the conceited. (4:36)

وَاتَّقُوا اللَّهَ الَّذِي تَسَاءَلُونَ بِهِ وَالْأَرْحَامَ

And fear God, in whose name you plead with one another, and beware of your relatives also. (4:1)

The word Raham originates from Rahman. Thus, God has addressed it and said: "He who has joined you, I will join him with Me, and he who severed you, I will also dissociate from him. (Sahih Bukhari, 5988)

A person asked: "O Messenger of God! Tell me something that can take me to Paradise." He replied: "Worship God and do not associate anyone with Him; be diligent in your prayer and pay zakah and fulfill the rights of the kindred." (Sahih Bukhari, 5983)

Those who care for the orphans financially, and I will be close to one another in Paradise, the way two fingers are close. (Sahih Bukhari, 6005)

"By God! He shall not be a believer; He shall not be a believer; He shall not be a believer." People asked: "Who? O Messenger of God!" The Prophet said: "A person whose neighbor is not secure from his mischief. (Sahih Bukhari, 6016)

Gabriel emphasized to me the rights of a neighbor so much that I thought he would soon make him a shareholder in a person's inheritance. (Sahih Bukhari, 6014)

O Abu Dharr! When you cook curry, add extra water and stay aware of your neighbors. (Sahih Muslim, 6688)

 ## 3 Spending your wealth

وَآتِ ذَا الْقُرْبَىٰ حَقَّهُ وَالْمِسْكِينَ وَابْنَ السَّبِيلِ وَلَا تُبَذِّرْ تَبْذِيرًا ۚ إِنَّ الْمُبَذِّرِينَ كَانُوا إِخْوَانَ الشَّيَاطِينِ ۖ وَكَانَ الشَّيْطَانُ لِرَبِّهِ كَفُورًا وَإِمَّا تُعْرِضَنَّ عَنْهُمُ ابْتِغَاءَ رَحْمَةٍ مِّن رَّبِّكَ تَرْجُوهَا فَقُل لَّهُمْ قَوْلًا مَّيْسُورًا ۚ وَلَا تَجْعَلْ يَدَكَ مَغْلُولَةً إِلَىٰ عُنُقِكَ وَلَا تَبْسُطْهَا كُلَّ الْبَسْطِ فَتَقْعُدَ مَلُومًا مَّحْسُورًا ۚ إِنَّ رَبَّكَ يَبْسُطُ الرِّزْقَ لِمَن يَشَاءُ وَيَقْدِرُ ۚ إِنَّهُ كَانَ بِعِبَادِهِ خَبِيرًا بَصِيرًا وَلَا تَقْتُلُوا أَوْلَادَكُمْ خَشْيَةَ إِمْلَاقٍ ۖ نَّحْنُ نَرْزُقُهُمْ وَإِيَّاكُمْ ۚ إِنَّ قَتْلَهُمْ كَانَ خِطْئًا كَبِيرًا

And give to the near of kin their due, the destitute and the traveler. And do not squander your wealth wastefully, for the wasteful are Satan's brothers, and Satan is ever-ungrateful to his Lord. And if you have to disregard [those in need] because you are seeking your Lord's bounty of which you are waiting, then speak to them affectionately. And do not be miserly or prodigal, that as a result of it, you should either earn reproach or be reduced to indigence. Indeed, your Lord gives abundantly to whom He pleases and sparingly to whom He pleases. He is aware of His servants and is observing them. And do not kill your children for fear of poverty. We also provide for them and for you because killing them is a heinous crime.

Spending in the way of God

- Spending in the way of God is a term used in the Quran for spending on fellow human beings (relatives and others).
- Our relationship with other human beings is manifested through our spending on them for the sake of God – ultimately, it also helps our relationship with God.
- Quran shifts the whole paradigm of ownership and possessions; it asks us to spend or share what has been given to us by God.
- Spending in the way of God is the right of one's relatives, orphans, and the needy.
- If we are unable to help these people for some reason at this time, we are asked to deal with them kindly until God blesses us with what we can share.
- We can spend on them publicly or in secret (2:270-271).
- God promised to bless this spending and increase it multifold (2:261).
- The reward for such spending is only guaranteed if it is done from one's legal wealth and does not accompany any hurting for the person whom one's spending (2:267).

> "Spend, for where your treasure is, will also be your heart". (attributed to Prophet Jesus)

Consequences of not spending

- The Quran gave many examples and similitudes to encourage people to spend in the way of God (2:265).
- Spending in the way of God something which a person does not like for himself is considered a very mean act (2:267).
- Amassing wealth while remaining indifferent to people's condition is considered hoarding, and the person will be punished on the day of judgment (9:34-35).
- The Quran states this fact in many verses: people who do not spend in this world, especially when the people around them (especially their relatives) need it, will regret it and wish to return to spend in the way of God (63:10).

وَالَّذِينَ يَكْنِزُونَ الذَّهَبَ وَالْفِضَّةَ وَلَا يُنفِقُونَهَا فِي سَبِيلِ اللَّهِ فَبَشِّرْهُم بِعَذَابٍ أَلِيمٍ

يَوْمَ يُحْمَىٰ عَلَيْهَا فِي نَارِ جَهَنَّمَ فَتُكْوَىٰ بِهَا جِبَاهُهُمْ وَجُنُوبُهُمْ وَظُهُورُهُمْ ۖ

هَٰذَا مَا كَنَزْتُمْ لِأَنفُسِكُمْ فَذُوقُوا مَا كُنتُمْ تَكْنِزُونَ

And those that hoard up gold and silver and do not spend it in the way of God give them glad tidings of a horrible punishment on the day when these [treasures of] gold and silver shall be heated in the fire of Hell, and their foreheads, sides, and backs branded with them. "These are the riches which you hoarded. Taste then what you have been hoarding." (9:34-35)

Quran encourages spending

إِن تُبْدُوا الصَّدَقَاتِ فَنِعِمَّا هِيَ ۖ وَإِن تُخْفُوهَا وَتُؤْتُوهَا الْفُقَرَاءَ فَهُوَ خَيْرٌ لَّكُمْ ۚ وَيُكَفِّرُ عَنكُم مِّن سَيِّئَاتِكُمْ ۗ وَاللَّهُ بِمَا تَعْمَلُونَ خَبِيرٌ

If you spend openly, that is good too, but giving to the poor secretly is better. [Through this], God will wipe out your sins, and [there is absolutely no doubt] that God has knowledge of all your deeds. (2:271)

وَأَنفِقُوا مِن مَّا رَزَقْنَاكُم مِّن قَبْلِ أَن يَأْتِيَ أَحَدَكُمُ الْمَوْتُ فَيَقُولَ رَبِّ لَوْلَا أَخَّرْتَنِي إِلَىٰ أَجَلٍ قَرِيبٍ فَأَصَّدَّقَ وَأَكُن مِّنَ الصَّالِحِينَ

And spend from that which We have given you before death approaches any of you and he says: "Lord! If only You would give me a brief respite so that I would be spending in charity and [as a result] could have been among your pious people." (63:10)

مَّثَلُ الَّذِينَ يُنفِقُونَ أَمْوَالَهُمْ فِي سَبِيلِ اللَّهِ كَمَثَلِ حَبَّةٍ أَنبَتَتْ سَبْعَ سَنَابِلَ فِي كُلِّ سُنبُلَةٍ مِّائَةُ حَبَّةٍ ۗ وَاللَّهُ يُضَاعِفُ لِمَن يَشَاءُ ۚ وَاللَّهُ وَاسِعٌ عَلِيمٌ

Those who spend their wealth in the way of God can be compared to a grain of corn which brings forth seven ears, each bearing a hundred grains. God [in accordance with His wisdom] provides in abundance [in this manner] to whom He wills; And [in reality] God is munificent and all-knowing. (2:261)

Discipline in spending

- In principle, the Quran states that people who adopt a balanced attitude toward spending can fulfill this directive.
- If wealth is a blessing of God and we are entrusted with it, then it cannot be squandered.
- People who spend most of their time in pursuit of their worldly desires and happiness will neither have time nor money to discharge this duty.
- People who squander their wealth are called Satan's brother, and he was ungrateful.
- When spending in God's way, we are asked to adopt a balanced approach.
- We cannot give away everything and end up in indigence, needing other people's help.
- Abundance or shortage of wealth can depend on someone's financial circumstances or a test from God.
- We should strive for it and avoid taking extreme measures out of fear of poverty.

④ Be chaste and Modest

وَلَا تَقْرَبُوا الزِّنَىٰ ۖ إِنَّهُ كَانَ فَاحِشَةً وَسَاءَ سَبِيلً

And do not even go near adultery because it is blatant lewdness and a very evil path.

- Adultery includes all premarital or extramarital sexual relationships.
- It is called 'blatant' because all human societies have acknowledged it as wrong.
- Due to its far-reaching impact, God asked us not to even go near it. It is considered one of the major sins in Islam.
- Keep away from things that may lead to it or ultimately entice a person to it.
- To keep a check on it, God provided the etiquette of gender interaction in Surah Nur.
- Islam gave many directions on how to maintain chastity and modesty to put a stop to things that lead to adultery.

> Without commitment and responsibility in this relationship, human society will be reduced to a herd of cattle.

- The institution of family is as essential to human societies as air and water are to them. But for this institution to be formed and maintained, any extramarital relationships must be condemned.
- The survival of the human race and society requires that neither a man nor a woman be free to gratify themselves and live without commitment.
- The institution of family can only be sustained through natural feelings and emotions with a sense of responsibility.
- The family is needed for the child. The care and support a child needs for several years cannot be guaranteed without a sound family founded on mutual love and trust.
- When Satan wants to corrupt society, its first aim is to break the family by making lewdness and extramarital affairs 'normal' in that society.

يَا بَنِي آدَمَ لَا يَفْتِنَنَّكُمُ الشَّيْطَانُ كَمَا أَخْرَجَ أَبَوَيْكُم مِّنَ الْجَنَّةِ يَنزِعُ عَنْهُمَا لِبَاسَهُمَا لِيُرِيَهُمَا سَوْآتِهِمَا ۗ إِنَّهُ يَرَاكُمْ هُوَ وَقَبِيلُهُ مِنْ حَيْثُ لَا تَرَوْنَهُمْ ۗ إِنَّا جَعَلْنَا الشَّيَاطِينَ أَوْلِيَاءَ لِلَّذِينَ لَا يُؤْمِنُونَ

Children of Adam! Let not Satan tempt you again the way he had expelled your parents from the orchard [in which they were living], stripping them of their garments to reveal their private parts to them. He and his associates see you from where you cannot see them. Indeed, We have made such devils associated with those who do not profess faith. (7:27)

Islam's prescription

- To protect society and individuals from the inclination to moral misconduct, God outlined the etiquette of gender interaction. The objective is to purify morals and the soul.
- God wants us to start with restraint in our gazes – this is the starting point for any immoral conduct. The attire of believing men and women must not be revealed to attract one another – our clothing, style, and actions must not be suggestive.
- Prophet Muhammad asked Muslim men and women to avoid meeting in seclusion and make dua.

قُل لِّلْمُؤْمِنِينَ يَغُضُّوا مِنْ أَبْصَارِهِمْ وَيَحْفَظُوا فُرُوجَهُمْ ۚ ذَٰلِكَ أَزْكَىٰ لَهُمْ ۗ إِنَّ اللَّهَ خَبِيرٌ بِمَا يَصْنَعُونَ

وَقُل لِّلْمُؤْمِنَاتِ يَغْضُضْنَ مِنْ أَبْصَارِهِنَّ وَيَحْفَظْنَ فُرُوجَهُنَّ وَلَا يُبْدِينَ زِينَتَهُنَّ إِلَّا مَا ظَهَرَ مِنْهَا

Tell believing men to restrain their eyes and guard their private parts. That is purer for them. And indeed Allah is well aware of what they do. And tell the believing women to restrain their eyes and to guard their private parts and not to display their ornaments publicly, but those which are normally revealed. (24:30-31)

اللهم إني أسألك الهدى والتقى والعفاف والغنى

O Allah, I ask for guidance, protection from sins, modesty, and self-sufficiency in life.

General advices

- The sin of Zina is at the core of prohibition, but it has its gravitational field, and if you go into it, the chances are that you will fall into it, so avoid getting into that field. Only you know where you are in the field, so keep a check on yourself.
- Satan will always suggest that it is OK to be in the field, and you will never get to that act – remember, that's how Satan works. It starts very simply and gradually, so you should know when to stop.
- Take the prescription of the Quran - guard your gazes because that's the starting point. Understand the difference between temptations and love – it is mostly temptations that grip us during a certain age period.
- Marry at an early age if you feel you are responsible and mature – financial stability should never prevent you from getting married.
- If you are making dua to avoid this sin, remember that God's help comes when you are making efforts to avoid it.
- Don't overjudge yourself when it comes to Zina; even the Prophet Yusuf asked God for help to avoid this temptation. Repentance is your best tool to get out of it; God loves the people who come back.

The adulterer is not a believer at the time when he is committing adultery. The consumer of alcohol is not a believer when he is consuming it. The thief is not a believer while stealing. The plunderer is not a believer when he is plundering. (Sahih Bukhari 2343)

There are seven whom Allah will shade on the Day of Judgment. They are a just ruler, a youth who grew up in the worship of Allah, one whose heart is attached to the mosques, two who love each other, meet each other, and depart from each other for the sake of Allah, a man who is tempted by a beautiful woman of high status. Still, he rejects her, saying, 'I fear Allah,' one spends in charity and conceals it such that his right hand does not know what his left hand has given, and one who remembers Allah in private and wept. (Sahih Bukhari 629)

 ## Do not kill a human life

وَلَا تَقْتُلُوا النَّفْسَ الَّتِي حَرَّمَ اللَّهُ إِلَّا بِالْحَقِّ ۗ وَمَن قُتِلَ مَظْلُومًا فَقَدْ جَعَلْنَا لِوَلِيِّهِ سُلْطَانًا فَلَا يُسْرِف فِّي الْقَتْلِ ۖ إِنَّهُ كَانَ مَنصُورًا

And do not wrongfully kill any person whose life has been held sacred by God and [remember that] if someone is slain unjustly, We have given his heir the authority. Then, he should not exceed the limits of his revenge because he has been helped.

- This is the declaration of a universally agreed directive from a religious and moral point of view. In the Abrahamic religions, this is considered the second biggest sin after Shirk.
- The Quran declared that killing one person intentionally and unjustly is like killing the entire humanity.
- Someone can be killed only through due process if they have killed someone or have become a nuisance or threat in society.
- The punishment in the Hereafter is eternal hellfire.
- In Islam, there are laws for Qisas and Diyat that suggest the procedure for retribution.

مِنْ أَجْلِ ذَٰلِكَ كَتَبْنَا عَلَىٰ بَنِي إِسْرَائِيلَ أَنَّهُ مَن قَتَلَ نَفْسًا بِغَيْرِ نَفْسٍ أَوْ فَسَادٍ فِي الْأَرْضِ فَكَأَنَّمَا قَتَلَ النَّاسَ جَمِيعًا وَمَنْ أَحْيَاهَا فَكَأَنَّمَا أَحْيَا النَّاسَ جَمِيعًا

That was why we laid it down for the Israelites that he who killed a human being without the latter being guilty of killing another or of spreading mischief in the land should be looked upon as if he had killed all of humanity, and he who saved one life should be looked upon as if he had saved all of humanity. (5:32)

وَمَن يَقْتُلْ مُؤْمِنًا مُّتَعَمِّدًا فَجَزَاؤُهُ جَهَنَّمُ خَالِدًا فِيهَا وَغَضِبَ اللَّهُ عَلَيْهِ وَلَعَنَهُ وَأَعَدَّ لَهُ عَذَابًا عَظِيمًا

And he who intentionally kills a believer, his reward is Hell. He shall abide therein forever, and the wrath and the curse of God are upon him. He has prepared a dreadful doom for him. (4:93)

6 Do not waste the orphan's wealth

وَلَا تَقْرَبُوا مَالَ الْيَتِيمِ إِلَّا بِالَّتِي هِيَ أَحْسَنُ حَتَّىٰ يَبْلُغَ أَشُدَّهُ

And do not approach the wealth of orphans except in a just and best manner, until they reach maturity.

- The wealth of orphans must not be misappropriated.
- The Quran used the same style it used for adultery and has asked us not to approach the wealth of orphans except for their welfare and betterment.
- One should use the orphans' wealth only for their development and protection until they reach an age when it can be handed over.
- Their wealth should be handed over to them only when they can be entrusted with it.
- It is considered one of the major sins in Islam.
- There are guidelines from God in the Shariah of Islam for handling such matters.

إِنَّ الَّذِينَ يَأْكُلُونَ أَمْوَالَ الْيَتَامَىٰ ظُلْمًا إِنَّمَا يَأْكُلُونَ فِي بُطُونِهِمْ نَارًا وَسَيَصْلَوْنَ سَعِيرًا

Indeed, those who devour the property of orphans unjustly, swallow fire into their bellies; and soon shall they be cast into the raging fire of Hell. (4:10)

7 Keeping promise

وَأَوْفُوا بِالْعَهْدِ إِنَّ الْعَهْدَ كَانَ مَسْئُولًا

And keep your promises because you shall be held accountable for promises.

Fulfilling a formal contract is the ultimate way to keep a promise.

- The promises (especially contracts) must be kept at all costs because we will be held accountable for them.
- The Quran called it an attribute of a believer: "When they make promises, they keep them" (2:177).
- Contracts/promises come in two types: written contracts that create a promise and unwritten contracts in our relationships.
- A believer has unwritten contracts with his Lord, the Prophet, his parents, family, relatives, neighbors, colleagues, tribe, etc, that bind him to fulfill their rights.
- Keeping promises is so critical in Islam that even in the middle of the battlefield (when God asked the Prophet to punish the disbelievers), the Prophet was asked to honor the treaties if they were time-bound until they expire.
- The Quran has emphasized this elsewhere as well. (5:1, 23:8, 70:32)

وَالَّذِينَ آمَنُوا وَلَمْ يُهَاجِرُوا مَا لَكُم مِّن وَلَايَتِهِم مِّن شَيْءٍ حَتَّىٰ يُهَاجِرُوا ۚ وَإِنِ اسْتَنصَرُوكُمْ فِي الدِّينِ فَعَلَيْكُمُ النَّصْرُ إِلَّا عَلَىٰ قَوْمٍ بَيْنَكُمْ وَبَيْنَهُم مِّيثَاقٌ ۗ وَاللَّهُ بِمَا تَعْمَلُونَ بَصِيرٌ

And to those who accepted faith but did not migrate [to Madinah], you owe no duty of protection until they migrate; but if they seek your help in religion, it is your duty to help them except against a people with whom you have a treaty; and [in reality] Allah sees what you do. (8:72)

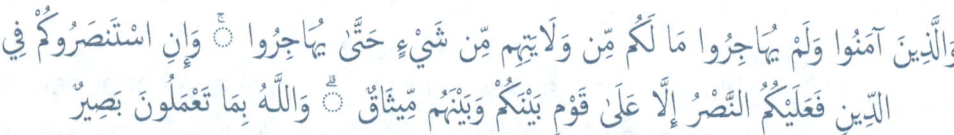

يَا أَيُّهَا الَّذِينَ آمَنُوا أَوْفُوا بِالْعُقُودِ

O believers, fulfill your contracts and promises (Quran 5:1)

وَالَّذِينَ هُمْ لِأَمَانَاتِهِمْ وَعَهْدِهِمْ رَاعُونَ

And those who protect the trust given to them and fulfill their promises and contracts (70:32)

Keeping promises in daily life

- Being on time is keeping a promise and should not be taken lightly. Punctuality pays back in ways you can never imagine.
- Keeping promises promotes trust, and trust plays a far-reaching role in our social affairs. Building trust is a gradual process, so do not take any of your promises lightly.
- Remember the old saying, "First impression is the last impression."
- Be very clear when promising and avoid habitual promising. The worst promise is the one that is made not to fulfill it – It's a LIE. Avoid promises when you are very happy or very sad.
- Learn to say NO. It is OK to hurt someone's feelings on the spot instead of making a false promise that you won't fulfill.

Be honest in business and dealings

وَأَوْفُوا الْكَيْلَ إِذَا كِلْتُمْ وَزِنُوا بِالْقِسْطَاسِ الْمُسْتَقِيمِ ۚ ذَٰلِكَ خَيْرٌ وَأَحْسَنُ تَأْوِيلًا

Give full measure, and weigh with the correct scales when you measure. This is better and fairer in terms of the consequences.

- This is an important directive and is not limited to weighing alone; it covers general business ethics when dealing with customers. This includes, but is not limited to, selling low-quality products with known defects, slacking off in the workplace, conflicts of interest, and other forms of shortchanging.
- God declared that He has set a balance in this universe, and everything is measured by a scale, so we should also keep our measurements just.
- When we deviate from the scale of justice in our dealings, it corrupts society's economic and social systems. (26:181-183)
- The nation of Prophet Shuaib engaged in this malpractice, and God chided them for it and punished them.

 Do no follow speculations about others

وَلَا تَقْفُ مَا لَيْسَ لَكَ بِهِ عِلْمٌ ۚ إِنَّ السَّمْعَ وَالْبَصَرَ وَالْفُؤَادَ كُلُّ أُولَٰئِكَ كَانَ عَنْهُ مَسْئُولًا

And do not go after what you know not, because eyes, ears, and heart – all of them shall be questioned.

- This directive puts us on the spot in our social lives and points out one of the main vices in our society.
- Do not take speculations and slander about other people lightly because every act of the eyes, ears, and heart, especially about other people, will be taken into account.
- This is necessary for a sound society.
- When it comes to other people, especially Muslims, we should not be judgmental, have bad estimations, or spread rumors merely based on speculations.
- If a matter does not concern us, it should be left or ignored.

Avoid speculation and suspicion

يَا أَيُّهَا الَّذِينَ آمَنُوا إِن جَاءَكُمْ فَاسِقٌ بِنَبَإٍ فَتَبَيَّنُوا أَن تُصِيبُوا قَوْمًا بِجَهَالَةٍ فَتُصْبِحُوا عَلَىٰ مَا فَعَلْتُمْ نَادِمِينَ

Believers! If a corrupt person brings you a piece of news, find out its true status, lest you inflict harm on others unwittingly, and then regret your action. (49:6)

يَا أَيُّهَا الَّذِينَ آمَنُوا اجْتَنِبُوا كَثِيرًا مِّنَ الظَّنِّ إِنَّ بَعْضَ الظَّنِّ إِثْمٌ ۖ وَلَا تَجَسَّسُو

Believers! Avoid being overly speculative, for some speculations are a blatant sin, and do not spy or be inquisitive about one another. (49:12)

- Be careful when acting on news given by people we do not trust. Although being judgmental quickly is not recommended anyway.
- All our words and actions must be backed by information that we trust to be truthful, so that we do not regret later.
- Our thoughts and opinions about people make or break our relationships; we should always think positively about others unless there is a clear reason to think otherwise.
- This creates an atmosphere of brotherhood and sisterhood in society, which Islam wants.
- If a matter or a person doesn't concern us, we don't need to be nosy or inquisitive about others.

Golden rule

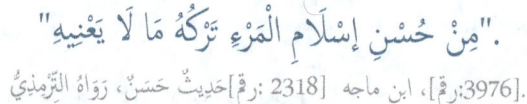

"مِنْ حُسْنِ إِسْلَامِ الْمَرْءِ تَرْكُهُ مَا لَا يَعْنِيهِ".

[رقم:3976]، ابن ماجه [رقم: 2318] حَدِيثٌ حَسَنٌ، رَوَاهُ التِّرْمِذِيُّ.

"Part of the perfection of one's Islam is his leaving that which does not concern him."

Note: This is not a particularly authentic hadith, but it outlines a golden rule for anyone seeking a carefree, peaceful life.

- Most people today in society speculate on matters that they have no concern with, meaning they are not related to them.
- Satan makes it sweet for people to talk about other people, speculate, and spread rumors.
- This golden rule given by Prophet Muhammad can save us from this widespread evil in society.

10   Do not be arrogant

وَلَا تَمْشِ فِي الْأَرْضِ مَرَحًا ۖ إِنَّكَ لَن تَخْرِقَ الْأَرْضَ وَلَن تَبْلُغَ الْجِبَالَ طُولًا

And do not walk conceitedly on the earth because neither can you split the earth, nor can you rival the mountains in stature.

- Wealth, authority, beauty, knowledge, power, and similar things produce wrongful pride and vanity in a person – this may lead to arrogance, the ultimate form of pride.
- Our style of walking on earth reveals the pride in our hearts, and this is what this verse is alluding to.
- On the other hand, it shows our weakness as human beings and a creation that, in terms of strength and power, is much inferior to other creations on earth, such as mountains.
- We must consider our position in the grand scheme of creation and always surrender ourselves to the majesty and splendor of God.
- The heart that has the perception of serving God and of His greatness only beats in the chests of people who have humility and humbleness.

"The person who has pride even to the measure of a mustard seed in his heart will not enter into Paradise" (Sahih Muslim 265)

What is pride or arrogance?

- Sometimes, it is difficult for us to figure out what pride or arrogance is and how it differs from other human traits that may seem like arrogance. This is explained in one of the Ahadith by Prophet Muhammad:

Abdullah ibn Masood reported: The Prophet said, "No one who has arrogance (even the weight of a seed) in his heart will enter Paradise." Someone asked, "But a man loves to have beautiful clothes and shoes." The Prophet said, "Verily, Allah is beautiful, and he loves beauty. That is not arrogance. Arrogance means:
1. Rejecting the Truth
2. looking down on people (belittling them)

Rejecting the Truth

- With arrogance in our hearts, we tend to reject the Truth when it is presented to us if it does not serve our interests.
- Sometimes, the messenger becomes a hindrance to our accepting the message (maybe we don't like them).
- This is a very visible sign of arrogance, which one should avoid.

إِنَّ الَّذِينَ كَذَّبُوا بِآيَاتِنَا وَاسْتَكْبَرُوا عَنْهَا لَا تُفَتَّحُ لَهُمْ أَبْوَابُ السَّمَاءِ وَلَا يَدْخُلُونَ الْجَنَّةَ حَتَّىٰ يَلِجَ الْجَمَلُ فِي سَمِّ الْخِيَاطِ ۚ وَكَذَٰلِكَ نَجْزِي الْمُجْرِمِينَ

Indeed, those who denied Our revelations and evaded them in arrogance, the gates of heaven shall not be opened for them, and neither shall they be able to enter Paradise except if a camel can pass through the eye of a needle. [This is their punishment] and thus do We punish the criminals. (Quran 7:40)

Belittling others

- The standard of nobility in the sight of God is very different from our standards.
- In God's sight, someone is honored or disgraced based on his faith and deeds, and their 'weight or value' is known to God alone.
- For the spirit of brotherhood to thrive within a community, people should avoid belittling other groups or individuals.
- People who enter into the folds of Islam become our brothers and sisters regardless of race, ethnicity, color, and geography.
- This kind of behavior towards others can extend to other vices, such as defaming, teasing, or even backbiting.

يَا أَيُّهَا الَّذِينَ آمَنُوا لَا يَسْخَرْ قَوْمٌ مِّن قَوْمٍ عَسَىٰ أَن يَكُونُوا خَيْرًا مِّنْهُمْ وَلَا نِسَاءٌ مِّن نِّسَاءٍ عَسَىٰ أَن يَكُنَّ خَيْرًا مِّنْهُنَّ

Believers! Let no people make fun of another people, who may perhaps be better than them and let no group of women make fun of another group of women, who may perhaps be better than them. (49:11)

Our behavior towards these directives

- All morals that we deal with in our lives are founded on these basic directives.
- What God calls "major sins and immoralities (especially in sexual behavior)" result from flouting these directives.
- Ignoring and breaching these directives have consequences in the Hereafter.
- These three aspects must be considered when looking at our behavior:
  - If the disobedience is unintentional or due to a lack of awareness, God will not hold us accountable for a misdeed committed in ignorance. (33:5)
  - If we do our best to abstain from breaching these directives, then God's promise is that He will forgive all minor sins without even looking at them; otherwise, they will be recorded. (4:31)
  - If we disobey any of these directives while overwhelmed by emotions, we should repent immediately and commit not to repeat it. God promises to forgive us for that sin. (4:17-18)

- What is that one directive that you think is hard to follow while living in a Western society?
- How can excessive use of social media easily trap us in breaching some of these directives?

Chapter 13

Modesty and Relationships

This is one of the most important chapters for teenage Muslims in the Western context. We will learn Allah's instructions on modesty and what Islam teaches about staying away from illicit relationships.

Islam's moral guidance

Introduction

- The Quran not only provides the foundation of morality and ethics but also explains them through the virtues one should adopt and the vices one should avoid.
- The Quran provided the guidance above on two occasions: 6:151-153 and 17:23-39. **Verses 17:23-39** explain them in detail.
- They are also referred to as the **Ten Commandments of the Quran**.
- We will discuss 17:23-39 to understand what the Quran considers morally sound and what it considers morally unsound.
- Humans tend to derive different conclusions from the same principle: the Quran's guidance.

Common word

- It is interesting to note that all major religions pretty much preach the same moral standards. The reason is that all man-made religions are deviations from the religion of God, and they are also compatible with human natural inclinations.
- These commandments begin and end with pure monotheism, which is considered the common belief among adherents of the Abrahamic religions.
- Besides monotheism, other commandments are also among the core teachings of Judaism and Christianity (in the Torah).
- These are well-known instructions revealed to Moses, who then passed these on to his nation.
- These commandments can serve as the basis for interfaith dialogue and mutually beneficial cooperation.
- That's exactly what the Quran argues when it invites the People of the Book to join Muslims.

قُلْ يَا أَهْلَ الْكِتَابِ تَعَالَوْا إِلَىٰ كَلِمَةٍ سَوَاءٍ بَيْنَنَا وَبَيْنَكُمْ أَلَّا نَعْبُدَ إِلَّا اللَّهَ وَلَا نُشْرِكَ بِهِ شَيْئًا

Say, O people of the book, let us come to a common word between us, that we will not worship anything other than Allah, we will not associate anything with Him. (3:64)

Islam and Modesty

Hijab and modesty (Haya)

- In the modern age, the hijab is a symbol of modesty (Haya) and dignity adopted by Muslim women. Although this word is not used in the Quran.

- In the Quran and Hadith, the word "Haya" is used as a broad term encompassing modesty and chastity, among other aspects.

- It must be reflected in our behavior, speech, appearance, and attitude toward people and God's directives.

- We only pay attention to the appearance part.

- It has both religious and cultural aspects, and must be examined separately.

- Islam regards modesty and chastity as fundamental values for both individuals and society.

View of the West

Faith has over 70 branches. At the top is monotheism, and at the bottom is removing harm from the road. Modesty is a branch of FAITH. (Hadith)

"Every religion has its distinct characteristic, and the distinct characteristic of Islam is modesty." (Hadith)

The basic unit of Family

- Man, as a social animal, loves to build relationships.

- We are not born in the prime of our youth, but we go through a life cycle – from a feeble infant to an old age, which is similar to being an infant.

- The family is the nucleus of civilization, the basic unit of society, and an important social concept in Islam.

- To God, the welfare of the child is the most important aspect of this unit of family.

- God wants to protect this unit of the family from all dangers that could jeopardize its survival, and hence He has given us detailed guidelines for gender interaction.

> The family is nature's established association for supplying mankind's everyday needs. (Aristotle)

Don't go near adultery

- All etiquette related to gender mixing in Islam emerged from this instruction.

وَلَا تَقْرَبُوا الزِّنَىٰ ۖ إِنَّهُ كَانَ فَاحِشَةً وَسَاءَ سَبِيلًا

And do not even go near adultery because it is blatant lewdness and a very evil path.

- Protecting the sanctity of family demands zero tolerance for any illicit relationship between a man and a woman before and after marriage.
- To make sure that the sexual relationship is limited to husband and wife, God declared any illicit relationship outside of marriage as prohibited.
- We can observe that, while living in the West, breaching this instruction from God, who also gave it in previous scriptures, can lead to a failed society at the social level.
- Children are struggling to find the peace and tranquility of a home that can only be provided by a family living in mutual love and commitment.
- Islam's guidance on gender interaction is given for two main reasons:
  - To save society from becoming one where sexual relations are taken casually and are morally bankrupt.
  - To protect the sanctity of the family.

Islam's guidance on etiquette of gender-mixing

قُل لِّلْمُؤْمِنِينَ يَغُضُّوا مِنْ أَبْصَارِهِمْ وَيَحْفَظُوا فُرُوجَهُمْ ۚ ذَٰلِكَ أَزْكَىٰ لَهُمْ ۗ إِنَّ اللَّهَ خَبِيرٌ بِمَا يَصْنَعُونَ
وَقُل لِّلْمُؤْمِنَاتِ يَغْضُضْنَ مِنْ أَبْصَارِهِنَّ وَيَحْفَظْنَ فُرُوجَهُنَّ وَلَا يُبْدِينَ زِينَتَهُنَّ إِلَّا مَا ظَهَرَ مِنْهَا ۖ
وَلْيَضْرِبْنَ بِخُمُرِهِنَّ عَلَىٰ جُيُوبِهِنَّ ۖ وَلَا يُبْدِينَ زِينَتَهُنَّ إِلَّا ....

[O Prophet!] Tell believing men to restrain their eyes and guard their private parts. That is purer for them. And indeed Allah is well aware of what they do. And tell the believing women to restrain their eyes, guard their private parts, and not publicly display their embellishments except those that are normally revealed, and to draw their coverings over their chests. And they should not reveal their embellishments to anyone except .... (24:30-31)

The etiquette

Instructions to both men and women

- Both men and women should have modesty in their gazes – restrain their gazes from staring at each other's physical attributes, especially body parts that stimulate sexual desires.
- Both men and women should guard their private parts in front of each other – the attire adopted on such occasions must be modest, covering all private parts and the surrounding area with due care.

Instructions specific to women

- Women should cover their chests adequately, as that is considered a private part for them.
- If women have adorned themselves with embellishments, they should not display them in public except within the circle of their close relatives – this excludes embellishments that are there or done on body parts usually visible, such as the dress, hands, feet, and face.

Note: The complete Social Shariah will be discussed in the second part of this course.

Islam does not dictate or prescribe a specific attire. Any attire or dress that fulfills the main requirements outlined in the instructions can be adopted in a given culture.

Discuss

In gender interactions, why has God given precautionary instructions in addition to the specific prohibition?

Concept of Guarding

- How do Muslim men and women understand the instruction of guarding their private parts?

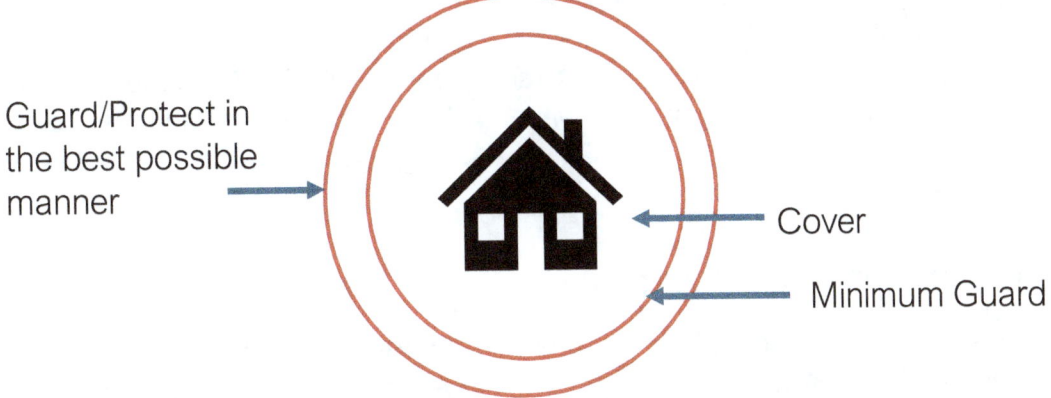

Guard/Protect in the best possible manner

Cover

Minimum Guard

Wisdom behind Allah's instructions

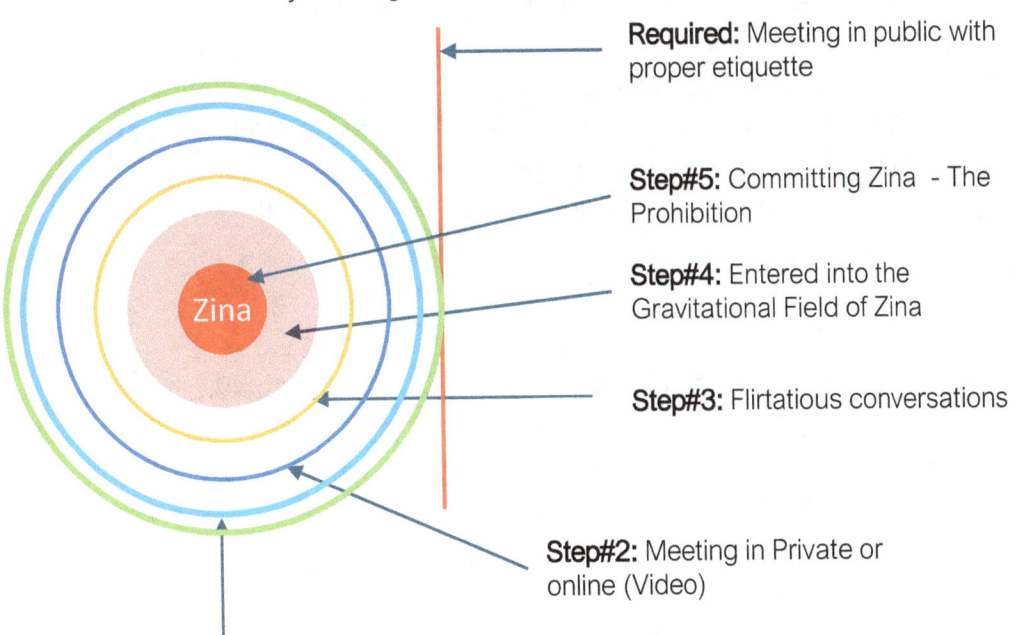

Allah SWT wants us to stop here when He says don't go **near** adultery.

Required: Meeting in public with proper etiquette

Step#5: Committing Zina - The Prohibition

Step#4: Entered into the Gravitational Field of Zina

Step#3: Flirtatious conversations

Step#2: Meeting in Private or online (Video)

Step#1: Meeting in Public in person or social media with bad intention

Purity is the objective

ذَٰلِكَ أَزْكَىٰ لَهُمْ

That is purer for them.

- The social etiquette outlined by Islam is poised magnificently between the extremes that human civilizations have witnessed between the East and the West.
- Like other objectives of Islam, the objective of this social etiquette is to purify the soul and purge the evil.

Dating and premarital relationships

- Until the early 1900s, men and women met to arrange matches in the presence of a chaperone, usually a woman.
- The new 'normal' of dating with pre-marital relationships is only about 50-60 years old. The 'rationale' behind the new form of dating is to "get to know each other before marriage."
- In reality, dating is not done with future marriage in mind. Today, people switch partners easily with mutual understanding, and dating is increasingly becoming a series of 'temporary relationships' until they marry (if they do).
- 'Temporary relationships' only expose the 'good side' of a person, which invalidates the rationale behind such a relationship in the first place. Seeing the 'other side' is usually shocking when people decide to live together permanently or marry.
- Due to societal pressure, people coming from conservative families resort to secret relationships, which create challenges for them later in their lives.

How to fight the temptations

- If we instill the concept of modesty from an early age, we may naturally feel uncomfortable moving toward such a relationship.
- Don't pretend to be superhuman, and find the right company of friends who have similar concepts on the morality of relationships.
- Block the urge at the outset, because the relationship is a process that starts with a "Hi" and moves on to the first meal, then to the first movie, and so on…
- Remember, what's 'appropriate' in morals should not be defined by society or movies.
- Remember, the opposite of modesty is shamelessness, and it creeps into a society slowly; over time, people get immune to it – that does not make shamelessness right.

- Avoiding such relationships early on saves young people from toxic relationships, unrealistic expectations, broken hearts, suicidal thoughts, stress, anxiety, and mental illnesses.
- Engaging your parents early in such relationships makes it easier to continue meeting in a safe, protected environment.

Modesty and purity in relationships are two of the defining virtues in the character of a believer.

Practical tips on following the guidelines

- Realize that it is a hard ask, especially in the time and society that you live in, and if you don't set certain rules for yourself about gender interaction, the chances of failure are high:
    1. When meeting, follow the fundamental rules: keep your gaze down and dress properly.
    2. Hang out with people who share your moral values.
    3. It is OK to develop "feelings" for someone, as long as you understand the limits and follow the guidelines God provides.
    4. Do not meet a person of the opposite gender in seclusion – even if you like someone, make the meeting a family or friend occasion.
    5. Make interaction purposeful (avoid just passing the time together).
    6. Avoid indulging in flirtatious conversations – we all know when that moment is.
    7. Watch your social media interactions and use them – meeting someone on a video call is the same as meeting in person (maybe with fewer consequences, only at that moment).

Remember, the goal of this etiquette is to remain outside the gravitational field of *Zina,* which is at the core of the prohibition and is considered one of the major sins in Islam after Shirk and murder.

"Whoever has faith in Allah and the Last Day, let him not be alone with an unrelated woman without her guardian. Verily, the third of them is Satan." (Ahmed: 14241)

- How does peer pressure make the virtues of modesty in relationships more challenging?
- What are some practical steps that can be taken to avoid getting into such relationships?

Chapter 14

Interacting with non-Muslims

This is an important chapter for students living in the West in a pluralistic society. We will learn how to interact with non-Muslims, anyone who does not call himself/herself a Muslim.

Interacting with non-Muslims

Introduction

- God never created human beings to belong either to the East or the West.
- We are all descendants of a single couple, our parents, Adam and Eve.
- Arabs, non-Arabs, blacks, whites, Westerners, and Easterners are all bound by a brotherhood rooted in humanity.
- Our identity as human beings comes first before our identity as Muslims.
- Fundamental principle: the life, wealth, and honor of every individual are as sacred as our own.
- The roles and responsibilities of Muslims living in the West should only be understood based on this mutual relationship among human beings.
- Only then can Muslims become an active component of the diverse fabric of Western societies.
- However, at no point, our identity as a Muslim should be compromised.

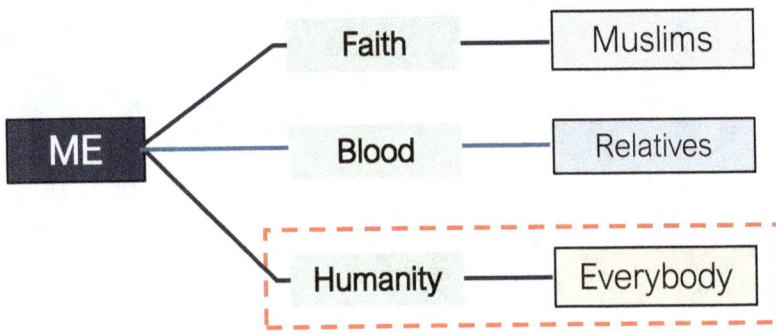

Misconception on dealing with non-Muslims

- Definition of *Kaafir*: A person who was given the message of Islam and they deny the truth in spite of being convinced in their hearts about the truth. A *Kafir* commits a crime against God.
- Misconception: All non-Muslims today are Kafirs and are worthy of condemnation and punishment.
- After revelation has ceased, we have no way to find out who is guilty of deliberately denying the truth (see the definition of Kafir below).
- The Quran termed Jews and Christians as "People of the Book" and chastised only those Jews and Christians who were living in the Prophet's time in the surroundings where the Prophet Muhammad was sent, and they rejected him.

- The idea that Muslims should never make friends with non-Muslims is due to not fully appreciating:
  - The special practice of God for the direct addressees of a Messenger when they reject him.
  - Ignoring the context of the verses.
- God categorically stated in the Quran that Jews and Christians of Prophet Muhammad's time recognized the Quran and Prophet Muhammad very well.
- They were committing the crime of deliberately denying a Prophet who was foretold in the scriptures given to them.
- That's why, when God revealed such verses, an *Alif-Laam* is added before *Yahood* and *Nasara* to indicate that they are the people addressed.

يَاأَيُّهَا الَّذِينَ آمَنُوا لَا تَتَّخِذُوا الْكَافِرِينَ أَوْلِيَاءَ مِنْ دُونِ الْمُؤْمِنِينَ أَتُرِيدُونَ أَنْ تَجْعَلُوا لِلَّهِ عَلَيْكُمْ سُلْطَانًا مُبِينًا

Believers! Do not make friends with these disbelievers, leaving aside the believers. Do you wish to offer God an open argument against yourselves? (4:144)

يَاأَيُّهَا الَّذِينَ آمَنُوا لَا تَتَّخِذُوا الْيَهُودَ وَالنَّصَارَى أَوْلِيَاءَ بَعْضُهُمْ أَوْلِيَاءُ بَعْضٍ وَمَنْ يَتَوَلَّهُمْ مِنْكُمْ فَإِنَّهُ مِنْهُمْ

Believers! Take not these Jews and the Christians for your friends. They are but friends to each other. And he, amongst you, who turns to them [for friendship] is of them. (5:51)

Relationship with people of other faiths

- With other Muslims, our relationship with them is one of sincere advice. And this is a mutual relationship. A father can advise a son, and the son can advise the father.

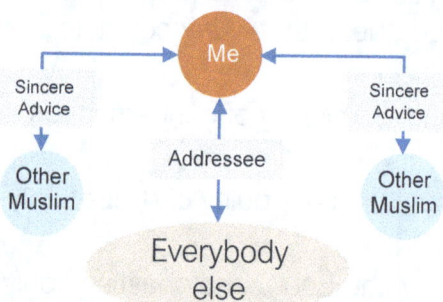

Our relationship with the people of other faiths is that of a caller with a message to an addressee.

- God wants human beings to have freedom of choice when it comes to religion, right and wrong, good and evil.
- Forcing our beliefs on others amounts to waging war against Allah because this is completely against His scheme for human beings.
- Principle: There will always be differences among human beings in creed, religion, understanding of God's law, application of human virtues … in almost every aspect of life.
- Learn to live with the differences in the most civilized manner.
- Never doubt the intentions of others, nor should we decide heaven and hell for anyone – we are not given any authority.

Calling others to Islam

- If we are convinced that we have the truth, then out of gratitude, it is our responsibility to share it with others within our capacity.
- Being a Muslim is not a privilege but a responsibility.
- Common beliefs and goodness are always a good starting point when discussing religion with others.
- For a common Muslim, sharing a copy of the Quran with others is more than enough.
- Sharing the message must be done wisely and intelligently with a good understanding of human psychology and circumstances.
- Our approach should be that of a well-wisher who is concerned about the well-being of others.

ادْعُ إِلَىٰ سَبِيلِ رَبِّكَ بِالْحِكْمَةِ وَالْمَوْعِظَةِ الْحَسَنَةِ ۖ وَجَادِلْهُم بِالَّتِي هِيَ أَحْسَنُ ۚ إِنَّ رَبَّكَ هُوَ أَعْلَمُ بِمَن ضَلَّ عَن سَبِيلِهِ ۖ وَهُوَ أَعْلَمُ بِالْمُهْتَدِينَ

Invite to the way of your Lord with wisdom and good advice and (if needed) to argue with them in the best possible way. Indeed, your Lord knows most who has strayed from His way, and He is most knowledgeable of who is [rightly] guided. (16:125)

Above all, we should be the flag-bearers of the moral character that Islam wants to inculcate in us.

Joining non-Muslims on social & moral issues

- Islam's emphasis on social justice is not limited to Muslims only but is related to all people in society.
- It is considered the manifestation of our belief when we uphold justice for all people, regardless of their ideological affiliation.
- In the life of Prophet Muhammad, he affirmed his commitment to the famous pledge known as Hilf-al-Fudul even before he was given the prophethood.
- As Muslims, we should not shy away from our responsibility in society, especially when it comes to social and moral issues that affect everyone regardless of creed and race.
- Instead of creating 'minority ghettos' within the society, we should be part of the society and play an active role in it as any other member.

وَتَعَاوَنُوا عَلَى الْبِرِّ وَالتَّقْوَىٰ وَلَا تَعَاوَنُوا عَلَى الْإِثْمِ وَالْعُدْوَانِ

And cooperate in moral virtue and piety, and do not cooperate in sin or transgression (5:2)

I witnessed a pact of justice in the house of Abdullah ibn Jud'an that was more beloved to me than a herd of expensive red camels. If I were called to it now in the time of Islam, I would respond. (Sunan Al-Kubra 12114, Sahih according to Ibn Al-Mulaqqin)

Attending social gatherings & festivals

- There is a common misunderstanding that Islam prohibits us from attending social gatherings or festivals of non-Muslims. However, that is not completely true.
- When it comes to socializing with or attending non-religious festivals (cultural or national), the principle that should be kept in mind is that we should not participate in any activity that involves:
  - polytheistic beliefs and practices.
  - immoral behavior and acts.
  - breaking the limits that God has asked us to remain within (related to the second point).
- This principle applies to any social activity, whether organized by Muslims or non-Muslims.
- The best way to deal with such a situation is to make your non-Muslim friends or acquaintances aware of Islam – this will allow them to be considerate when they invite you to the gathering.

- If none of the above is involved, then we are encouraged to attend any social activity, as this is the best way for non-Muslims to learn about Islam and Muslims.
- Our identity as Muslims should not stop us from being patriotic (in a positive sense) and law-abiding citizens.
- Creating bonds with our fellow citizens is highly desirable, and these cultural and national festivals offer a great opportunity to do so.

Celebrating religious festivals with non-Muslims

- This is not a new situation when Muslims are living with non-Muslims in the same geographical area or country. When Muslims migrated to different lands outside of Arabia, they lived with non-Muslims for centuries, who used to celebrate their cultural, seasonal, and religious festivals in those lands.
- The principle outlined on the previous slide also applies to religious festivals or occasions.
- If the religious festival or custom is enforcing a belief that goes against the principle, then it is recommended to avoid attending such an occasion.
- However, it does not stop us from greeting, wishing, or congratulating them on their joyous occasion.
- If the event is related to religion but does not involve any activity that goes against the principle, then there is no harm in attending such an event.

Inviting non-Muslims to your home or festivals

- One of the main reasons non-Muslims are largely unaware of Islam and Muslims is that most of us do not have social ties with non-Muslims, especially with our neighbors and colleagues.
- Our circle of friends and acquaintances is usually limited to people who belong to the country of our parents or who we meet in the mosque.
- Both the Quran and Prophet Muhammad have stressed being kind and generous to our neighbors and not harming them in any way – none of the instructions from the Quran and Sunnah distinguishes between Muslim and non-Muslim neighbors.
- Our neighbors have special rights to us when it comes to sharing food with them or inviting them to festivities.
- This is the best way Muslims can foster understanding and trust with non-Muslims and be able to break the wall of misunderstanding and phobia.

وَاعْبُدُوا اللَّهَ وَلَا تُشْرِكُوا بِهِ شَيْئًا ۖ وَبِالْوَالِدَيْنِ إِحْسَانًا وَبِذِي الْقُرْبَىٰ وَالْيَتَامَىٰ وَالْمَسَاكِينِ وَالْجَارِ ذِي الْقُرْبَىٰ وَالْجَارِ الْجُنُبِ وَالصَّاحِبِ بِالْجَنبِ

And Worship Allah and do not associate anything with Him, and be kind to your parents, blood relatives, orphans, poor, and neighbors who are relatives and who are not, and to your travel companions. (4:36)

From the life of Prophet Muhammad

On one occasion, Prophet Muhammad repeated three times, "By Allah, he does not have faith!" It was said, "Who is it, O Messenger of Allah?" The Prophet said, "He whose neighbor does not feel safe from him." (Sahih Al-Bukhari 5670)

Angel Jibrael kept telling me about treating my neighbors well so many times that I thought he would tell me to make him one of my heirs. (Sahih Al-Bukhari 6014)

He is not a believer who eats his full while his next-door neighbor goes hungry. (Sahih Al-Bukhari 112)

O Abu Dharr, when you cook a stew, put more water in the broth and take care of your neighbors. (Sahih Muslim 2625)

A funeral passed by the Messenger of Allah, and he stood up. It was said to him, "It is of a Jew." The Prophet said, "Was he not a soul?" (Sahih Al-Bukhari 1250)

A delegation of around 60 Christians, headed by a bishop, once visited Prophet Muhammad in Medina. Prophet Muhammad hosted them in the mosque. While they were discussing the matters with Prophet Muhammad, the time for their prayers approached, and they requested to pray. While honoring his guests, Prophet Muhammad permitted them to pray in the mosque however they wanted to. Prophet Muhammad respected their religion (knowing that they were on the wrong path) and their religious practices. (Source: Books of Seerah)

Dealing with Islamophobia

What is Islamophobia?

- In simple terms, Islamophobia is "the fear, hatred of, or prejudice against Islam and Muslims". (Wikipedia)
- Islamophobia is not a new term for us, and it's rampant in the society that we live in, mostly enabled by organized groups associated with political powers and media for their benefits.
- Other reasons for its normalization in society are:
- A minority of people who do not represent Islam have been representing Muslims in the world.
- Instead of learning directly from us, most non-Muslims learn about Islam through the statements and actions of these groups.
- The interpretation of Islam that we are presenting to the world does not make sense to them and is not compatible with God's word in the Quran.

How to respond to Islamophobia

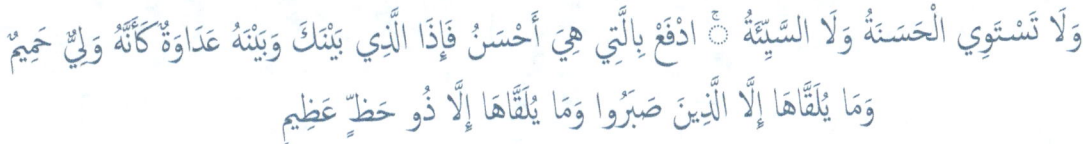

Good and evil cannot be the same; respond badly with good, and you will see that the person you have enmity with becomes a close friend. But this wisdom is not granted to anyone except those who are patient and those who have mighty aims. (41:34-35)

- Integrating well within society in every facet of life will allow non-Muslims to learn Islam from us through our character and dealings.
- Develop alliances with people of other faiths and collaborate on the causes for upholding social justice and moral values – Islamophobia is a kind of racism, and we can always join forces with good people out in the society (a majority).
- Get educated about true Islam, which is purely based on the Quran and the Sunnah.
- Engage people at a personal level in a civilized discourse (face to face or through social media) when we hear about Islamophobic comments from someone – eliminating misunderstanding of one person can go a long way.

Be the ambassador of Islam

- When living in a multi-faith society, we should be the ambassadors of Islam through our character and actions – no one sees our prayers or fasting, but they see what we do.

- The first interaction people have with Islam is through us.

- Prophet Muhammad was known as truthful and trustworthy among his people even before he received his first revelation.

- Contrary to what people believe, in the early days of the Islamic civilization's boom, Islam spread due to the simplicity of its message, persuasive arguments, and the moral conviction it brought to the population.

- Unfortunately, Muslims are not known for their best character as they used to be, and young Muslims in America have the opportunity to change this perception and revive that Islamic character.

فَبِمَا رَحْمَةٍ مِّنَ اللَّهِ لِنتَ لَهُمْ ۖ وَلَوْ كُنتَ فَظًّا غَلِيظَ الْقَلْبِ لَانفَضُّوا مِنْ حَوْلِكَ

So it is from the Mercy of God that you have been very lenient to them (companions) if you had been rude in speech and harsh in heart, they would have deserted you (3:159)

إِنَّ مِنْ خِيَارِكُمْ أَحْسَنَكُمْ أَخْلَاقًا

Verily, among the best of you are those with the best character. (Sahih Al-Bukhari 3366)

- What role can you play in fighting Islamophobia?
- What activities can we introduce in our mosques to build bridges with people of other faiths?
- What role have Muslims played in general in normalizing Islamophobia in the West?

Chapter 15

Course Summary

This chapter summarizes this course and the Quran's 10 commandments.

Course Summary

1 - Content of Islam

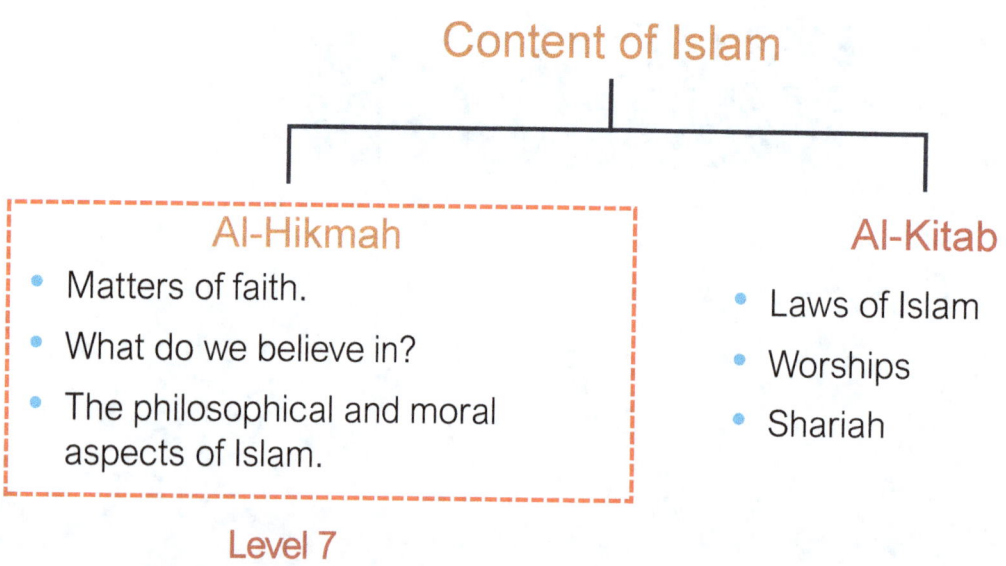

Content of Islam

Al-Hikmah
- Matters of faith.
- What do we believe in?
- The philosophical and moral aspects of Islam.

Level 7

Al-Kitab
- Laws of Islam
- Worships
- Shariah

2 - The Essence of Islam

Muslims generally think of Islam as a collection of rituals and practices. These are just symbolic expressions of the actual "worship".

Worship = Inner sense of Humility and Servility

Results of humility and servility	
Arrogance ✗	Humbleness ✓
Pride & Vanity ✗	God Consciousness ✓
Disobedience ✗	Trust ✓
Oppression ✗	Goodness ✓
Ungratefulness ✗	Gratefulness ✓

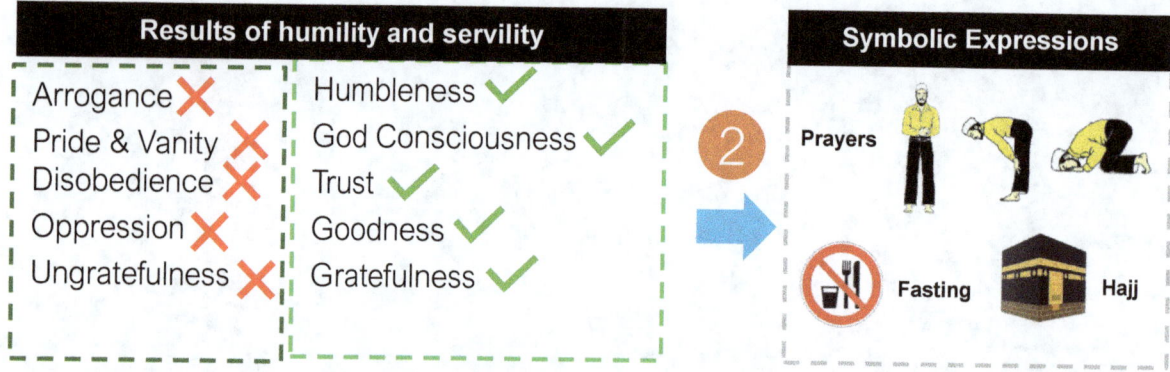

Symbolic Expressions

Prayers

Fasting   Hajj

3 - The Sources of Islam

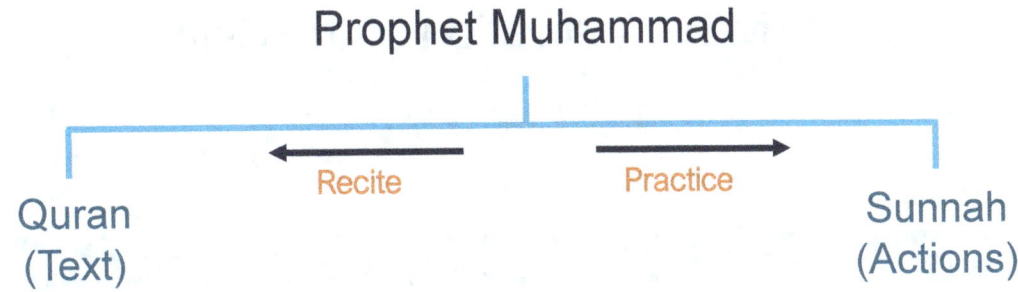

4 – The status of Hadith

Hadith does not add anything to the corpus of Islam and only explains and demonstrates what's already given in the Quran and Sunnah.

Quran and Sunnah - *Religion*	What does hadith provide? *Exemplary way*
Prayers	How did the Prophet pray?
Fasting	What did he eat in the morning, and what were his daily activities during the fast?
Sacrifice animal	What animal he sacrificed and how did he do it?
Perform Hajj	How many times he did do it, and how did he perform the steps already mentioned in Sunnah?
Punishment for Adulterer	How did the Prophet perform it as the head of the state

5 - Purpose of Prophets and Messengers

- Chosen by God, after receiving divine revelation, teaches the truth to his direct addressees.
- Gives glad tidings of a good fate in the Hereafter to those who accept it – *Bashaarah*.
- Warns those who reject it that a bad consequence awaits them – *Indhar*.
- With the signs of the truth that they have directly observed, they present the truth and the guidance to the people with full certainty, and that is called *Shahadah (Direct Witness)*.

6 - The Main Objective of Islam

Tazkiyah (Purification of the Self)

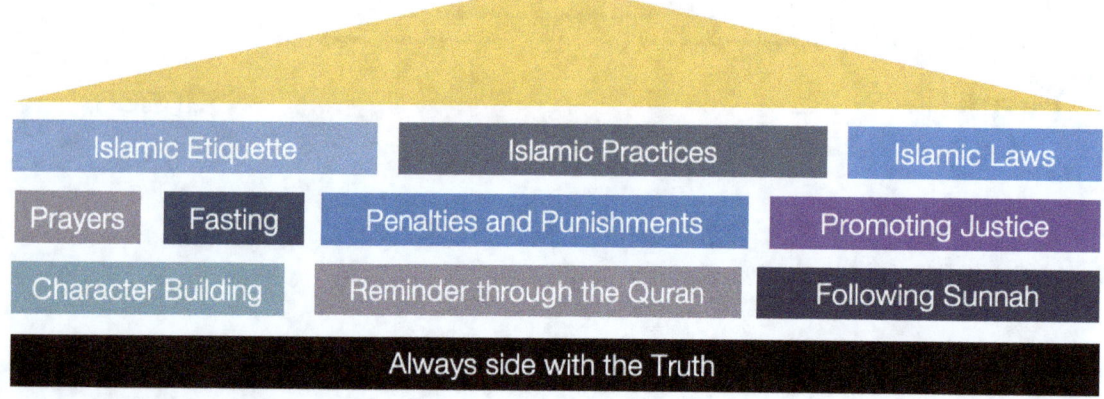

Islamic Etiquette	Islamic Practices	Islamic Laws
Prayers / Fasting	Penalties and Punishments	Promoting Justice
Character Building	Reminder through the Quran	Following Sunnah

Always side with the Truth

7 - The Requirements of Faith (Eeman)

Permanent Requirements of *Eeman* (Required all the time)

- Righteous Deeds
- Urging one another toward truthfulness and steadfastness.

Contingent Requirements of *Eeman* (Based on Circumstance)

- Migration to another land due to religious persecution.
- Supporting the causes of Islam.
- Adhering to Justice.

8 - Faith and Action

Light attests to the existence of the sun

9 - Islam, Judaism and Christianity

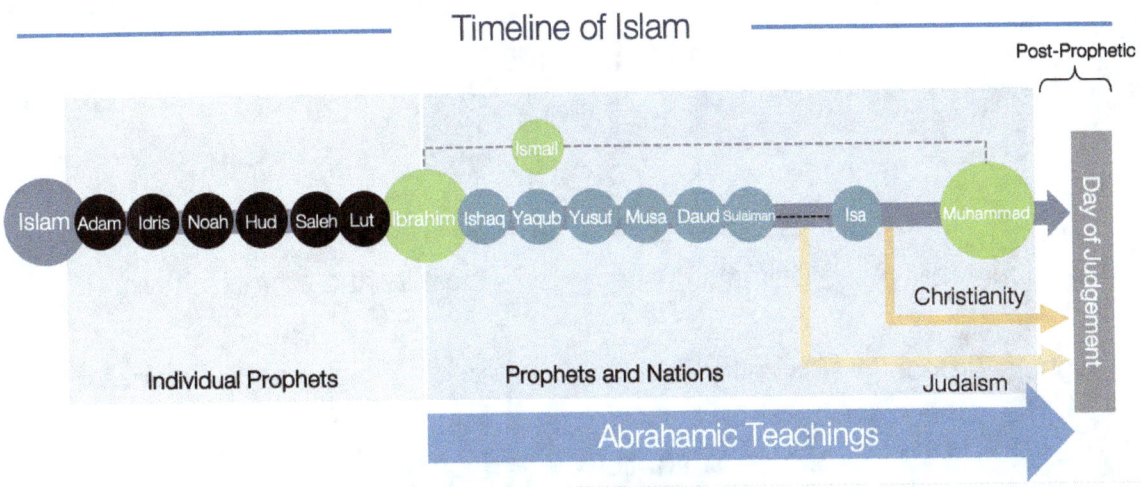

From an Islamic point of view, Judaism and Christianity are misguided groups of Islam. God never sent any other religion other than Islam on Earth. Islam is never associated with a group of people.

10 - Islam is a revealed religion

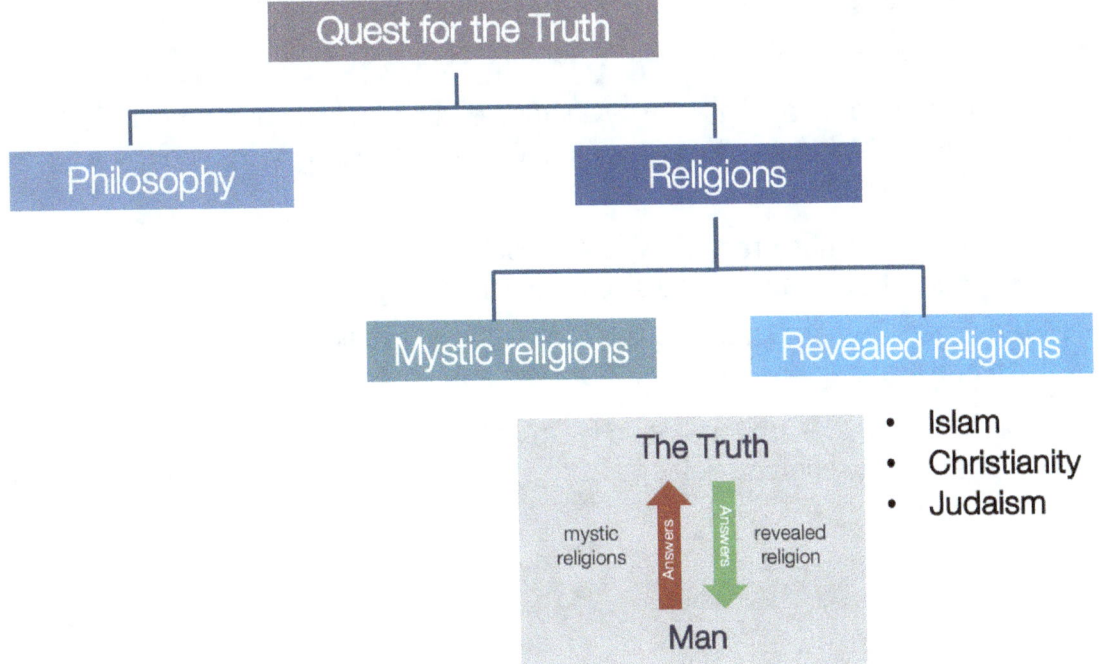

11 – Why do we need religion?

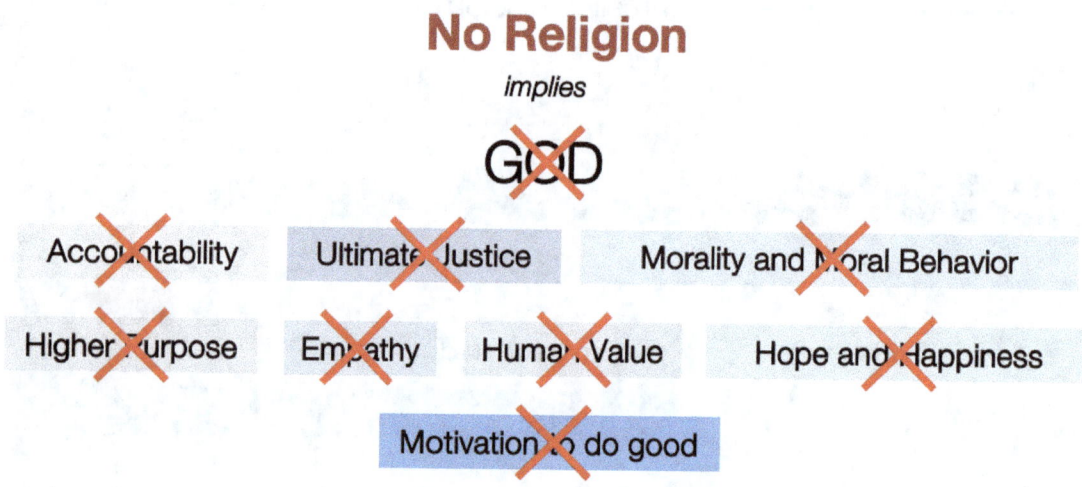

No Religion

implies

G~~O~~D

~~Accountability~~   ~~Ultimate Justice~~   ~~Morality and Moral Behavior~~

~~Higher Purpose~~   ~~Empathy~~   ~~Human Value~~   ~~Hope and Happiness~~

~~Motivation to do good~~

Believing in no religion is a recipe for existential disaster.

12 - Why is Islam the only Divine Religion

- FINAL practices and religious text exist in its original shape and form in the light of history.

- It claims to be given from the first human until the day of judgment.

- Teachings are closest to the nature of human beings.

- Quran – a living miracle given to Muhammad, a bedouin, over a period of 23-years with no sign of progression in thought and message, with zero inconsistency.

- Prophet Muhammad predicted certain results at the beginning of his mission, which came true exactly as he said in less than 20 years.

- Messengers demonstrated multiple times a manifestation of God's judgment in this world – last one happened 1400 years ago.

- Basic human values that the world is struggling with today were part of Islam 1400 years ago – human rights is just one example (see the next page for more).

13 - Difference between Prophet and Messenger

Prophet (Nabi)

The Prophet's responsibility is to deliver the message in the best possible way, give glad tidings to the believers, and warn the people who reject the message.

Messenger (Rasool)

Messenger practically enforces the sovereignty of the truth upon their people by implementing God's Judgment in this world on them—the righteous will be rewarded, and the wicked will be punished.

14 – Punishment for the disbelievers of the Messengers

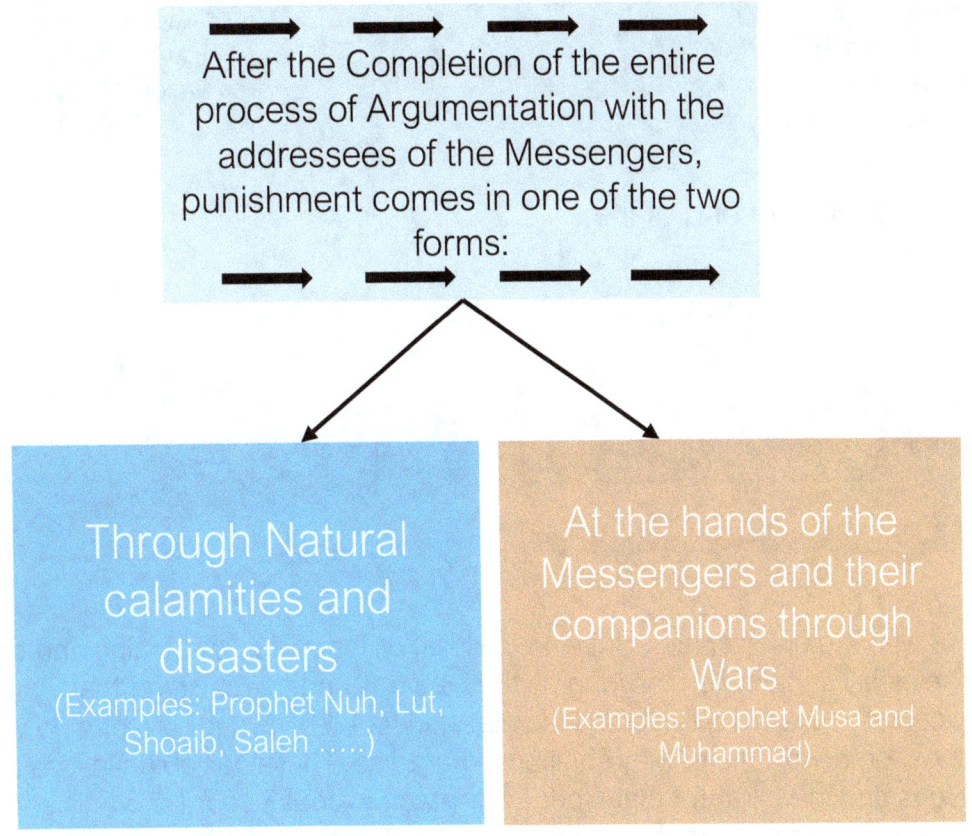

15 - The Quran is Divine

The collective human knowledge that we have so far is <u>not aware of</u> any human thought, philosophy, or literary writing:

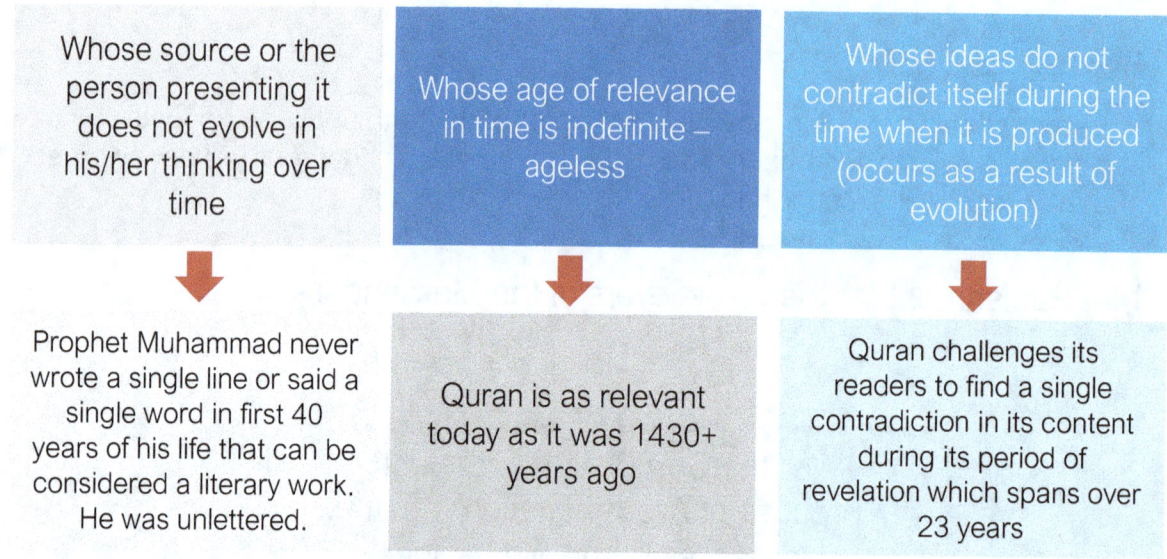

Whose source or the person presenting it does not evolve in his/her thinking over time	Whose age of relevance in time is indefinite – ageless	Whose ideas do not contradict itself during the time when it is produced (occurs as a result of evolution)
Prophet Muhammad never wrote a single line or said a single word in first 40 years of his life that can be considered a literary work. He was unlettered.	Quran is as relevant today as it was 1430+ years ago	Quran challenges its readers to find a single contradiction in its content during its period of revelation which spans over 23 years

16 - This is not the end of life

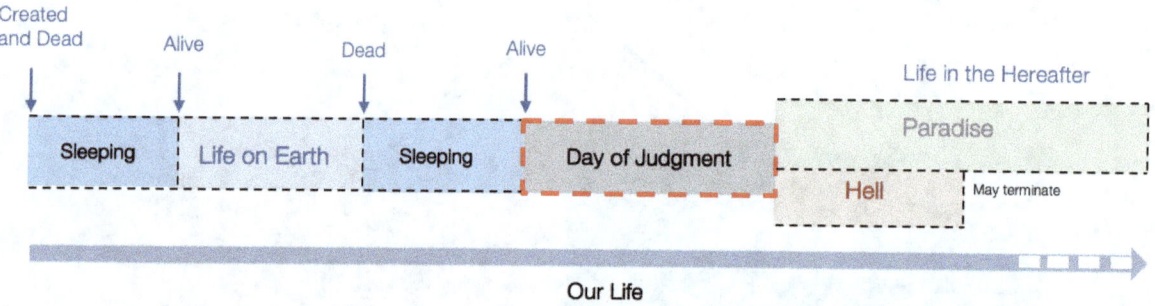

So, those who are unfortunate shall land in Hell. For them, it is screaming and crying there. They shall remain there as long as the heavens and the earth [of that world] are intact except if your Lord wills something else. Undoubtedly, your Lord can do whatever He wills. As for the fortunate, they shall be in Paradise. They shall abide in it as long as the heavens and the earth [of that world] are intact, except if your Lord wills something else – as a grant from Him that shall never cease. (Surah Hud:106-108)

17 - The foundation of good and evil

The foundation of all good morals one wants to acquire, and the evil traits one wants to avoid, are described in this verse of the Quran.

إِنَّ اللَّهَ يَأْمُرُ بِالْعَدْلِ وَالْإِحْسَانِ وَإِيتَاءِ ذِي الْقُرْبَىٰ وَيَنْهَىٰ عَنِ الْفَحْشَاءِ وَالْمُنكَرِ وَالْبَغْيِ ۚ يَعِظُكُمْ لَعَلَّكُمْ تَذَكَّرُونَ

God enjoins you to justice, goodness, and spending on the kindred and forbids vulgarity, evil, and rebellious arrogance. He admonishes you so that you may take heed. (16:90)

Positives	Negatives
Justice, goodness and spending on the kindred	Vulgarity, evil and rebellious arrogance

10 Commandments of the Quran

Do **NOT** associate partners with God.

It is like a defensive wall around our moral conduct. If this defensive wall is breached, every commandment will be breached.

Worship God alone.

Worship does not just mean praying; it's about an attitude of humility and obedience toward God. For example, spending time with family is worship when done in obedience to God.

Be kind to your parents.

Kind and respectful in every situation, even when you disagree with them. They are keys to heaven, especially when they reach old age.

Spend on relatives, the poor and needy, and be moderate in spending

God asked you to share what He has given you. There is a reason you have it, and they don't. You will never have anything to share if you do not moderate spending. Remember, a spendthrift is called the brother of Satan.

Do not go near illicit relationships.

When Satan wants to destroy the fabric of a society, its first objective is to make illicit affairs 'normal' in that society. Do not play in the hands of Satan.

Do not kill anyone.

God has given sanctity to human life, wealth, and honor. The punishment for this is eternal hellfire.

Do not misappropriate the wealth of orphans.

God wants people to be highly sensitive to the needs of orphans and to protect their welfare in society.

Keep your promises and contracts.

Do not take this lightly. God has warned that He will hold us accountable for our verbal or written promises on the Day of Judgment.

Be honest in your business dealings

When we deviate from justice and honesty in our dealings, it corrupts society's economic and social systems and erodes trust among people.

Do not go after things which we do not certainly know of.

Avoid speculation and do not pursue things with which we have no concern. This causes disharmony in society. Give everyone the benefit of the doubt and think positively of them. You will have a peaceful life ☺.

Islam is all about building a relationship with Allah SWT in such a way that when you meet Allah SWT on the Day of Judgment, you should hear this:

Oh, <your name>,
you are here!
Welcome!